THE HOUSE OF WORTH: PORTRAIT OF AN ARCHIVE
Amy de la Haye & Valerie D. Mendes

V&A Photographer
Ken Jackson

V&A Publishing

First published by V&A Publishing, 2014
Victoria and Albert Museum
South Kensington
London SW7 2RL
www.vandapublishing.com

Distributed in North America by Abrams, an imprint of ABRAMS
© Victoria and Albert Museum, London

The moral right of the authors has been asserted.

ISBN 978 1 85177 774 7

Library of Congress Control Number 2013945503

10 9 8 7 6 5 4 3 2
2018 2017 2016 2015

A catalogue record for this book is available from the British Library.
All rights reserved. No part of this publication may be reproduced, stored in a
retrieval system, or transmitted in any form or by any means, electronic, mechanical,
photocopying, recording or otherwise, without the written permission of the publishers.

Every effort has been made to seek permission to reproduce those images whose
copyright does not reside with the V&A, and we are grateful to the individuals and
institutions who have assisted in this task. Any omissions are entirely unintentional,
and the details should be addressed to V&A Publishing.

Front jacket illustration: Evening gown, white satin with an overlay of embroidered
blue tulle, 1899-1900. AAD/1982/1/41
Back jacket illustration: Evening gown or déshabillé, chiffon, lace and embroidery,
1097. AAD/1982/1/52
Image spread captions (pp. 24-5, 48-9, 74-5, 118-19): see p.172

Design: Charlie Smith Design
Copy-ed tor: Denny Hemming
Index: Hilary Bird

New phctography by Ken Jackson
V&A Photographic Studio

Printed in Singapore

V&A Publishing

Supporting the world's leading
museum of art and design,
the Victoria and Albert
Museum, London

INTRODUCTION
Amy de la Haye & Valerie D. Mendes — 6

CHAPTER 1
THE HOUSE OF WORTH 1858-1914 *Amy de la Haye* — 11

CHAPTER 2
PHOTOGRAPH ALBUMS *Valerie D. Mendes* — 27

CHAPTER 3
TAILORING *Valerie D. Mendes* — 51

CHAPTER 4
DRESSMAKING *Amy de la Haye* — 77

CHAPTER 5
FANCY DRESS *Amy de la Haye* — 111

CHAPTER 6
CLIENTS *Amy de la Haye* — 121

CHAPTER 7
THE HOUSE OF WORTH 1914-1956 *Amy de la Haye* — 135

APPENDICES
01 THE WORTH ARCHIVE AT THE V&A *Alexia Kirk, Victoria Platt and Daniel Milford Cottam* — 156
02 THE WORTH ARCHIVE AT THE FASHION MUSEUM, BATH *Rosemary Harden and Ben Whyman* — 158
03 THE PENNINGTON-MELLOR COLLECTION *E-J Scott* — 160
04 PERFUME *Ben Whyman* — 162
05 THE WORTH PARIS ARCHIVE *Ben Whyman* — 163

CHRONOLOGY *Valerie D. Mendes* — 166
ACKNOWLEDGEMENTS — 168
GLOSSARY *Valerie D. Mendes* — 168
BIBLIOGRAPHY — 169
INDEX — 173

The House of Worth was pre-eminent among Paris couturiers – clothes with the Worth label were the ultimate in luxury indicating taste, status and wealth, be it *haut* or *demi-monde*. Founder of the company, Charles Frederick Worth (1825–1895) (heralded variously in his obituaries as fashion's high priest, king and autocrat) is widely acknowledged to have established the template for haute couture as we know it today. He was among the first to produce a 'brand' by labelling his creations; he cultivated an international clientele; favoured seasonal collections and welcomed new technologies and distribution methods. As Paris trade directories and fashion journals testify, Worth et Bobergh (subsequently Worth) did not exist in a couture vacuum, though the house clearly outshone competition to lead the field. Worth triumphed thanks to Charles Frederick's work ethic, enormous energy, innovations and a hard-won prestigious clientele encompassing an international array of royals, aristocrats, *grande bourgeoisie*, actresses and courtesans. Wealthy Worth devotees attracted a healthy stream of fresh customers in their wake. The company rarely advertised but fashion's grapevine rapidly spread the news about Worth's desirable creations. Other designers were quick to emulate his methods, such as selecting a garment together with its fabric and trimmings under one roof, and were influenced by the arrangement of his salons. Rivals included Empress Eugénie's dressmaker, the long-established Madame Roger, and later the salons of Laferrière, Pingat and Doucet followed by Raudnitz, Rouff, Félix and Paquin. Gradually other couturiers opened in and around rue de la Paix and the *grands boulevards*, created by Haussmann as part of Napoleon III's vision for an imperial Paris. The extravagant confections of these designers satisfied the needs of La Belle Époque's most fashionable women. In 1895 Gaston-Lucien Worth (1853–1924), Charles Frederick's son, asserted that the industry known as 'la couture et de la confection pour femmes' was barely 50 years old and that it had two broad divisions – made-to-measure garments and ready-made clothes. Using Bottin's trade directories, he tracked the rise of Paris couture in the second half of the nineteenth century – in 1850 there were 158 couturiers and 67 *maisons de nouveautés confectionnées* (occasionally an establishment was listed in both categories) but by 1895, 1,636 couturiers and 296 *maisons de nouveautés confectionnées* were vying for trade.[1] Four years after the death of Charles Frederick, Marie A. Belloc (journalist, author and sister of Hilaire Belloc) wrote, 'Although he has many rivals, each with their train of faithful patrons, and, it may be added imitators, the present head of Maison Worth is still king of fashion-land'.[2] *La Collectivité de la Couture*, a brochure commemorating creations by 20 Paris couturiers displayed at the Exposition Universelle of 1900, is a reliable turn-of-the-century guide to the leading fashion houses. Along with Worth, Callot Soeurs and Paquin survived well into the twentieth century, whereas the likes of Bonnaire and Ney Soeurs fell by fashion's wayside.

Dress historians and curators are influenced by trends (just as fashion is itself). Until the end of the 1960s historical dress and haute couture were traditional research areas but within 20 years fashion studies had been embraced by the broad-based university sector and an academic shift occurred. Everyday dress, radical fashions, world and regional clothing, as well as sub-cultural styles became popular topics and 'modern' was the watchword. This study is part of a revival of interest in the roots of haute couture and brings a little known, key collection into the public domain. It adds a new dimension to Worth studies and to the wider history of late nineteenth-century and twentieth-century fashionable dress. Central to this monograph are black and white fashion photographs, dating from 1889 to 1914, which have been selected from the V&A's unique collection of over 8,000 photographs of newly completed garments, fresh from the Worth ateliers. They document the output from one of the company's most prolific and financially successful periods. Later material from the Archive brings the narrative up to the 1950s and includes some notable survivals, including a sequence of 54 photographs surveying the entire couture house at work in 1927. The photographer was given free rein and captured behind-the-scenes activities in the kitchens, staff dining rooms and ateliers as well as front of house salons with mannequins parading in the latest Worth creations.

Over the past 25 years the photographs have been consulted to trace specific garments and fabrics but this is the first time that these remarkable and informative visual records have been considered in their own right, minutely scrutinized and evaluated as a collection. Their importance is multi-faceted, offering insights into photography, the operation of a great haute couture establishment, the history of fashion mannequins (live and inanimate) and, most significantly, they spotlight the splendours of long vanished couture.

Made *sur mesure* (the costliest of beginnings), each ensemble was the result of skilled craftsmanship and painstaking attention to detail – celebrated here by close-ups of Worth hallmarks, from artificial flowers and elaborate embroideries to complex sleeves and eye-catching collars. The fact that the back of a garment was as important and invariably as intricate as the front enhanced the stylish value of a Worth creation and, of course, increased its price. One minor concession to cost was documented in the photograph albums – Worth garments with fur collars, cuffs or borders could be bought with or without (therefore cheaper) fur trimmings. Nevertheless, couture from the house was the most expensive there was – within the reach only of an international, ultra-wealthy elite. In *The History of Haute Couture 1850–1950* (1980) Diana de Marly devoted an enlightening chapter to the cost of fashion, which included useful comparative data. The question of prices charged by Worth is not straightforward and is complicated by international exchange rates at any given date, in addition to the issue of old francs and new francs. In his retrospectively published interview (1895) with Charles Frederick Worth, journalist F. Adolphus quoted the designer on expenditure: 'There are very respectable women in Paris who don't spend more that £60 a year on their toilet [*sic*], and who, for that really don't look bad. But you mean, of course, the women who come to me, who are of a different class. Well, they get through anything you like from a minimum of £400 to a maximum of £4000… Why, some of them especially the Russians need £150 a year for shoes alone, without counting boots.' Of American clients he added: 'I like to dress them, for, as I say occasionally, "they have faith, figures and francs" – faith to believe in me, figures that I can put into shape, francs to pay my bills. Yes, I like to dress Americans.'[3] Accurate or not, *The Westminster Gazette* for 11 March 1895 claimed that Charles Frederick said this of his prices: 'My charges are high of course but then my *modes* are exclusive. A Worth costume is a Worth costume. If my fees were lower I should be simply unable to execute the dress… My usual charge for an ordinary silk evening dress is from £50 to £75, but of course this sum may be considerably augmented by special trimming. I once made a court gown, the train of which alone cost £1,000. This was largely owing to its being covered with superb silk embroidery. One of the most expensive dresses I have ever made came to nearly £5,000.'

Works on Charles Frederick Worth and the Worth dynasty are now out of print, thus this book begins with a preliminary chapter outlining the history of the company and establishing a context for the photographs. In the shadow of its world-renowned founder, subsequent designers and business managers including second generation Jean-Philippe Worth (1856–1926) and Gaston-Lucien Worth, and third generation Jean-Charles Worth, have been somewhat neglected but here their achievements are given due recognition.

The Worth family almost certainly issued a notice upon the death of Charles Frederick as specific information, such as the number of employees and details about the roles of Jean and Gaston Worth, is repeated verbatim in newspaper after newspaper. Some of the claims are credible whereas other 'facts' have to be treated warily. Obituaries compiled by those who were familiar with the world of fashion, or drew on first-hand experience of Worth, are the most dependable of death citations. It is unlikely that letters of condolence contain deliberate misinformation apart from an occasional exaggeration or slip with dates. Clearly Gaston and Jean were awed by their father's achievements. In their respective publications they describe and praise his success in the fashion industry, emphasizing his support of French textile manufacturers. Gaston's report[4] was commissioned by the French government and contains painstakingly assembled factual tables whereas Jean's history[5] is a free-flowing collaborative venture compiled when he was ailing and his recall was not perfect. Although it was published many years after his visit to Suresnes, the location of the Worth family home, there is little reason to doubt the veracity of Adolphus's interview with Charles Frederick Worth. That the literary luminaries Emile Zola, Charles Dickens and Hippolyte Taine wrote about Charles Frederick indicates his iconic status. Memoirs by observers and autobiographies by notable clients (from Madame Carette to actress Lillie Langtry) as well as sometimes gushing reports by fashion journalists throw light on the House of Worth but must be assessed with due care.

The text is faithful to the photographs' original chronological order and division into day and evening wear (including fancy dress). Just a brief mention is made of theatre costumes by Worth as the Archive contains a mere handful of references to this lucrative and high profile speciality. However, actresses (who wore Worth both on and off stage) feature in the chapter considering illustrious clients, whose patronage helped to make Worth a world famous name.

Five invaluable appendices add new material: details of the Worth collection at both the V&A and at Bath's Fashion Museum; an exploration of a rare, newly discovered collection of Worth garments; an outline of the history of Worth perfume; and a summary of the albums held by the recently revived company.

The Archive poses various currently unanswerable questions, among them, when exactly did the Worth photographic records begin, who were the photographers and what equipment did they use? The company left no papers defining the purpose of these photographs – the First World War brought this systematic programme to an apparently abrupt end and it was never revived. The many-layered significance of this extraordinary Archive was recognized immediately by the far-sighted curator and polymath James Laver. Thanks to his tenacity, it was secured for the V&A and posterity.

PREVIOUS STUDIES

The number of learned publications and exhibitions on the subject of the House of Worth, written and curated over the past 100 years, are testimony to the importance of the Worth dynasty to the world of fashion.

It is rare to find a history of twentieth-century fashion that does not take Charles Frederick Worth as its starting point. To cite just a few, in *Paris Fashion* (1972) Alison Settle stated that 'It was due to his efforts that the haute couture found itself at the beginning of this century, at the heights of its power and influence'; Elizabeth Ewing agreed with this assertion in her *History of 20th Century Fashion* (1974); while in *Magic Names of Fashion* (1980) Ernestine Carter crowned him 'Monarch of the Belle Epoque'. In *Couture: The Great Designers* (1985) Caroline Rennolds Milbank named him first among 'The Founders'. Yvonne Deslandres and Florence Müller in *Histoire de la Mode au XXe Siècle* (1986) and Charlotte Seeling in *Mode, das Jahrhundert der Designer 1900–1999* (1999) begin their excellent histories in 1900 with, of course, Monsieur Worth. His position seems unassailable.

Charles Frederick Worth gave very few interviews and, like his Swedish partner Otto Bobergh, never wrote an autobiography. The first company biography, *A Century of Fashion*, was written by the founder's son, Jean Worth, with the translator Ann Scott Miller, and published posthumously in 1928. Jean's objective was to identify his father as *the* first fashion leader – as a creative genius who, unprecedentedly, dictated the style of dress worn by the international society elite of elegant and moneyed women. The writer's grandiose narrative style has been dismissed by Diana de Marly as consisting of 'rambling memories and not of definitive research'.[6] Nevertheless, it provides valuable insights into the working of the company and throws light upon Jean, himself a notable designer. Another, apparently related, text – *A History of Feminine Fashion* – is a rare and more modest publication, which, again in spite of its title, focuses upon the House of Worth. It is not dated or attributed; it was also published *c*.1928 and written in the style of Jean Worth. Exceptionally, it is illustrated with examples of photographs from the Worth photograph albums.

In 1954, two years before the V&A acquired the Worth Archive, a socio-historical monograph *The Age of Worth: Couturier to the Empress Eugénie* by the novelist, translator and historian Edith Saunders was published. James Laver, reviewing the book, considered the author to be a writer of distinction. *The Age of Worth*, an authorized biography fully supported by the family, was based upon extensive research into contemporary sources and memorabilia provided by Charles' great-grandsons, the sons of Jacques, Roger and Maurice. Saunders presented Worth in the context of his times, as an exemplar of the 'upright', nineteenth-century self-made man, set against the backdrop of the extravagances of Second Empire Paris. Two years later, in *Kings of Fashion* (first published as *Magier der Mode* in 1956), historian Anny Latour explored the circumstances underpinning Parisian fashion leadership and documented the largely neglected history of haute couture and its designers. Latour heralded Worth as the 'Founder of Parisian Haute Couture',[7] having defined an haute couturier thus: 'He is an artist who signs his work like a painter or a sculptor; he is an industrialist who employs hundreds of workers and employees, and his creations have become one of the most important items of the French export trade.'[8] Undoubtedly Worth's later appearance contributed to this definition. Once the company was firmly established, Worth, perhaps to distance himself from 'trade', eschewed the customary strictly tailored frock coat in favour of an 'artistic' flowing coat over a bohemian, straight-cut jacket and completed the look with a 'Rembrandt' beret and flowing cravat.

Rich clients in the United States formed a major part of Worth's business and in their benevolence they gave or bequeathed their Worth dresses to American museums. Unsurprisingly, all major exhibitions on Worth have been staged in America. In 1962 the exhibition *The House of Worth* (accompanied by a succinct catalogue with black and white illustrations) opened at the Brooklyn Museum, New York. This show presented a chronological survey of Worth garments from 1860 to 1908. Exhibition curator Robert Riley made a telling observation that, 'Worth's real contribution was his progress and far-sighted organization of French dressmaking and its attendant industries. The powerful French couture stands as a monument to him.'[9] Sixteen years later, Elizabeth Jachimowicz organized *Eight Chicago Women and Their Fashions 1860–1929* at the Chicago Historical Society. In accordance with the remit of her institution, Jachimowicz explored, by means of a socio-historical approach, the distinctive tastes and buying habits of women from wealthy, Chicago-based, entrepreneurial families. In 1982, the Museum of the City of New York's *The House of Worth, the Gilded Age*, curated by JoAnne Olian, opened. Its excellent collection is also city-specific and the exhibition showed garments worn by fashionable New Yorkers, dating back to the 1860s. Jan Glier Reeder's lavish survey *High Style: Masterworks from the Brooklyn Museum Costume Collection at The Metropolitan Museum of Art* (2010) includes a visually rich and rigorous textual analysis about this important collection of Worth's creations.

In her preface to *Worth: Father of Haute Couture* (1980), updated in 1990 with new research based on American collections and endorsed by the Worth family, Diana de Marly bemoaned the 'surprising dearth of original material.' She reported that 'Material disappeared, for example, when the House changed its premises in 1935, and again when the whole business was bought up by Paquin in 1954 – only to be closed down in 1956.'[10] To her credit, she overcame these hurdles to achieve a thoroughgoing monograph. Following up in *The History of Haute Couture*, she summarized the story of the House of Worth to the closure of its Paris headquarters in 1956.

Curator Elizabeth Ann Coleman's major work, *The Opulent Era: Fashions of Worth, Doucet and Pingat* (1989), is an invaluable, scholarly, sound catalogue. Her erudite, object-led, narrative documents the history of the house and, by providing important comparative analysis, considers Worth's competitors. Her biographical accounts of the Worth men, their creations and their textiles, together with the distribution of Worth's products and most significantly the clientele, cannot be bettered. However, the V&A Archive made only minor impact upon her extensive studies. Coleman's book was published to coincide with the opening of the exhibition she organized at the Brooklyn Museum.

Though Worth was not their main focus, a number of ground-breaking exhibitions in Paris examining nineteenth-century dress featured fine Worth pieces from the Musée de la Mode and Musée de la Mode et du Costume. Three took place at the Palais Galliera – *Femmes fin de siècle 1885–1895* (1990), *Au paradis des dames* (1992) and *Sous l'Empire des*

Crinolines (2008). These accompanying catalogues set Worth in context, displaying key garments and documents. Most recently, the wide-ranging exhibition *Impressionism, Fashion & Modernity*, first shown at the Musée d'Orsay, Paris, has made new inroads into the synergy between fashion, painting and photography, and inevitably included Worth. Art historian Françoise Tétart-Vittu's contributions to these exhibitions reveal the academic rigour with which she unearthed papers and records in the Paris archives that add immeasurably to the early history of Worth.

The House of Worth continues to form the focus of new research and discoveries. In 2012 a small privately run exhibition in Worth's home town of Bourne, Lincolnshire, was opened to the public to honour his achievements.[11] Across the Atlantic, curator Phyllis Magidson has created a notable web presentation comparing and contrasting designs by Worth and the couturier Mainbocher (1890–1976). It features detailed photographs of the insides and outsides of garments, dating from 1860 to 1953, all from the Museum of the City of New York's impressive collection. And an exciting discovery of Worth garments that had not seen the light of day since the 1940s was made in 2006 (Appendix 03). A large trunk, containing fashions and fancy dress by Worth dating from *c.*1880 to 1920, worn by a mother and her daughter, was packed and dispatched across war-torn Europe for safekeeping. It came to light in a London attic.

In 2010 at Paris Fashion Week, the House of Worth hit the headlines once more. The fashion house had been re-invented for the twenty-first century, its appearance on the catwalk marked by an haute couture collection designed by Giovanni Bedin (previously with Karl Lagerfeld and Thierry Mugler), whose aim was to create modern pieces inspired by Worth's style. British entrepreneur Martin McCarthy purchased the intellectual property to the label, and business partner Dilesh Mehta became chairman of the House of Worth in 2005 and CEO of Designer Parfums (which includes Worth perfumes). Mehta has become fascinated by the brand's heritage and his researches into the Worth legacy in spring 2012 resulted in renewed contact with Worth's descendants. He is now Guardian of the two bound volumes of Worth obituaries and letters of condolence that form part of the Worth Archive (Appendix 05).

NOTES
1. G. Worth 1895.
2. Marie A. Belloc, 'French Fashion-Land', *The Woman at Home*. Annie S. Swan's Magazine, July 1899, pp.952-61.
3. F. Adolphus, 'Mr Worth', Blackwood's *Edinburgh Magazine*, vol. CLVII, May 1895.
4. Worth 1895.
5. J-P. Worth 1928.
6. De Marly, *Worth: Father of Haute Couture* (London, 1980), p.11
7. Latour 1958, p.75.
8. Latour 1958, p.x
9. Riley, 1962, p.13.
10. De Marly, cited note 6, p.xiii.
11. The Worth exhibition is the work of the Bourne Civic Society, Baldock's Mill, South Street, Bourne, Lincolnshire, PE10 9LY.

1

THE HOUSE OF WORTH
1858-1914

AMY DE LA HAYE

LEFT – Jacket, blue grey wool embroidered with silver, 1899–1901. AAD/1982/1/40

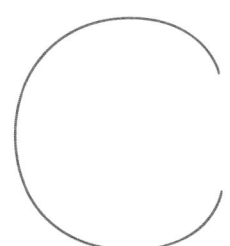

Charles Frederick Worth was born in Bourne, Lincolnshire in 1825. When just 11 years old, he was apprenticed to a printer (a job he loathed) and then he became attracted to the business of haberdashery and the sale of fabrics, trimmings and ready-made accessories such as shawls. Here he was to find his métier. In the spring of 1838, the ambitious and intrepid young Charles Frederick (now 13 years old) travelled to London, where he became an apprentice (for seven years, according to his son Gaston) in the department store Swan and Edgar. Later (according to his son Jean), he may have worked briefly for the more exclusive silk mercer, Lewis and Allenby. In his leisure hours, he explored the collections at the National Gallery, being particularly fascinated by the historical portraits. Worth became convinced that the textiles and gowns portrayed were stylistically superior to prevailing fashion trends of the day. It appears that he also enjoyed studying reproductions of famous paintings. 'Those whose subjects flaunted elaborate costumes fascinated him before all others. One in particular, that of Queen Elizabeth in her velvet gown embroidered with the ears and eyes, signifying that she saw everything and heard everything, was destined to become the love of his life.'[1] Worth would become renowned for elaborate garments based upon historical styles.

Worth was determined to pursue a career in the world's most exclusive dressmaking industries and so, in 1845, with minimal funds, he set sail for Paris. Two years later, after struggling to find work and learn the language, he was appointed as a sales clerk at Maison Gagelin-Opigez, Chazelle et Cie, purveyor of luxury silks, shawls and mantles (capes), where he became a great asset. The company was awarded a gold medal for dressmaking at London's 1851 Great Exhibition: although it has been variously reported that Worth was responsible for the winning design, this is not certain. However, it is acknowledged that – four years later – he designed the lavish court train made in a fine, white, watered silk embroidered in gold thread that won Gagelin-Opigez first prize at the Exposition Universelle in Paris (1855). Breaking with tradition, Worth had raised the train to the shoulder line, rather than suspending it from the waist as was customary, in order to showcase a greater sweep of Gagelin's luxury fabric. The style was soon adopted by the courts of Europe and in Russia. In June 1851 Worth had married Marie Augustine Vernet (1825–1898), a fellow employee, and henceforth made dresses for her to wear – both on and off the premises – using Gagelin-Opigez cloth and trimmings. As women admired and placed orders for the styles Marie wore with such panache (she has been described as the first professional mannequin), Worth's reputation started to grow. The timing could not have been better. During the glittering Second Empire (1852–70) under Napoleon III, courtly life, with its luxurious and ceremonial lifestyle, was resumed and the demand for luxury goods – including fashionable dress – flourished.

By 1857 Worth's creative talents were finely tuned, he had experience of making clothes for private clients and had forged relationships with the suppliers of fine fabrics and trimmings. That year Charles Frederick and Marie left Gagelin and Worth entered into a partnership with Otto Gustaf Bobergh (1821–1882), a Swedish national who had business skills and capital to invest. Operating as Worth et Bobergh, they rented premises on the first floor at 7 rue de la Paix in the 2nd arrondissement, with an initial staff of 20 workers. At this time the street was mainly residential with just a few purveyors of luxury fashion goods: Doucet's lingerie salon was based at No.17; fine gloves were sold at No.20 and Chez Grafton millinery was situated at No.25. The premises of the exclusive dressmakers – Madame Leroy, Madame Bonnard, Alexandrine and the Mademoiselles Laure – were located on the *grands boulevards*.

WORTH ET BOBERGH: A FASHION PARTNERSHIP

When Worth and Bobergh opened their Paris fashion house in winter 1857–8, it was unusual for a man to design dresses. Until the seventeenth century, the making of luxurious clothing in France was a profession undertaken by male tailors, but in 1675 a law was passed that permitted women to become dressmakers upon completion of a three-year apprenticeship. Dressmaking soon became an occupation dominated by women, the most famous being Mlle Rose Bertin, dressmaker to Marie Antoinette. From this point, until the mid-nineteenth century, clients selected and purchased their own textiles and trimmings, which they then took to a dressmaker, specifying their requirements. This process – dressmaking for the individual – was known as *couture à façon*. In contrast, the haute couture system that Worth was to inaugurate comprised all-inclusive seasonal collections (sample models of dresses as well as tailored garments and accessories), which clients were invited to view in order to make their selection.

One of Worth's former clients from Gagelin described retrospectively, for *Harper's Bazar* magazine (this is the title by which the magazine was known until 1929), her visit to the newly opened premises of Worth et Bobergh. The first room she entered was hung with brown velvet ornamented with steel decorations and had as its centrepiece a huge display of camellias. The second was equally luxurious and contained 'such a scene of fashionable excitement that it was impossible to pay much attention to anything else. On all the sofas, chairs, tables and pianos of this room, and several beyond, were heaped piles of cloaks, shawls, and jackets, and even dresses, laces, and *lingerie*.' The clientele was altogether impressive – a Russian grand duchess, half a dozen English peeresses and several Spanish families among others – but it was the appearance of Worth's staff that the writer found most noteworthy. 'These shop-girls were dressed up in clothing, jewels, and laces fit for the gala wear of so many empresses, queens, and princesses of the blood. To complete the picture they were superbly *coiffées*, and one of them, in addition, wore a splendid diamond ornament resting on her forehead. This proved to be the wife of Worth… I shall never forget her dress. It was a superb black silk heavily wrought with flowers of gold, evidently embroidered by hand; the skirt cut with a fine sweeping train such as is indispensable to every elegant dress nowadays, but which at the time was quite an innovation. The rest of the *corsage* was perfect; and the remainder of the toilette was of equal costliness and taste.'[2]

As Worth explained to the writer, each model wore a dress within a particular price range, so that when a client specified what she wished to pay, he could show her a suitable model. Meanwhile, she reported, 'Wearied of our long stay, some of the Duchesses and Princesses approached and began talking to him in a coaxing, pleading way, which struck me as being in strange contrast to the imperious manner in which women of their rank are wont to address tradespeople. But this man had made himself a wonderful reputation as master of that art which is dearest of all others to the feminine heart…'. Before leaving she purchased a ready-made cloak 'which struck my fancy on the spot': the price was $60.[3] By 1867, when this article was published in the newly launched American fashion magazine, Worth et Bobergh was the most famous fashion house in the world.

HAUTE COUTURE

Histories are often written in terms of 'firsts' and Worth et Bobergh has been credited with a great many of these. Among the most significant was the role Worth created for himself as a dictatorial couturier, who designed and determined the styles of dress his clients were to wear. His business provided all the necessary accoutrements for a complete wardrobe of fashionable and ceremonial dress, together with the requisite accessories. One newspaper reported that, 'Worth's lead in the world of fashion was due in large measure to his sense of composition in costume. He "saw" every feature, every detail, and harmonized them. With every order for a gown were designed all the accessories – numbers of pairs of gloves, slippers or shoes, hosiery, handkerchiefs, parasols, fans, bonnets, wraps, etc., according to the use to which the gown was to be put. Even to jewels and card cases his aesthetic sense extended.'[4]

The practice of showing collections in advance of the season was another of Worth's initiatives. He recognized that as clients were in the country in the summer it made sense to show them his Spring/Summer collection in January. By the early 1860s, the firm was stamping its name onto the petersham waist-stays of its skirts, thus endorsing the importance of the designer fashion label.

The sewing machine was vital in the democratization of fashion and Worth (like many couture houses) employed this innovative technology to complete long runs of seaming and later (as the Archive's photographs indicate) immaculately executed rows of parallel topstitching. In keeping with haute couture tradition, garments were embroidered, trimmed and variously finished by hand – this was labour-intensive, time-consuming and highly skilled. From the outset, the firm instituted new working practices, organizing the supply of the costly materials and external services they required. Crucial to their success were the collaborative working relationships they forged with French textile manufacturers, particularly the silk weavers of Lyons, who were commissioned to make runs of exclusive textiles and revive historical designs. Charles Frederick's son Jean, who joined the company in 1874/5, stated that his father was responsible for developing the production of fine, lustrous silk satin, which became a mainstay fabric for luxurious evening gowns. He reflected: 'It is absurd to think that in 1858 there was no satin to be had except a kind of lustrine used to line candy boxes and cover buttons.'[5] The house was also responsible for presenting existing materials in new fashion contexts: jet, which had traditionally been confined to mourning dress, was used as a smart fashion trim and – bizarrely – Worth has been credited with introducing chamois (leather) underwear.[6]

EARLY CLIENTS

Histories of Worth, relying on Princess Pauline von Metternich's *Souvenirs*, relate that in 1860 Marie Worth persuaded the Princess, wife of the Austrian Ambassador to the French Imperial Court, to view her husband's portfolio. The Anglo-American conman, socialite and writer Julian Osgood Field described the impact the lively Princess made in Parisian society: 'The most prominent lady in the social world of Paris in those days – after the Empress, of course – was Princess Pauline von Metternich… She had, like the Empress, that really rare gift – for it is a *gift* – like poetry, music, cooking and like them, cannot be acquired – the "*sentiment de la toilette*" to a degree approaching genius, and could wear the most amazing dresses, both as regards material, make and colouring – so exquisitely put together… so grouped that the effect was always charming. She generally wore quiet colours but I have seen her in marvellous vestments, once in a dress of yellow, red and blue of the most glaring shades, and yet the whole harmonized most admirably. It was, of course, she who discovered at Gagelins in the rue de Richelieu, that young Englishman from Lincolnshire, Worth, and soon recognizing in him a fellow genius, took him up and made his fortune. Imagine a poor youth from the Fen country becoming, thanks to his lucky meeting with the Austrian Ambassadrice, the High Priest of ladies' dress in the capital of Fashion!'[7] Whatever the sequence of events, the Princess recorded that she placed an order for a morning and an evening gown, on the understanding that they would cost no more than 300 francs each.[8] She was so delighted with the results that she wore the evening gown to the Salle des Maréchaux state ball at the Palais des Tuileries – one of most prestigious events of social calendar. The dreamy confection of white tulle, spangled with silver and decorated with daisies with pink hearts, placed in bunches of wild grass veiled in more white tulle, caught the eye of the Empress Eugénie and thus Worth secured the patronage of the most desirable of all fashion clients.

THE CRINOLINE

The history of Worth is inextricably entwined with the history of the cage crinoline. It was a style Charles Frederick only reluctantly adopted and apparently came to loathe. By 1856 the term was appropriated to describe the new, lightweight, flexible cage structure, initially made from whalebone and eventually from sprung steel, which replaced cumbersome, layered and heavy horsehair (*crin*) petticoats. Though probably apocryphal, it was rumoured that after suffering a miscarriage, and keen to conceal her new

WORTH. — Photographie Nadar.

J. P. WORTH
About 1908

CLOCKWISE FROM LEFT – Portrait of Charles Frederick Worth, c.1892 Bridgeman Art Library

J.P. Worth, c.1908. Brooklyn Museum Libraries

Gaston Worth, c.1908. Brooklyn Museum Libraries

OPPOSITE, ABOVE AND BELOW –
Watercolour designs for evening gowns from an album marked 'Worth 1863'. V&A: E.22392-1957, p.61

Watercolour designs for evening gowns and a wedding dress, from an album marked 'Worth 1863'. V&A: E.22392-1957, p.62

pregnancy, the Empress implored Worth to adopt the crinoline. In his hands, the style became the height of chic and was captured eloquently in Franz Winterhalter's romantic portraits. The skirt's silhouette remained dome-shaped until 1859, when it became an ovoid. Between 1862 and 1867 Worth reduced the size of the crinoline and in 1868 he designed dresses that were flat at the front, with the fullness swept round to the back: these gowns were supported at the rear by the new half crinoline, or *crinolette*, that Worth favoured until 1873.

According to Jean, the house retained artists on the premises to make 'water-colour drawings' of the designs, which could then be sent to clients.[9] Dress historian Françoise Tétart-Vittu, in agreement with curator Elizabeth Ann Coleman, identified some of these as gouaches by Charles Pilatte and further suggested that the accompanying pencil sketches were by Worth himself.[10] She speculated that the gouaches were collected for Worth's records, or 'to guide customer choice'. It has not been determined if any were made up into garments for Worth et Bobergh's seasonal collections. Two large and fragile albums of watercolour designs, titled 'Worth, 1863', are housed in the V&A's Word and Image department, although some designs are later and probably date from around 1868, when the cage crinoline began to give way to a flatter silhouette. A design for a white gown features a striking trompe l'oeil design of a barbaric-looking branch with pairs of floral forms that increase in dimension down the skirt. To contemporary eyes it looks surreal: at the time it would have been exceptional. An aproned gown, accented with pink ribbon bows and white lace trim, was much more typical. A shorter model, embellished with self-fabric trim and pretty pink ribbon, was designed for a young woman to wear prior to her marriage. Demure ingénue white gowns would become a Worth speciality and appeared frequently in the later photographic albums. Likewise, bow motifs became a house signature.

PRICES AND PRODUCTION

Though Worth's prices were often considered exorbitant, even by his richest clients, he continued to seduce them by his clever marketing strategies and personal authority. In the late 1850s, a writer accompanied an American client – 'a great social personage at home and abroad' – to preview the collection before other customers and claimed, 'No one who had not the undeniable cachet of high social and fashionable rank could ever hope to possess of these priceless invitations.'[11] In 1867 Miriam Folline Squier, an American client, wore a purple gown of such magnificence that it was reported to have cost $20,000.[12] In the 1890s Worth told a reporter, 'It is impossible to make a dress itself worth above a certain value, but the trimming can increase the cost to any amount. Suppose that you string solitaire diamonds around the corsage? Gold and silver thread and jewels make heavy cost. Several years ago we were paid $24,000 by a Peruvian lady for a single gown, but the laces alone cost $23,600. A cloak we sold for $9,000 had $2,800 value of fur. It is an error to suppose that our gowns all cost fabulous sums. We have many patrons of comparatively moderate means. We make dresses costing from $200 upward. I rather think we make more for less than $200 than above that sum.'[13] Clearly the house did not want to divulge how they calculated their prices and so they devised a secret costing code, relating letters to numbers that only staff understood. Dress historian Diana de Marly suggests how the final price of an ensemble was arrived at (see p.33).[14] Clients were unaware of Worth's cost-effective, 'mix and match' methods of production, which are evident from the V&A's collection.

Worth's 'flair for engineering' has been noted by curator Robert Riley, who astutely pointed out that many of Worth's garments were made using standard interchangeable pattern pieces. 'Each pattern must have done yeoman work at the House of Worth. An oblong skirt drapery introduced in the late Sixties continues basically unchanged into the late Eighties. It may be trimmed with fringes, bands or fluting, or finished with rosettes, but the pattern remains the same. The gracefully pointed edges of an 1870 skirt are used again and again in the Eighties and Nineties until it disappears under the skirt to trim a turn-of-the-century petticoat.'[15]

A FAMILY BUSINESS

At the peak of its success in 1870, Worth et Bobergh was compelled to cease trading following the outbreak of the Franco-Prussian War. Bobergh decided to retire and, after offering his business premises for use as a military hospital, Worth allegedly made a dramatic escape from Paris in a hot air balloon: 'Worth, the dressmaker, once found himself in a very perilous position. His balloon landed him near the enemy's camp, and Bismarck insisted on having him shot, but Von Moltke intervened and saved the life of the Lincolnshire genius... The great couturier never tired when peace came of telling the story... and I really think he believed it to be one of the most important incidents of the war.'[16] France was defeated and in the spring of 1871 the Worths returned to scenes of devastation and a city without two of his greatest clients – the Princess Pauline von Metternich and the Empress Eugénie, now in exile. The house re-opened, using a new label that simply read 'C. Worth', and along with the other luxury industries struggled valiantly to survive amidst the political turmoil of the ruling Commune. When Maréchal MacMahon (1st Duke of Magenta) was voted President in 1873, elite social life was gradually resumed, but never returned to its former glories. Worth had always been resourceful and astute in business and over the next decade he opened special departments for maternity and mourning wear, as well as sportswear, the latter selling yachting suits and riding habits.[17] It is perhaps by this expansion that Worth managed to maintain a workforce of some 1,200 people throughout the 1870s and 1880s, though staff numbers have been disputed.[18]

Between 1874 and 1875 Worth's sons, Jean-Philippe and Gaston-Lucien (referred to in the current work as Jean and Gaston) officially joined the company that they were to develop and expand. Jean stated that there was never any discussion about the brothers entering the firm; it was always considered an inevitability. Gaston took charge of administration and management while the more artistic Jean (who had studied with the French landscape painter Camille Corot) gradually followed in his father's footsteps as a designer. He observed, 'Is it any wonder, having known nothing from my birth but crinolines and laces, velvets and tulle, dresses half made and finished ready to be worn by a queen, frivolous dresses for famous courtesans and nun-like dresses for brides, that I became a *couturier?*'[19]

The early 1880s witnessed another period of economic decline in Paris and it was reported that by 1886 Worth's business had suffered so badly that he employed just one-tenth as many workers as he had previously.[20]

Watercolour designs for an evening gown, riding habit and winter dress, from an album marked 'Worth 1863': V&A: 22392-1957, p.67

A NOVEL ACTION

In 1879, Miss Carlsen (soon to marry a Captain Hubert Bradley) was making and selling corsets from premises in Hanover Street, London, under the name of Worth et Cie. Two years later Worth (Paris) complained about the appropriation of the company's name but on Bradley's promise to sell only corsets (which Worth [Paris] did not make) the matter was dropped and Worth et Cie continued trading. However, Worth et Cie began to make dresses and costumes, and in May 1883 participated in an exhibition promoting women's dress reform held at the Prince's Hall in London's Piccadilly. The exhibits – a curious 'trousered' evening gown and a knickerbocker costume – entered in a 'Dress of the Future' section would have horrified the Worth family. In 1884 Worth et Cie relocated to 134 New Bond Street. Seven years later a customer sent Gaston a cutting from *The Times* announcing that the Paris house was suing a client in London. Gaston had this error corrected in court – the case was in fact that of Worth et Cie v. Tilden. At this point Gaston decided that the confusion had to be stopped and began proceedings against Worth et Cie. In 1893 Gaston, representing Charles Frederick Worth, sued Mrs Bradley (now a widow) in the Queen's Division of London's High Court – the case was described by *The Times* on 18 March 1893 as a 'novel action'. The plaintiff Gaston Worth alleged that garments sold by the defendant Mrs Bradley were often 'badly made, badly fitted and in bad taste' and consequently his name and reputation suffered. The defendant countered that her goods were not badly made and that the plaintiff had long acquiesced in her trading as Worth et Cie. Lord Justice A. L. Smith warned Mrs Bradley, 'You take a name with a world-wide celebrity, and nine persons out of ten would be misled by it and suppose it means Worth of Paris'. Eventually, the litigants were persuaded to come to an agreement whereby Mrs Bradley was ordered to amend her signage in the New Bond Street premises. The sign above her entrance had to be changed from Worth to Worth et Cie, the term 'corsetier' was to be displayed in her windows and the announcement 'no connexion [*sic*] with Worth of Paris' was to be printed on all her bill heads and circulars. The Lord Justice announced that *The Times* report would make the settlement 'known to the whole world' and Gaston was satisfied that this publicity would dispel any future misapprehensions that there was a link between the two establishments.

Following a visit to the rue de la Paix couture house in 1894, a journalist reported that, 'A stranger would be specially struck with the constant, attentive supervision over all departments by M. Worth and his two sons; the unpretentious appearance of the reception and fitting rooms, the beautiful finish and refined daintiness of all the work and the daring originality which every model exhibits, which only a creative, artistic mind could possibly think of. Above all, all the workrooms that I was freely permitted to visit, as well as the kitchen, where the food is cooked for the many employees, show the care and forethought of the master for those who work for him.' The author also noted, 'Several young women are dressed in the latest style of morning, visiting, dinner and reception toilets, and are paraded in turn, this way and that, before clients, to enable them to judge of the effect of the garments when worn.'[21]

DESIGN PIRACY AND THE FASHION PRESS

The proliferation of fashion magazines was a huge boon to manufacturers and retailers, who could copy with ease the detailed line drawings of Worth's latest designs. This made Worth wary of the press who, in turn, did not always report on his collections as extensively as one might have expected – this seems to be especially true of the French publications. Writing in 1895, one journalist noted that, 'For many years they [the House of Worth] have made it a rule there to show nothing to newspaper reporters or correspondents; and although the attendants always treat every visitor with courtesy, this rule, unless one can bring strong influence to bear, is strictly adhered to. Indeed some of the fashion magazines buy Worth's gowns for their illustrators to copy: just as the fashionable American dressmakers buy his gowns every season to serve as models for their own designers and to show their customers. In fact, the big American houses are among the best customers of many of the Parisian *couturiers*. Worth's objection to newspaper publicity of late years has made first-hand accounts of his gowns or his ideas of the coming *modes* very hard to get; and greater prominence has been given to two, or perhaps three, other houses in Paris, who court, rather than avoid, seeing their names in print.'[22]

In American museum collections, Elizabeth Ann Coleman has identified three copies that were based on a Worth original design of 1874 for a high-necked, long-sleeved bodice, as advertised in *Harper's Bazar*.[23] She also found evidence that clients obtained lengths of fabric used by Worth, which they then took to their own dressmakers to have made up.[24] Unscrupulous traders not only copied the design and materials of haute couture designs illegally; they also made fake Worth labels to deceive customers. Surviving examples confirm this illegal practice was taking place in the early 1870s.[25] One reporter noted that, 'So much a fad did he [Worth] become that the trademark on the belts of his mantles and gowns has been cut from cast-off garments and placed upon articles made in inferior establishments in order to delude buyers into paying fancy prices.'[26] Although the specialist trade organization, the Chambre Syndicale de la Couture Parisienne, was effective in clamping down on piracy where it could be proved, in reality Worth could do little to monitor or prevent this fraud. However, Worth was able to reap some of the commercial rewards from the reproduction of his own models.

ORIGINAL VERSUS REPRODUCTION

While not every single garment by Worth was unique, the house liked to emphasize the 'originality' of their work for each client. In 1908 Jean wrote that, 'Not only must the maker of modes maintain a reputation for "exclusive designs", given to one customer solely for her own beautification – the silks woven for us by the Lyons looms are copyrighted as though they were paintings…'.[27] In *Couture Culture* (2003) Nancy Troy observed that 'Worth's business, and haute couture generally, were forged out of seemingly incommensurate elements: on the one hand, extremely expensive items destined for elite patronage and, on the other models described as unique creations that were nevertheless subject to endless adaptation and repetition: the original and the reproduction at one and the same time.'[28]

At the top end of the market, copies of Worth's designs could be purchased at reduced prices from high class dressmakers in Europe and America, who had purchased the rights to reproduce certain models. Indeed, many couture clients supplemented their exclusive wardrobes with cheaper garments ordered from refined local dressmakers or department stores. However, the distribution of designs was not always carefully orchestrated. Lady Paget noted in her diary in May 1892 that, 'When a dressmaker brings back a *modèle* from Paris she proceeds to make one or two dozen dresses exactly like it and you meet it everywhere on the backs of your friends, at parties, on actresses at the theatre…'.[29] Certain dressmakers were known for reproducing designs by particular couture houses. Writing about her presentation at court in around 1899, Lady Angela Forbes Hamilton recalled, 'I had a lovely white frock made by Mrs. Mason. She was "it" in the dressmaker line; all her models came direct from Jean Worth, and everyone who had any pretension to dressing well in those days bought their frocks from her.'[30]

PARIS STYLE FOR THE AMERICAN MARKET

Worth also sold models that were translated into paper pattern format. The earliest patterns for the tailoring trades have been dated back to the sixteenth century, but it was not until 1854 that tissue paper patterns for garments became commercially available. They were developed by an American, Ellen Curtis Demorest, who initially sold them in periodicals such as *Godey's Ladies Book*, before she and her husband launched their own quarterly publication *Mme. Demorest's Mirror of Fashions* in 1860. From this point paper patterns became widely available – Butterick was launched in 1879 and McCalls patterns were available by the 1880s. Mme Demorest had scouts in Paris and also travelled there herself to visit the couture houses. In 1867 she advised readers that French fashions were taken from two sources: the ceremonial dress worn at court and designs for the *demi-mondaine*. The couple's biographer states that they drew the best from each, avoiding both extremes and turning out gowns that they knew the American woman would like and find wearable – 'Worth translated into Americanese'.[31] While the Demorests (along with America's fashion press) bowed to Parisian fashion supremacy, their aim was to adapt Paris style for the home market.

DEATH OF THE FOUNDER

By 1890 Charles Frederick Worth had virtually retired from the business and his sons took the helm. He died of pulmonary congestion on 10 March 1895. *The Times* reported that, 'For a generation M. WORTH has been supreme in his own domain. He has known how to dress woman as nobody else knew how to dress her.'[32] *Vanity Fair*'s tribute was less formal, 'In his prime Mr. Worth was a bit of a poseur, and owed some of his success to his Aberthenian manner, but he possessed real taste, artistic sense of colour and outline, and a kindly heart.'[33] Obituaries across the Western world reflected variously upon Charles Frederick Worth's innovations, creativity, business acumen and personal qualities and some, aware of possible anxieties, reassured their readers that the future of the house was in good hands. San Francisco's *Report* finished its eulogy with: 'In conclusion the *Report* wishes to assure the ladies of San Francisco that Worth's mantle will fall on worthy shoulders and there need be no fear that style will receive a death blow by the dressmaker's death.'[34] This forecast was entirely accurate: Gaston and Jean were to lead the House of Worth successfully into the twentieth century. Elizabeth Ann Coleman asserted that, 'The best years for the house, in financial terms, aside from the initial ones (i.e. during Charles Frederick Worth's triumphant years), must have fallen in the decades flanking 1900. Monied maidens and matrons coveted a Worth confection, whether it was *"en gros ou en détail"* – ready- or custom-made'.[35]

THE SECOND GENERATION

Jean and Gaston had complementary skills with Jean controlling the firm's creative component and Gaston steering its management. They embraced technologies such as the telephone, now installed in most affluent houses enabling clients to place, and discuss, their orders from the comfort of their own homes. Likewise, the brothers preferred photography at a time when many houses still relied upon fashion drawings. Gaston's keen analytical business mind was recognized by the Minister of Commerce and Industry when he commissioned Gaston to compile *La Couture et la Confection des Vêtements de Femme* (1895), which proved to be an exemplary study of all levels of the French fashion industry in the years immediately before 1895. It is wide-ranging and packed with valuable information. Methodically minded, Gaston divided his treatise into five chapters:

1. *Origine de la mode avant 1818 – Qu'est ce que la mode?*
2. *Transformation et création de l'industrie de la confection*
3. *Comment se fait la mode*
4. *Influence exercée par l'industrie de la confection sur les fabriques et réciproquement*
5. *Organisation et production*[36]

He described how his own father, with inspiration, energy, and perseverance, played a lead in the mid-to-late nineteenth-century transformation of French dressmaking. Sadly, he was unaware that within three weeks, just as the book went to print, his father would die. A footnote was hurriedly inserted. It cited the letters of appreciation received on the announcement of Charles Frederick's death and regretted that he had not been given due official recognition for his achievements in his lifetime. Gaston's report emphasized the extensive and geographically widespread nature of the French fashion industry. He stressed that, as a whole, it was economically important, providing employment for a considerable workforce (this he illustrated with a model analysis of two broad types of mid-1890s fashion house including staff details). He collated an admirable range of facts including import/export tables (the export of women's clothes more than doubled between 1890 and 1894) and an exhaustive list of materials used in dressmaking (textiles of all kinds including essential *garnitures* lace, embroidery, ribbons and passementerie) and exactly where in France these goods were made.

Watercolour designs for skirts, from an album marked 'Worth 1863'. V&A: E.22392-1957, p.50.

Jean's prime concern was top to toe elegance and leaders of the *haut monde* turned to him for expert guidance. His published opinions reveal his knowledge of historical dress plus an overriding interest in all contemporary fashion issues. One example – the manufacture of dressmaking figures and mannequins – serves to indicate his forward-looking preoccupations. 'Of late years the lay figure has been brought to an extraordinary state of perfection, and in many cases we have *mannequins* exactly reproducing our foreign customer's peculiarities of form etc. Indeed this system of fitting has many advantages, especially when, as not unfrequently [*sic*] happens, a client requires twenty or thirty dresses'. He continued to describe an amusing experimental figure and another that seems rather cumbersome: 'The most successful and newest lay figure is made on the same principle as an india-rubber cushion, and with the help of a pattern bodice, or even the measurements, can be made to express exactly the size and shape required. Another and more usual mannequin is that worked by a series of buckles and straps, which also expands till it exactly fits the lining placed over it'.[37]

Clients visiting the Paris house, to view the collections and undertake fittings, now arrived at the epicentre of luxury fashion goods. Its reputation for *suprême bon ton* endured. In 1906 *Femina*'s pseudonymous reporter, 'La Parisienne', considered a day in the life of the rue de la Paix, one of Les Quartiers Elégants. Walking the street, she gives a pen picture of each deluxe establishment: 'We are in front of Worth, the great couturier. The entrance is sober with a majestic aura; a thoroughly French house of good taste'.[38] Jacques Doucet (whose family business was shirt-making, lingerie and lace-making) had opened his fashion house in the rue de la Paix in 1875 and Mme Paquin (whose company later acquired Worth) took premises there in 1891. They were joined in nearby central Paris locations by the British firm Redfern, established in Paris in 1881; Félix (Félix Poussineau, listed as *Félix: Robes, modes et coiffures*) in 1889; Lanvin (who originally worked as a milliner) in 1890; Callot Soeurs in 1895; and Doeuillet in 1899. In 1899 the exclusive jeweller Cartier (established in 1848), with whom Worth shared a clientele, opened its premises at 13 rue de la Paix. Among many innovations, Cartier was celebrated for its elegant use of platinum set with diamonds and monochromatic jewellery. In the depressed years following the Franco-Prussian War, Charles Frederick Worth and Cartier's founder, Louis-François Cartier, had worked closely together to revive the luxury trades. Worth sold Cartier sumptuous dress silks against which Cartier displayed his jewellery. Recognizing that Cartier's elegant, precious jewellery enhanced the desirability of his evening gowns, Worth showed Cartier's jewels and dress ornaments – diamond pins, belt buckles, clasps and buttons – in the salons at 7 rue de la Paix. The two families also became joined by marriage: in 1898 Louis Cartier, the founder's son, married Jean's daughter Andrée and Louis's sister Suzanne later married Gaston's son Jacques.

1900 EXPOSITION UNIVERSELLE IN PARIS

Fashion was well represented at the 1900 Exposition Universelle in Paris, the world fair that celebrated a century of achievements and heralded Art Nouveau as the modern style to mark the new century. Altogether some 50 million visitors attended. The Chambre Syndicale co-ordinated the installation of its members' designs. The Fashion Hall was divided into four sections, each representing a season-specific location or event. Autumn was represented by the Longchamps races; the great hall of a luxurious private house evoked Winter; Spring featured a *défilé* (fashion show); and Summer depicted the seaside resort of Deauville. Each couturier drew lots to determine in which spaces they would display their fashions: Worth was allocated the Longchamps and Deauville displays.

Jean was irked that these daytime settings would not display effectively his eveningwear designs and urged his fellow exhibitors to incorporate artificial light. He also wanted them to utilize wax mannequins to display their clothes to best advantage on body forms. He was to recall bitterly, 'However our colleagues would have none of it, declared it to be bizarre, a masquerade, undignified and not to be considered.' Whilst Gaston complied with the Chambre's concept, Jean staged an independent scheme in the Hall. 'In this I put a copy of a Louis XVI drawing-room and staged therein incidents from English life. The models represented a great lady dressed in the regulation court costume, three feathers and all, with her young sister whom she was to represent to the queen; a lady reclining in a sofa in a splendid tea gown, her tiny sister offering tea to her guests: a maid holding a *manteau de soirée*; a lady in a white *tailleur*… These fragments of scenes allowed the use of all materials from cloth to brocade, and all styles from the most elaborate to the uniform of the maid. Yet they were fitted altogether with due regard to reality that those who saw the set could not exclaim enough over it. Its sensation was such that it became necessary to station a policeman before it in order to keep the crowd moving and during the six months the Exposition endured it was necessary to replace the floor twice.'[39]

In addition to the modern fashion displays at the Exposition Universelle, the couturier Monsieur Félix organized Le Palais du Costume, for 'le costume de la femme à travers les âges' in a building at the foot of the Eiffel Tower. Reproduction costumes were meticulously constructed on realistic mannequins and Félix also included a display of the history of hairdressing. The costume palace was heralded as one of the most interesting features of the Exposition, being described as the 'Museum of Modes' in *The Queen*.[40] Félix, the fashion house on the rue du Faubourg Saint Honoré, was perhaps Worth's chief competitor. A profile of Monsieur Félix – 'A Parisian Prince of Dress' – and his establishment by a reporter with the pen name 'Intime' noted that, 'There are few, if any, leaders of fashion who do not go to him for their dresses'. There followed a long list of clients including Worth devotees Comtesse de Greffuhle and Lillie Langtry. 'Intime', suggesting that Worth's evening *salon de vente* was no longer unique, went on to describe Félix's 'little room cut off from the ordinary showrooms… [which] contains some of these evening dresses… They are arranged on lay figures, and the room is aglow with dozens of little incandescent lights, to enable the customer to judge of the exact effect as seen in a ball room flooded with electric light.'[41]

ARRIVAL OF PAUL POIRET

While Jean tended to safeguard the traditions of couture and championed classic design, Gaston recognized that the House of Worth also needed to plan for the future. With this in mind, in 1901 he engaged the talented young designer Paul Poiret (1879–1944) to work alongside Jean. Poiret had worked as a designer before his military service and went on to become a leading force in twentieth-century fashion. In his autobiography *King of Fashion* (1931), Poiret refers to Worth as one of his former 'clients', which suggests he had sold designs to the house (on a freelance basis) before joining the company in 1901. Poiret's narrative is full of swagger but is nonetheless illuminating in relation to his reported experiences at Worth, starting with the job offer made by Gaston: '"Young man, you know the Maison Worth, which has always dressed the Courts of the whole world. It possesses the most exalted and richest clientele, but today this clientele does not dress exclusively in the robes of State. Sometimes Princesses take the omnibus, and go on foot in the streets. My brother Jean has always refused to make a certain order of dresses, for which he feels no inclination: simple and practical dresses which, none the less, we are asked for. We are like some great restaurant, which would refuse to serve aught but truffles. It is therefore, necessary for us to create a department for fried potatoes." I perceived immediately what interest I might have in becoming the potato frier for this great house, and I at once accepted the position that was offered me. Its terms were, in any case, most flattering, and I began to make models that were severely criticised by the vendeuses (who reminded me of the Furies at Doucet's) but which pleased the public'. Poiret clearly admired Jean's work, stating that in his hands the house designs had 'much evolved' and were 'models of art and purity'. He records that 'He [Jean] was surrounded by very highly skilled women, and by one, in particular, who moulded corsages as in the Great Century, out of plain or figured satin, which stood up stiff like armour, giving at the waist in charming folds to disclose the suppleness of the thighs. And he would make a sleeve out of a long tulle scarf held above the elbow by a row of diamonds and finished by two emerald tassels. (For he could not conceive that a dress could be made without some opulence.)' Poiret felt he was 'hated' by Jean, who, he believed, regarded the younger man's modernistic designs as sweeping away his own romantic notions of how a woman should look. In contrast, 'Gaston Worth, who thought only of commercial results, foresaw the present day, and the threat that already overhung the Courts of Europe.'[42]

At the outset of Poiret's appointment, in 1901, Gaston Worth was awarded the Légion d'honneur in recognition of his contribution to the French luxury trades (including his 1895 report and the 1900 Exposition displays) and the house was granted the prestigious status of Ancien Notable Commerçant. Gaston had served as President of the Women's Tailoring Union from 1885 to 1888 and became the third President of the Chambre Syndicale (established in 1868), which had evolved from and became entwined with a series of smaller trade organizations. Its functions and codes were multifarious including strict membership criteria, the minimum number of permanent staff each house must employ, and how many models should be presented in each collection. A significant and difficult role was to protect the couturiers from design theft.

WORTH OPENS IN LONDON

In 1902 Worth expanded its operations by opening a London branch at 4 New Burlington Street, in the heart of the capital's elite dressmaking area. Jean credited Gaston with this initiative: 'At first his idea had been to have a sort of office in that city, where our British clientele might come and order gowns to be made in Paris. But he found out that our London customers wanted to be shown models, and so the office developed into an establishment that included not only salons where models were shown, but elaborate workrooms where these models might be copied. Owing to the fact that materials are rather cheaper and general expenses are lighter in England – we need display only twenty or thirty models there, whereas we must present five hundred in Paris – and that the models copied are not exclusive, we are able to make dresses about five or ten per cent cheaper in England than in Paris. The chief attraction this has for our clientele is that it makes it unnecessary for those on a flying trip to Paris to spend four or five days at the *couturiers* for fittings.'[43] Along with other designers, Worth's presentation gowns for the London Court were governed by dictates from the Lord Chamberlain's office. Some models in the Worth photographic albums, now in the V&A Archives, are annotated 'Londres'.

PARIS COUTURIERS IN THE TWENTIETH CENTURY

In the years leading up to the First World War a new generation of Parisian couturiers opened fashion houses including Premet (1902), Poiret (1903), Martial et Armand (1905), Beer (also 1905), Cheruit (1906) and Beschoff (1912). Some Worth monographs have interpreted this as a period of decline and stagnation for the firm, supposedly suffering adversely in the face of new competition. Elizabeth Ann Coleman states that, by 1903, 'signs of design rigor mortis' had set in[44] and observes that the photographic albums from this period show repetition of designs created a decade earlier. However, examining each album, page by page, some 20 years later, it can be argued that Worth catered for an existing traditionally minded clientele while simultaneously presenting entirely modern designs that withstood competition from newly established houses. Without surviving comparative sales data, the real state of affairs has to remain a matter of speculation, however.

FASHION IN PRINT

Offering a lively commentary as well as an invaluable photographic survey of Paris couture during La Belle Epoque, *Créateurs de la Mode* was published in 1910. It includes photographs of Worth's couture *salon de vente*, showing vendeuses presenting and describing to clients an ensemble worn by a mannequin, and the behind-the-scenes room where silks were stored, considered and measured.

Pochoir prints of Worth's designs appeared in the fashion journal *La Gazette du Bon Ton* (1912–15 and 1920–5). Launched by Lucien Vogel, it was famed for its lyrical evocations of Paris high fashion (see pp.152–3). Vogel gathered together a group of talented artists – Boutet de Monvel, Pierre Brissaud, Georges Barbier, Jean Besnard, A.E. Marty, Paul Iribe and George Lepape – and ran the journal on a profit-share basis. Each luxurious issue was illustrated with pochoir (literally 'stencil') prints, characterized by bold lines and vibrant colours, initially painted in watercolours and later in gouaches, laboriously produced on handmade paper. Initially the deluxe publication was sponsored by seven of the top Paris houses: Cheruit, Doeuillet, Doucet, Lanvin, Poiret, Redfern and Worth, all of whose fashions were featured in each issue.

BELOW — Interior of Worth's *salon de vente*, rue de la Paix, from *Les Créateurs de la Mode* (Paris, 1910)

Presented in a variety of settings, seasons and times of day, Worth's designs are captured in a romantic, idealized format, forming full-colour companions to the V&A Archive's monochromatic photographs. *La Gazette du Bon Ton* was available by annual subscription and distributed by Condé Nast. The final issues were printed in 1925. Possibly because of anxieties about copyists, images and reports on Worth's collections in contemporary French fashion magazines are hardly plentiful. *Les Modes* has about ten references in as many years (1903–13) and *Femina* is without a single lead article on the House of Worth. Fashion journalists writing for *The Queen* offered detailed descriptions of the seasonal collections, but clearly favoured Félix and Laferrière over Worth, while *Vogue* (American and British) and *Harper's Bazar* (American) reported on the House of Worth more extensively.

At the outbreak of the First World War in August 1914 Gaston Worth's sons Jean-Charles (1881–1962) and Jacques (1882–1941) were called-up for military service, along with fellow couturiers Poiret, Doeuillet and Beshoff. Throughout the hostilities Jean worked as a designer and – with the exception of the Spring 1914 collection – the house continued to operate. Towards the end of the war, some of the Worth workrooms in the rue de la Paix were turned over to emergency wards for the wounded.[45]

This chapter has explored the history of the House of Worth within the time frame that predates and corresponds with the photographic albums forming the focus of this book. The final chapter resumes this chronology, situating other archival items with the context of two world wars and up to 1956, when the business closed and the Archive was acquired by the V&A.

NOTES
1. J-P. Worth 1928, pp.7-8.
2. Unnamed author, *Harper's Bazar*, December 1867, p.22.
3. Ibid.
4. *Times Herald*, Chicago, 14 March 1895.
5. J-P. Worth 1928, p.26.
6. Picken 1956, p.197.
7. Julian Osgood Field, *Uncensored Recollections* (London, 1924).
8. Princesse Pauline de Metternich, *Souvenirs 1859-1871* (Paris, 1922), pp.135-45.
9. J-P. Worth 1908, Part II, pp.0-4.
10. Tétart-Vittu 1992, pp.40-5.
11. *The Washington Post*, 14 March 1895.
12. Ross 1963, p.163.
13. *Commercial Gazette*, Cincinnati, 16 March 1895.
14. Diana de Marly, *Worth: Father of Haute Couture* (London, 1980), pp.141-2.
15. Riley 1962, p.10.
16. Osgood Field, cited note 7, p.730.
17. De Marly, cited note 14, p.140.
18. De Marly, cited note 14, p.101; see also *The Times*, 12 March 1895, p.9.
19. J-P. Worth 1928, p.73.
20. Ross 1963, p.251. This would suggest 120 employees instead of 1,200 but these figures are impossible to corroborate.
21. *Milwaukee Sentinel*, 14 March 1895.
22. *Home Journal*, Boston, 30 April 1895.
23. Coleman 1989, p.36.
24. Ibid.
25. Troy 2003, p.25.
26. *Times Herald*, Chicago, 14 March 1895.
27. J-P. Worth 1908, pp.0-4.
28. Troy 2003, p.21.
29. Paget 1923, vol.11, p.536.
30. Forbes Hamilton 1922, pp.58-9.
31. Ross 1963, p.24.
32. *The Times*, 12 March 1895.
33. *Vanity Fair*, 14 March 1895.
34. *Report*, 11 March 1895.
35. Coleman 1989, p.20.
36. Gaston Worth 1895: 1. The Origins of fashion before 1818 - What is fashion? 2. Production and changes in the fashion industry. 3. How fashion works. 4. The influence of the fashion industry on textiles and vice versa. 5. Organization and production.
37. Jean Worth, quoted in Belloc 1896, p.142.
38. 'La Parisienne', *Femina*, 15 April 1906: 'Nous voici devant chez Worth, le grand couturier. Entrée sobre, grand air, maison de bon ton bien français' (XVII).
39. J-P. Worth 1928, pp.187-8.
40. *The Queen*, 10 March 1900, p.387.
41. 'Intime', *The Lady's Realm*, November 1900, pp.21-6.
42. Paul Poiret, *King of Fashion* (London, 1931), pp.61-3.
43. J-P. Worth 1928, pp.181-2.
44. Coleman 1990, p.23.
45. The Worth workrooms were designated 'Hôpital militaire auxiliaire no. 152', as recorded in photographs taken by the press agency Meurisse, now in the Bibliothèque Nationale, Paris.

2
PHOTOGRAPH ALBUMS
VALERIE D. MENDES

OPPOSITE – Gown, silk chiffon with 'pompadour' floral print, trimmed with lace and embroidery, 1905-6. Shown at the International Exhibition, Milan, 1906. AAD/1982/1/7

The extensive collection of Worth photographs appears to be the earliest surviving large-scale evidence of a leading couture house systematically photographing its output; both by type of garment as well as season by season. Over 8,000 photographs are contained within 81 albums. The earliest photographs were taken in 1889 and the last images are of eveningwear in an album stamped with the years 1913 and 1914. Chief player in recognizing the significance of this collection and securing it for the Victoria and Albert Museum was the eminent curator and dress historian James Laver, Keeper of Engraving, Illustration and Design (EID). After the Second World War he turned down the post of Keeper of the Textiles Department (which included the dress collection), claiming that his interest in fashion was 'purely technical and utilitarian', to help him date pictures. This did not deter him from making important dress-related additions to the collections. Towards the end of his autobiography *Museum Piece* (1963) he describes the acquisition of the Worth Archive with some pride and slight dramatic exaggeration: 'One of my last actions before retiring from the Museum was yet another fashion-foray. A letter arrived from the firm of Worth-Paquin announcing the closing of their Paris house and offering us the entire records of the combined establishments. We were given four days to make up our minds. Next day I took the early plane and by noon was in the Rue du Faubourg St Honoré and knocking at the door.

'Inside was a chaos of abandoned workshops, offices and showrooms. Ancient *vendeuses* with red eyes were standing about uncertain what to do next. I saw Worth's portrait upside down in a corner. I was shown into the room where the archives were kept and satisfied myself that they were worth having. Worth having! There were about 20,000 original designs for dresses, some of them going back to the 'sixties. Worth being no draughtsman, had, I was interested to note, worked on the ready-made lithographs of head and arms, filling in his designs for the crinoline dresses of the period. What an astonishing career it was, that of the Lincolnshire youth, the shop assistant at Swan and Edgar's, who went to Paris in the 'fifties and, in ten years, was the unchallenged dictator of the mode!

'Some of the account books were fascinating, in particular one huge leather-bound volume labelled "*Debiteurs*". I flicked over the pages and found the names of *La Belle Otéro* and other famous ladies of half a century ago; what they bought, who paid for it, and how much! I decided to accept the entire collection on behalf of the Museum and before the day was out I had arranged for its transport to South Kensington. I knew that my friend François Boucher would have liked the collection for his *Société des Amis du Costume*; but, after all, Worth *was* an Englishman and I felt justified in grabbing the lot. The House of Worth had lasted in Paris for just a hundred years.'[1]

In 1954, during a time of gloomy post-war austerity, the House of Paquin (founded in 1891) took over Worth – by combining forces it was hoped to revive the fortunes of both houses. However, two years later, in the face of a changing and diminishing clientele, together with increasing competition from recently founded couture establishments with more contemporary appeal, such as Dior, Givenchy and Pierre Cardin, it was decided to close the Worth-Paquin Paris premises at 120 rue du Faubourg Saint-Honoré. Lieutenant-Colonel F.W. Pay, chairman and managing director of Worth (London) Ltd, made the inspired approach to the V&A about a possible donation of these joint archives.

Though Laver claimed that, in response to this remarkable offer, he flew over to Paris immediately to inspect the collection, in fact he moved with due curatorial care and considered pace – the offer was dated 22 May and 15 days later, on 7 June, he arrived in Paris. However, when Worth (London) Ltd in association with Paquin alerted the Museum to the fact that 120 rue du Faubourg Saint-Honoré had to be vacated that month, and that possession of various documents had to be taken before the 15th, events started to

(Exposition de Milan) 1940. Robe mousseline pompadour
Mousseline pompadour fu
Dentelle cao crem cff9
Broderie cor (coutant)
Liberty blanc ca

move quickly. The collection had to be stored temporarily in a Paris holding warehouse. It was a sign of economically stretched times that the V&A asked the shippers for a reduction in transport costs (the final bill was £157 10s 7d with a £12 discount) and requested the usual museum deal of 'special' (i.e. non-commercial) entry through customs. This meant inspection of only 10 per cent of the goods in order to reduce the custom fee. Finally, the collection in 33 hefty packing cases, weighing almost five tons, was delivered to the Museum at the end of August 1956.[2]

SPLITTING THE ARCHIVE

The complicated exercise of splitting the collection was spearheaded by Laver who broke it into four broad categories: 1. Drawings 2. Engravings 3. Photographs 4. Press cuttings. He then had the parts delivered to the V&A's Library; the Department of Engraving, Illustration and Design, or EID (subsequently the Department of Prints and Drawings, then Prints and Drawings, Paintings and Photography, and currently Word and Image); and the Fashion Museum (formerly the Costume Museum), Bath. By 1957, after noting that some 'engraved plates may be duplicates… in which case they will probably be destroyed'[3] (happily none were), EID had accepted the Worth and Paquin original designs, historical costume plates, textile designs and designs for Worth advertising, swiftly assigning each work a Museum number. The departmental catalogue provides an admirable summary of this remarkable collection amounting to some 23,000 works: 'Designs for costume and accessories, some with additional sketches, and examples of fabrics used; and designs for fancy dress, theatrical costume etc. *c*.1865–1956. Also a reference collection of fashion plates of men's and women's costume, and miscellaneous engravings, chiefly French, late 18th century and 19th century. Most mounted in volumes. Many of the costume designs are inscribed in ink or pencil with the title identifying the dress, with notes etc. And in some cases, with the name of the client'.[4] Materials and techniques are not forgotten: 'Pencil, pen and ink and water-colour; engravings, etchings, lithographs and process engravings, coloured by hand. Various sizes'.[5] Together with the books and works on paper transferred to Bath, this reference collection reveals where Charles Frederick and Jean found the ideas for their creations based on historical dress. They would have turned to their own rare copy of *Mascardes recueillies et mises en taille douce* by Robert Broissard (1597) to be inspired by fanciful masquerade costumes, or leafed through their equally rare plates from *Gallerie des Modes et Costumes français* (1778–87) for enlightenment about eighteenth-century dress.

MARKING THE WORTH CENTENARY

A year after the collection was formally accessioned, Worth (London) Ltd in association with Paquin persuaded Laver to mount an exhibition of designs for dresses celebrating the company's centenary. Laver assigned three Prints and Drawings galleries for the purpose and, liaising with Crawfords (a prestigious public relations and advertising company), went about organizing the event. Lady Olivier (Vivien Leigh) was approached to open the exhibition but was unavailable. Laver (due to retire in 12 months) had inadvertently neglected to share details about the exhibition with colleagues, which got him into hot water with the Keeper of the Department of Public Relations, the redoubtable polymath Charles Harvard Gibbs-Smith. In a typical curatorial spat, Gibbs-Smith pointed out that Worth was a going concern in a highly competitive market and would be getting maximum publicity from a government office. A cardinal sin at that time. The row abated and *The House of Worth: A Centenary Exhibition of Designs for Dresses (1858–1958)* received excellent reviews. There were no hard feelings. On the occasion of Laver's death in 1976, Gibbs-Smith wrote an obituary for the journal *Costume* in praise of his considerable achievements, asserting that 'He actually became the man in England who made the study of costume respectable – no mean achievement at that time'.[6]

A CHEQUERED HISTORY

The fate of the photograph albums, remnants of the Worth library, Paquin papers and press cuttings was not straightforward. In the spirit of sharing, duplicate albums, the remains of Worth's library, volumes of Paquin-registered designs, press cuttings and five volumes of bridal gown photographs were all offered (by Laver) to Mrs Doris Langley Moore for the Costume Museum, Bath (see Appendix 02). The remaining Worth photographs, pasted into their unwieldy albums, were retained by the V&A where, for quarter of a century, they yo-yoed between departments and storerooms. From the Department of Engraving, Illustration and Design, they were assigned to the Library, where they stayed until the 1970s. There is no doubt that the albums will always be a physical challenge. Each cumbersome volume has an average weight of 7 kilograms and dimensions of 20 x 35 x 45 cm; they consume over 15 metres of valuable lower shelf space. The study of fashion had not yet become the academic force it is today and the space-guzzling albums were not exactly perceived as assets. Thus, as a collection of historical photographs, they were transferred to back to EID (by then known as the Department of Prints and Drawings and Photographs). Though the acquisition of individual fashion pictures by outstanding photographers was covered by museum guidelines, evolutionary records on the enormous scale of the Worth had escaped the net. However, the albums remained in their new home for some years until they became a space liability once more. Their future was always endangered by the fact that they had not yet been assigned Museum numbers. The next ignominious move was to a basement in South Kensington before consignment to an offsite store, after which they endured further temporary accommodation, this time in a mannequin and fittings store administered by the Textiles Department. Finally, their long precarious journey ended in the haven of the Archive of Art and Design. Laver is to be applauded for 'saving' the Worth-Paquin records in 1956, and in recognizing their enormous archival value he was far ahead of his time. In the catalogue of the exhibition *The House of Worth* (Brooklyn Museum, New York, 1962), Robert Riley, paying homage to a fellow curator, wrote: 'The alert critic and historian James Laver collected what remained of the great houses' records and sketches and delivered them to the safe-keeping of the Victoria and Albert Museum'.[7] However, at the time of delivery the V&A's traditional departmental structure was not geared to dealing with extensive records in an all-embracing manner. It was not until 1978, some 22 years later, that the Museum's Archive of Art and Design was established under Sir Roy Strong's directorship, precisely to deal with such eventualities. It recognizes the integrity of archives such as the multifarious Worth 'papers'; it has the expertise to curate large collections and the space to accommodate them. In 1982, 26 years after its arrival at the V&A, the collection was finally assigned Museum numbers, catalogued, and housed in protective conservation boxes.

THE CASE OF THE ABSENT LEDGERS

During the unavoidably speedy removal and relocation of the entire contents of the couture house, there were inevitable casualties. Charles Frederick Worth and his successors had amassed 100 years of design records and considerable design resources, including a wide-ranging library centred upon fashion, textiles and the arts. No catalogues or listings (if they ever existed) have been discovered. Fortunately, part of the library survived, some of the works remaining with the V&A, others being passed to Bath. They give a clear indication of the family's knowledge of the fine and decorative arts, and fashion-related interests. What became of the bulk of the library is a matter of speculation. Perhaps the most frustrating loss was that of the accounts books. Inspecting this vast amount of material, as disconcerted staff hurried about clearing and packing, was no easy task. Laver had hinted at the mêlée within 120 rue du Faubourg Saint-Honoré but, nevertheless, in this chaos he made a point of mentioning the accounts books – in particular the big *Débiteurs* accounts ledger. The name La Belle Otéro (the Spanish-born Carolina Otéro) caught Laver's eye. In addition to this star of the Folies-Bergère (she was also an actress and infamous courtesan), what other names of European aristocrats, American heiresses, actresses and *femmes du monde* did this volume contain? It is tantalizing to consider that here were key financial records naming clients, listing their orders and documenting how much they paid – or, crucially, what they owed as not paying one's bills was a habit of the rich and famous throughout the late nineteenth century and early 1900s. As the rascally Julian Osgood Field testified: 'Many a time I have heard Worth tell his amusing yarns about ladies he honoured with his patronage, and how very often he would be forced to writ the richest of them before they could be brought to realise they could not be immortalised by him for nothing. One lady, a Scottish peeress, whose husband was famous for his wealth… would never dream of paying until legal proceedings were begun… She would not pay until she was compelled to do so; then she settled up without a murmur and would begin immediately running up a fresh bill for a few more thousand pounds at Worth's establishment. She bore not the slightest malice, and fully recognised there was only one Worth in the world. This farce went on, I believe, for years – indeed until the death of the great dressmaker'.[8]

Jean Worth asserted that 'the majority of our clientele either paid cash or met the bill presented to them within the year without question' but described the case of Lord Dudley, who was very particular about his wife's dress. Lord Dudley wrote to Worth, 'ordering a dress for Lady Dudley and describing it minutely even to the hand-painted orchids with which he wished it trimmed. Owing to his desire that this exotic flower, hand-painted at that, be used among several other rather expensive items, the cost of the frock mounted and when Lord Dudley received our bill he refused to pay it'.[9] Worth took Lord Dudley to court in London and won. Another famous name likely to have figured in these accounts was that of Louise Ramé, the hugely popular novelist working under the pseudonym 'Ouida'. Eileen Bigland (biographer, travel writer and novelist) noted the extent of the writer's debts in her biography *Ouida: The Passionate Victorian* (1950): 'M Worth and his fellow dressmakers in Paris had sent ominous letters to the effect that unless their bills were settled by return they would be obliged to take "other steps".'[10] In her novel *A House Party* (1887), Ouida had her character Lord Usk observe: 'Women get into debt up to their eyes for their toilets [*sic*]… Hundred guinea gowns soon make up a pretty total when you change 'em three times a day'.[11] The name Worth, as a synonym for exclusive and expensive fashion, appeared increasingly in the literature of the day, including the novels of Emile Zola, who alludes to the perennial pitfalls of the reckless pursuit of fine clothes when writing of his spendthrift heroine Madame Renée Saccard: 'She was far more alarmed by her debt to Worms, which now amounted to nearly two hundred thousand francs. He insisted on a deposit, and threatened to stop her credit. She shuddered at the thought of the scandal of a lawsuit, and especially of a quarrel with the illustrious dressmaker' (*La Curée*, 1872).[12] The 'illustrious dressmaker' in question, 'Worms', was a thinly disguised Worth. It may well be that these vanished ledgers contained confidential client information (some famous customers were still alive), deemed in 1956 too sensitive for the public domain; consequently, they did not make the journey to London. Their fate is a matter of surmise and regret.

CLASSIFYING AND CONSERVING

For the most part the photographs are in fair to good condition. Just occasionally they have degenerated becoming faded, foxed, discoloured, scratched or variously marked. A conservation report in 1989 mentioned that some volumes were warped (all were tightly bound) while some of the photographs were fogged, their brittle acidic card mounts frequently chipped. Dust was seeping into the pages and it was recommended that boxing would eliminate this hazard. Most volumes are dated and have numerical indices giving page and design numbers, presumably a quick reference system. At some unrecorded point the V&A had the albums rebound by Her Majesty's Stationery Office in regulation dark blue buckram; unfortunately the original covers were not documented and were discarded, though some existing marbled boards were retained. One original brown cloth binding (AAD/1982/1/6, *c.*1910) has survived and its distressed, badly water-marked rear cover is almost certainly indicative of the sad state of the other bindings. Provenance notes state that 'the albums were rebound after they came to the Victoria and Albert Museum; the titles and dates on the new bindings may be a copy of those on the original bindings but they do not appear to be entirely accurate'. Elizabeth Ann Coleman echoed this in her publication *The Opulent Era* (1989): 'These volumes are not the chronological record that their bindings would indicate'.[13] Indeed, errors occurred at the bindery, the major fault being a bewildering lack of synchronization when transferring information and numbers to the new covers and catalogue entries. However, apart from a few misplacements, anomalies and inexplicable duplication of outfits, most garments seem to fit within the assigned dates and the pagination is, on the whole, reliable. It was hoped that the albums assumed to be duplicates, which

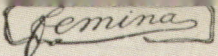

COSTUME TAILLEUR (Création de la maison PAUL POIRET.)

Jaquette de drap noir, revers de moire. Petit gilet de tussor « gazon ». Jupe à larges carreaux noirs et blancs.

OPPOSITE – Tailored costume, black lightweight wool jacket with silk moiré revers, silk tussore waistcoat and black and white checked wool skirt. Designed by Paul Poiret (*Femina*, 1 April 1906)

ABOVE, LEFT TO RIGHT –
Costume, green lightweight wool with a pinned seam, 1909-10. AAD/1982/1/12

Gown, embroidered blue silk tussore, the skirt's box pleats held by long tacking stitches, 1909-10. AAD/1982/1/12

had been transferred to Bath, might be in their original state and would help resolve any inconsistencies in the V&A set but they, too, have been rebound. At times the broad, often fluid, typological classification into 'costumes', 'manteaux', 'jaquettes', 'robes de bal' and 'blouses', each arranged more or less chronologically, can prove frustrating to research. However, this division reflects the organization of the Worth ateliers and accords with the way in which clients selected and ordered their clothes.

PHOTOGRAPHING THE COLLECTIONS

Without doubt, the value of these fashion photographs is their veracity. Each original print gives an accurate and reliable depiction of the clothes photographed. There has been no retouching and no manipulation of the ensembles (with pins, stitches or clamps) to achieve an ideal. The garments were for the most part immaculately mounted on traditional dressmaking forms, such as the standard linen-covered torsos manufactured by the well-known company Stockman Frères, established in Paris in the late 1860s. The upright dress forms are inanimate, neutral and anonymous, and almost transcend period. Without limbs or heads there are no gestures, no facial expressions, no accessories or hairstyles to draw attention away from the garments. The few wax and live mannequins scattered throughout the albums show how faces and intriguing poses add further meaning or associations but obviously divert attention from the clothes. The photographers did not have the freedom enjoyed by fashion illustrators, who could improve or elaborate or even completely transform an ensemble. They faithfully recorded a wide spectrum of fashionable dress over a period of 25 years. Occasionally there was a need to hurry and some ensembles were photographed unfinished, showing pinned seams, tacked pleats (above) and temporary muslin bands around floor-length hemlines, which provided protection from dirt and friction (p.54 left). After 1907 the standard of display became erratic and clearly the photographic sessions were rushed. Clothes were often mounted in a slapdash manner; some garments were hugely overpadded on stands that lurched sideways. Most photographs are annotated and only the seasonal albums (AAD/1982/1/63 to AAD/1982/1/77) are without descriptions beyond date, season and model number. Though the photographs are monochrome, the annotations usually give a clear idea of colour and of the plethora of dress fabrics and trimmings. The pin-sharp photography permits close scrutiny of cut, construction and decoration. Especially useful are the evocative names of textiles such as 'drap chamois' and 'mousseline glacée'. Descriptions were painstakingly handwritten with a metal-nib dip pen and black ink. At first it was thought that the initials at the end of each descriptive line referred to employees responsible for particular parts of each ensemble but in fact they are code for the prices of the materials and skilled labour. Discovered by Diana de Marly, the code was used by the house until it closed.[14] Not one price is apparent to customers perusing the photographs but Worth staff knew exactly how much each ensemble cost. According to de Marly, 'In arriving at the final price of a gown, the cost of the material was doubled and that of the handwork trebled'.[15] The albums reveal the range of desirable clothes that a woman of considerable wealth could have custom-made by Worth in the years flanking 1900: tea gowns and déshabillés; tailored costumes and blouses; coats and jackets; afternoon, dinner, theatre, casino and ball gowns; *sorties de bal*; furs and those specialities of the house, *robes de cour*, wedding gowns and fancy dress.

MULTI-PURPOSE PHOTOGRAPHS

It is probable that the photographs were multi-purpose, acting as design protection, as a seasonal catalogue for clients and, when orders were received, as a quick guide to Worth's craftsmen and women who had cut, assembled and decorated each ensemble. In 1896 Jean Worth explained that photographs were also used for mail order transactions:

BELOW LEFT — Travelling coat, plum-coloured wool bordered with fur, 1912. AAD/1982/1/36

BELOW RIGHT — Wedding gown, white satin, lace, tulle and taffeta with a trailing corsage of waxed artificial orange blossom, 1901–2. AAD/1982/1/43

OPPOSITE — 'Van Lao', afternoon gown, cream lace and charmeuse, 1913–14. AAD/1982/1/19

4762. Robe en dentelle crème, gar. mfg.

Van Lao

LEFT — Tailored jacket, beige wool over taffeta (*decoupé*) trimmed with cream guipure and emb-oidery, 1889-1900. AAD/1982/1/21

'One curious development of modern life is that so many people order their clothes in Paris who have perhaps never been within sight of France. People write to us from all over America. We often send photographs of some of our newest creations to all parts of the world'.[16]

The photographs fall into four broad categories. 1. Garments against a dark ground with back and front shot separately. 2. Garments against pale wooden panelling in salons (shot in the original Worth building at 7 rue de la Paix) with front and back shot separately. 3. Garments positioned at an angle before a full-length mirror to show front and back in one shot (the majority). 4. Garments placed against a painted backcloth of lace curtain draped to the left of a fanciful Rococo table. Photographs taken in the salons reveal hooks attached to the panelling and contemporary photographs of Worth salons published in fashion periodicals and publications such as *Les Créateurs de la Mode* show how luxurious capes and shawls were draped on them to tempt customers. There is no evidence of photographic equipment, or photographers. In her enlightening chapter 'Photography, Fashion and the Cult of Appearances' in the exhibition catalogue *Impressionism, Fashion and Modernity* (2012), Elizabeth A. McCauley remarked that 'The absence of scholarly literature on the early history of fashion photography has resulted in confusion over the definition of the genre and its origins'. According to curator of photography Nancy Hall-Duncan, 'Though the name of the photographer of these Worth pictures is unknown, there were several studios which "documented" fashion, such as Maurisse [*sic*], which called itself an *Agence de Reportage Photographique*.'[17] Whereas curator of film and photography Valerie Lloyd wrote of such documents: 'Clothes and photography alike stood rooted in the Victorian age. Clothes hung on dummies or static mannequins against painted backdrops. In Paris, already established as the centre of the couture business, the greatest houses like Worth made their own in-house photographic record'.[18] A client's letter, following her visit to the house, originally printed in *The Strand Magazine*, confirms Lloyd's assertion: 'At the top of the house is a studio, where all the models are photographed, and looking over the albums of costumes, extending back for many years, I had the pleasure of examining the most interesting…'.[19] Unfortunately, this customer neither stated how far back the albums extended, nor did she describe the layout or contents of the studio. Obviously photography had started under the aegis of Charles Frederick but as to when is a matter of speculation – the earliest V&A albums record late 1880s fashions.

LIGHTING EFFECTS

Worth's photographers worked in both the studio and the salons, presumably with a heavy bellows glass plate studio camera, probably mounted on a wooden tripod. It is not known if artificial lighting was used to supplement natural light but in the salons daylight from the long windows and possibly skylights would have provided illumination. Though ever-changing natural light and dull days must have presented problems, the photographers cleverly used available, sometimes raked, light to capture the characteristics of fabrics and trimmings. V&A photographer Ken Jackson has described how photographers angled reflector sheets of white linen or cotton to bounce daylight onto garments and he is familiar with late nineteenth-century glass plates showing such fabric reflectors.[20] Some were small, easily moved and stretched on light wooden frames – Nadar's photographic studio in Paris used small paddle-shaped reflectors handheld by young assistants. McCauley states that Félix Nadar and his contemporaries experimented with artificial light in the early 1860s but even after the introduction of electric lighting in the 1870s, commercial photographers continued to employ natural light until the end of the nineteenth century. She describes studios on the top floors of buildings with side and overhead windows fitted with roller blinds to control sunlight and goes on to note that (for portraits) supplementary 'portable screens were used to bounce light off the side of the face farthest from the light source'.[21] While copying the original Worth photographs Jackson observed that they have been variously trimmed and probably came from 12 x 10 in or 10 x 8 in glass plates, which were printed on different types of paper by photographers experimenting with new materials, processes and chemicals. Worth's photographers caught the lustre of crêpe de Chine (p.47), charmeuse and other soft silks perfectly, as well as the glitter and glisten of beaded embroideries, the three-dimensional nature of frail laces and heavy guipure, and the velvety texture of furs.

The light from high windows that bathed the rue de la Paix salons was in turn reflected by long mirrors, set on most available walls (p.44). Mirrors are fashion's accomplices and were essential to the art of a couturier; during fittings clients would be set in front of such a mirror, so the master could consider his creation all round. Zola described such a fitting in his novel *La Curée* (1872): 'He [Worms] made Renée stand before the mirror which rose from the floor to the ceiling, and pondered with knit brows while Renée, overcome with emotion, held her breath, so as to remain quite still'.[22] They were also effective in shop window fashion displays, as Zola observed: 'Mirrors on either side of the windows had been skilfully arranged to reflect the dummies, multiplying them endlessly' (*Au Bonheur des Dames*, 1883).[23] The mirrors used by the Worth photographers were practical and undecorated; they were there to record 'products'. Photographer Paul Nadar took the process to a new level in his formal portrait of Comtesse de Greffuhle (1896), posing her before an elaborate swivel mirror to capture both the front and back of her magnificent Worth ball gown, made in black velvet embroidered with lilies in white satin, glistening gold thread and sequins (p.38).

The archive of the Wiener Werkstätte's fashion department in the Österreichischen Museums für Angewandte Kunst reveals that from 1911, to give an all-round view of new creations by Werkstätte designers (especially Eduard Josef Wimmer-Wisgull and Max Snischek), the ensembles were worn by mannequins and photographed against free-standing mirrors. Jean Worth was keenly aware of the importance of mirrors: 'The reason the French woman is so well dressed is that she is immensely critical and makes very good use of the triple mirror… in which she can see at once the back and side views of her figure. She never remains foolishly gratified with her appearance after a cursory glance at the front view, but remembers that all the world does not bow *before* her; to many it is her back view that must be mainly visible'.[24]

MANNEQUINS AND MODELS

In a few albums (without any apparent logic or explanation) wax or live mannequins suddenly appear in the middle of a

LEFT — Elisabeth, Comtesse de Greffuhle, in a Worth ball gown of velvet with an appliqué of trailing lily stems in satin and metal threads. Photographed by Paul Nadar, 1896. © Ministère de la Culture – Médiathèque du Patrimonie, Dist. RMN – Grand Palais / Paul Nadar.

OPPOSITE, LEFT TO RIGHT — Evening coat or déshabillé, lightweight sky-blue wool and velvet trimmed with guipure and bordered with mink, c.1900. AAD/1982/1/23

Dust or travelling coat, heavy silk, Summer 1907. AAD/1982/1/63

Evening gown or déshabillé, chiffon, lace and embroidery, 1907. AAD/1982/1/52

run of dressmaking forms. The earliest use of a live model in the Archive dates from about 1900 (below left). She is swathed in a mink trimmed evening coat with enormous flared sleeves and high collar. Like the dressmaking stands, she is posed against a mirror to reflect the coat's elaborately embroidered back. With her full figure, she represents an ideal of the time: a languid pose, a wistful faraway gaze and abundant hair, piled up in a chignon. A series of live mannequins, in photographs dated 1907–8, epitomize the look. Dressed in floating, pale coloured deshabillé, they adopt elegantly lyrical attitudes. Again, hairstyles are full and piled on top of the head. A photograph of a *cabine de mannequins* in *Les Créateurs de la Mode* (1910) shows a young woman preparing the false hairpiece (*postiche*) used to achieve such coiffures. In one of the Worth photographs the mannequin gives a provocative sideways glance; she appears to be wearing heavy make-up and leans nonchalantly against a chinchilla stole. No mention is made of the fact that the clothes are worn by live mannequins, who will forever remain anonymous.

Occasionally garments were photographed on a wax mannequin, characteristic of the figures sculpted by the famous Paris-based Pierre Imans of Mannequins et Cires Artistiques. The company was renowned for its supremely realistic representations of beautiful women (and handsome men) from the 1900s to the 1930s. Immaculately constructed, the figures were praised for their grace and sophistication – by 1920 Imans was using the by-line '*chic, grace, elegance*' in advertisements. The studios perfected extraordinary tableaux of groups of mannequins representing the beau monde at their leisure pursuits. Like Worth, Imans exhibited at the 1911 Turin International Exhibition, where he won a gold medal for a diorama of a boating party of 12 fashionably attired men and women embarking upon Lake Como. In 1907 Worth used a wax mannequin (possibly by Imans) with a full, slightly dishevelled hairstyle (each human hair was sewn individually into the wax head), glass eyes and full make-up, capturing the then popular romantic, dreamy look. Heads were moulded to the torso, which was articulated at the waist. Arms slotted into the shoulders and were available in various positions. Most unusually for the period, Worth's photographer devised an informal pose with arms akimbo and hands thrust deep within the pockets.

HISTORICAL INSPIRATION

The albums reveal that under the aegis of Gaston and Jean, the second Worth generation, the high standards and design innovation established by their father were maintained. The reputation of Maison Worth was safe in their hands. Photographs indicate that, like Worth père, Jean, the firm's artistic director, made full use of the Worth library, which was stocked with key works on costume, art and related topics. He was further inspired by historical textiles (p.116, left) and dress, and explained that ideas came from 'a piece of old Church embroidery or a scrap of Louis Quinze brocade picked up in an old curiosity shop'.[25] He commissioned weavers in Lyons to create fabrics based on fragments from patterned vestments or court dress. He was especially fond of lustrous velvets, with long meandering designs adapted from Italian Renaissance silks and velvets (p.41 left). Inspired sleuthing by Elizabeth Ann Coleman has linked a magnificent embroidered wool riding cape of 1570–80 in the Germanisches National Museum, Nuremberg, with a Worth copy in silver soutache on velvet in the Metropolitan Museum, New York. She further traced its illustration by Adolf Sandoz on the cover of *Harper's Bazar* (13 April 1895).[26] At Maison Worth they were adept at reworking historical and regional dress in opulent ensembles, which appealed to clients desiring the unusual. For a privileged coterie, life was tantamount to a masquerade with Worth providing suitably extrovert designs for their 'on parade' appearances. So successful was this ploy that at times it is difficult to distinguish between fancy dress, theatrical costume and off-stage clothes. A velvet riding costume for Lillie Langtry in the role of Marie Antoinette in *A Royal Necklace* (April 1901) (p.40, left) is closely related to a 1904 redingote (p.54, left), while a green velvet with silver lace 'Louis XIII' gown would have been in perfect company at a fancy dress ball (p.40, right).

ABOVE, LEFT TO RIGHT — Stage costume, violet velvet redingote worn by Lillie Langtry as Marie Antoinette in *A Royal Necklace*, April 1901. V&A: Lafayette collection 2642

'Louis XIII', costume, green velvet trimmed with silver lace, based on a seventeenth-century riding habit, 1900. AAD/1982/1/42

OPPOSITE, LEFT TO RIGHT — Afternoon or dinner gown, voided silk velvet with a design based on Italian late fifteenth-century velvets, 1908-9. AAD/1982/1/10

'Matador', costume, blue ribbed wool trimmed with braid and fur. Blouse and cummerbund in pleated voile, 1913-14. AAD/1982/1/19

40 — PHOTOGRAPH ALBUMS

41

ANTICIPATING THE FUTURE

While many Worth creations made reference to the past, a number anticipated designs of the future. Embroidered faux collars and tassels bring to mind the inventive embroideries of Elsa Schiaparelli (1890–1973) in the 1930s (opposite, right). A three-quarter-length leopard swing coat could have stepped out of a 1940s Hollywood film noir (p.46), while a pert costume titled 'Matador', 1913–14, recalls the smart black and white couture of the later 1950s (p.41, right). A deeply pleated sleeve of about 1904 (p.43, left) is a precursor of Balenciaga's pleated mantle cloak of 1950 and a coat of 1904–5 (p.46, right) shares the high waist and immaculate finish of a Jean Muir jacket. The back of a karakul and ermine jacket is adorned with an amusing pair of wings – a decorative ploy much favoured on 'little angel' baby grows and printed adult T-shirts throughout the 1990s and 2000s. The provocative notion of underwear as outerwear (much used by recent designers including Dolce & Gabbana and Jean Paul Gaultier) was tried out by Worth in the Winter collection for 1904–5 (p.90), while for sheer fantasy and volume some evening extravaganzas bring to mind the work of Vivienne Westwood and the exuberant designs of the late Alexander McQueen and his successor Sarah Burton.

THE IMPORTANCE OF THE PHOTOGRAPH ARCHIVE

From the late nineteenth century onwards the method of regularly recording production photographically was not confined to Maison Worth and was adopted by other top couture establishments. Regrettably, the greater part of these archives has vanished, making the Worth albums all the more significant. The search for haute couture repositories comparable to those of Worth in extent, comprehensiveness and date has, so far, proved fruitless. The ever shifting and volatile fashion industry has always emphasized the validity of the new and next season's collection. Though companies were, to varying degrees, aware of the usefulness of their 'old' designs and records, preserving their history was not a primary concern. Designs, photographs and records in heavy bindings required much valuable space and were expensive to maintain. In times of recession or conflict the luxury industries are always among first to suffer and remedial cutbacks often require smaller premises, involving the disposal of non-essentials such as archives. The situation improved after the First World War, when a number of important photographic archives were assembled and have survived, though many are incomplete.

Paul Poiret's short time designing for Worth (Winter 1901 – Autumn 1903) obviously acquainted him with the company's photographic programme and indeed, the Worth albums for these years must record some of his work. Unfortunately, designers are not acknowledged in the albums. In his autobiography Poiret recognized the importance of early modes, describing his insatiable curiosity and forays into the Worth records: 'I got to know a type of dress that I had never before met with. I wanted to know everything that had been done before me, and several times I examined all the models successively. I even looked through the albums which told of the exuberances of good Father Worth the *couturier* of the Tuileries. They were full of samples and watercolour sketches, which spoke eloquently of the taste of the Court of the Empress'.[27] It is likely that Poiret's own inspirational 'museum' of mainly ethnographical textiles and accessories (formed after he launched his own label) was sparked off by Charles Frederick's personal 'collection of ancient costumes and old materials, lengths of lace and trimmings etc., gathered together by dint of much care and insight into their historical value. By studying these and other such relics M Worth would peruse and select his colors [*sic*] and arrange his patterns'.[28] The Worth establishment evidently had a considerable effect upon Paul Poiret's methodology and creative output, though Poiret himself glossed over the impact this great fashion house had upon him. Subsequent fashion historians (perhaps swayed by Poiret's eloquent self-promotion and undeniably startling innovations) have barely acknowledged Worth's influence on his output. A glance through the albums, however, confirms that Worth was a springboard for so many of Poiret's dazzling creations. Inevitably Poiret's first independent collections are stylistic echoes of gowns with the Worth label, featuring flowing *manteaux* and trim, tailored costumes with trailing gored skirts (p.32). There can be little doubt that Jean Worth's penchant for high waisted, Directoire-styled tea gowns and floating deshabillés, together with his delight in striped and large-scale patterned fabrics, had a significant influence on the rising star of Paris couture. From 1910 the Empire silhouette came to dominate Poiret's output and he manipulated all manner of stripes and giant patterns for dynamic decoration. Following Worth's example, his collections were recorded but on live mannequins and a group of these photographs (dated after 1918) survive in the Musée de la Mode et du Textile, Paris.

The same museum houses an impressive list of fashion archives including the extensive collection (in 79 albums) of fashion designer Madeleine Vionnet's copyright photographs dating from about 1919 to the 1930s. Vionnet was keenly aware of the iniquities of profit-sapping copying and won several lawsuits against offenders (one case was aided by the testimony of the third generation Jacques Worth). Vionnet's creations were photographed being worn by live mannequins, turned in different poses to show salient views of each garment. Vionnet also used mirrors as Worth had done in earlier years (p.45). Mannequins were positioned between mirrors angled to capture an all-round record of each garment. Like the Worth photographs, Vionnet's records were accomplished shots, in sharp focus, clearly illustrating cut and decorative details. To avoid the blur of any inadvertent movement, the mannequins were provided with a vertical bar to hold and so steady themselves. Again as in the Worth photographs, a design number was placed in the foreground but to assert unequivocally her creative rights, Vionnet always included her name and an exact date.

In the Musée de la Mode de la Ville de Paris, in the 16th arrondissement, the Palais Galliera has both a major couture collection and library. Recognizing the growing importance of designer, press and agency photographs, and fashion-related paper ephemera, in 1984 the then director Guillaume Garnier established the Department d'Arts Graphiques et Photographies. It houses an abundant diversity of rare fashion ephemera and designer archival material, such as photographs of the work of the eminent couturiers Boué Soeurs (*c*.1899–1935). Later in the twentieth century, following in the footsteps of Charles Frederick Worth, a number of couturiers – most notably Cristobal Balenciaga – set examples of good archival practice by documenting their output meticulously. *Croquis* (or sketches), client

LEFT — Blouse, khaki voile trimmed with passementeries c.1904. AAD/1982/1/20

RIGHT — Jacket, embroidered velvet, 1906-8. AAD/1982/1/31

ABOVE — Worth salons with two models from the *cabine de mannequins* (Léon Roger-Milès, *Les Créateurs de la Mode*, Paris, 1910)

OPPOSITE — Copyright photograph of an evening gown, silk and tulle with velvet appliqué. Designed by Madeleine Vionnet, 1938. Musée de la Mode et du Textile, Paris. Photo Les Arts Décoratifs, Paris

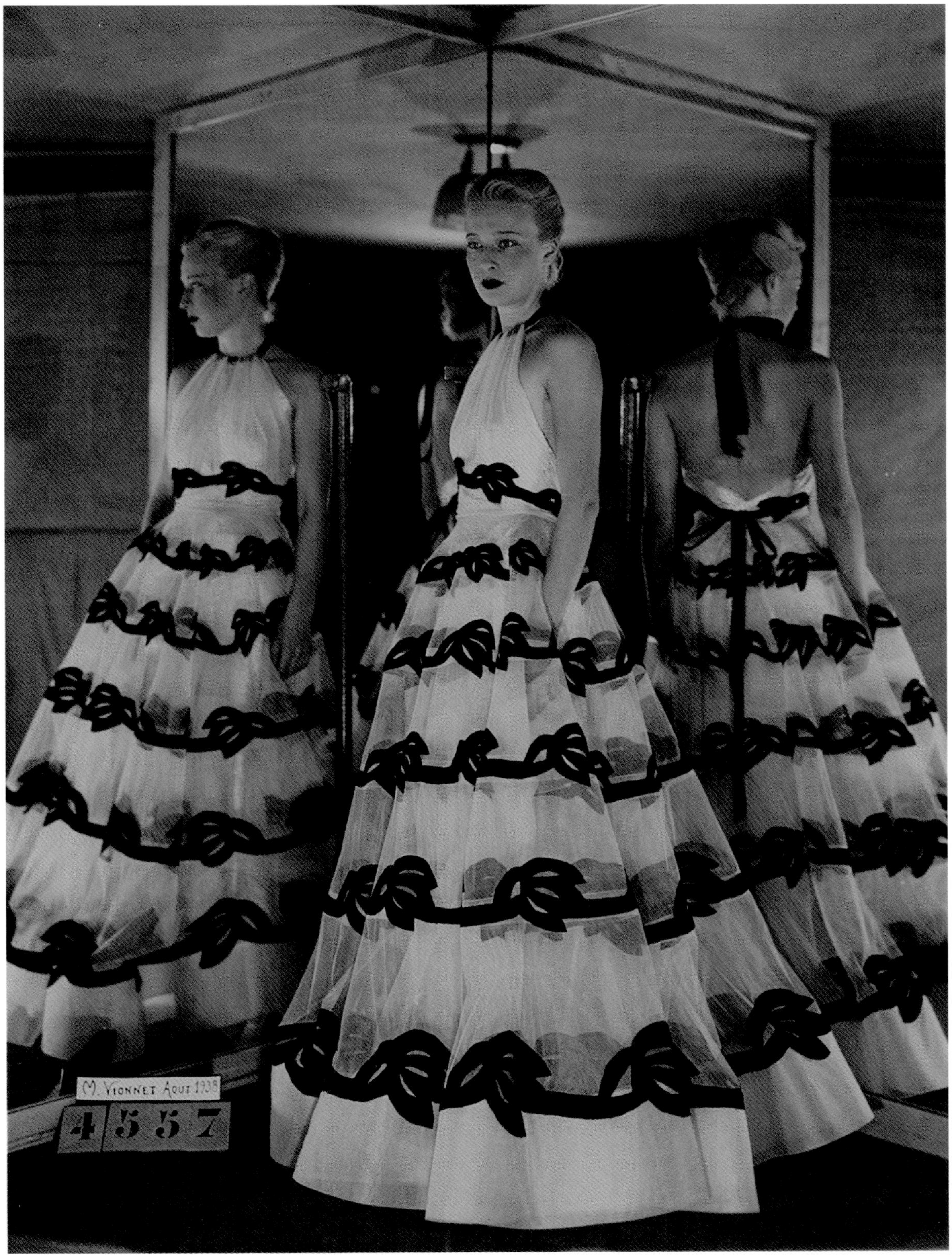
M. VIONNET AOUT 1938
4557

BELOW, LEFT TO RIGHT –
Paletot, leopard skin, 1906-8. AAD/1982/1/31

Jacket, lightweight blue wool, 1904-5. AAD/1982/1/29

OPPOSITE – Evening mantle, yellow crêpe de Chine bordered with fur, 1912. AAD/1982/1/36

notebooks, fabric and trimming samples, and house photographs were used to record each collection. Photographs include catwalk mannequins brandishing cards with model numbers, as well as house models with the by now traditional label giving designer, date and design number. The House of Balenciaga continues to care for and extend this exemplary archive. Survival in precarious recessionary times compelled fashion businesses to change and adapt. In the sometimes frenetic pursuit of 'must have' styles, companies became increasingly aware of the wealth of ideas residing in their archives. Karl Lagerfeld for Chanel led the way with his inspired reworkings of clothes originally conceived by Coco Chanel. At Balenciaga, Nicolas Ghesquière captured the essence of Cristobal Balenciaga's classic designs in works with up-to-the-minute appeal. In the hands of Christopher Bailey the revisionist Burberry check and trench coat became international best sellers. Fashion companies safeguarded and expanded their archives, even employing curators to care for and add to varied collections of drawings, photographs, textile samples, film, garments and accessories. Thus, the likes of Chanel, Dior, Lanvin, Pierre Cardin, Yves Saint Laurent, Hermès, Capucci, Valentino, Armani, Ferragamo and Calvin Klein own multifarious archives that instantly provide a wide range of company information and, most significantly, feed into their latest designs.

NOTES

1. James Laver, *Museum Piece* (London, 1963), pp.248-9.
2. V&A Registered Papers, Archive of Art and Design.
3. V&A Registered Papers, Archive of Art and Design.
4. Engraving, Illustration and Designs Departmental catalogue, V&A.
5. Engraving, Illustration and Designs Departmental catalogue, V&A.
6. Charles Harvard Gibbs-Smith, *Costume* (Journal of the Costume Society), no.10, 1976.
7. Riley, 1962, p.12.
8. Julian Osgood Field, *More Uncensored Recollections* (London, 1926), p.73.
9. J-P. Worth 1928.
10. Eileen Bigland, *Ouida: The Passionate Victorian* (London, 1950), p.193.
11. Ouida [Maria Louise Ramé], *A House Party* (London, 1887), ch.5.
12. Émile Zola, *La Curée* [1872] (Oxford, 2004), p.170.
13. Coleman 1989, p.202.
14. Diana de Marly unearthed the in-house price code, which was based on the phrase 'Chers Frères Worth, on gagne Dieu mais avec volonté-reflechissez'. The first letter of each word represented a number from 1 to 0. Thus c=1, f=2, w=3, o=4, g=5, d=6, m=7, a=8, v=9, r=0. *Worth, Father of Haute Couture* (London, 1980), p.141.
15. Diana de Marly, cited note 14, p.142.
16. Jean-Philippe Worth, *The Lady's Realm*, November 1896.
17. Nancy Hall-Duncan 1979, p.30
18. Valerie Lloyd, *Fashion 1900-1939* (London, 1975), p.22.
19. From unnamed client's letter, originally published in *The Strand Magazine* and quoted in the *Milwaukee Sentinel*, 10 March 1895, when reporting the death of Charles Frederick.
20. Email correspondence with the Author, April 2013.
21. Elizabeth Anne McCauley, 'Photography and the Cult of Appearances', in Groom 2012, p.200.
22. Émile Zola, *La Curée* [1872] (Oxford, 2004), p.91.
23. Émile Zola, *Au Bonheur des Dames* [1883] (Oxford, 2008), p.6.
24. J-P. Worth 1908, n.p.
25. J-P. Worth, as cited note 14.
26. Coleman 1989, p.60.
27. Paul Poiret, *My First Fifty Years* (London, 1931), p.62.
28. *The Post*, Chicago, 11 March 1895.

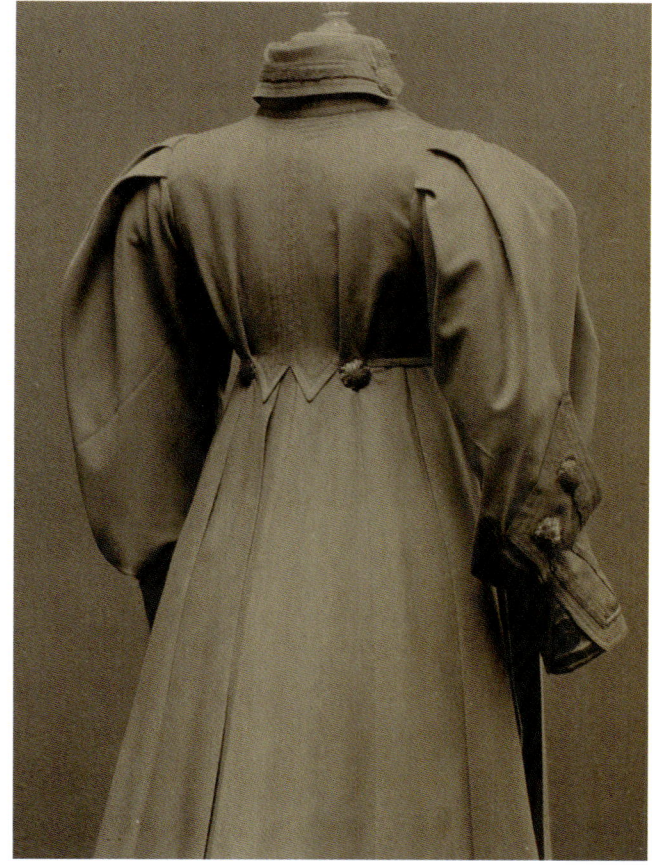

8554. Manteau Crêpe de chine jaune garni Skungs
j.br   crêpe de chine jaune fwb
b.or   Liberty noir   ocr   agr
         mro   avec fourrure: xcmg

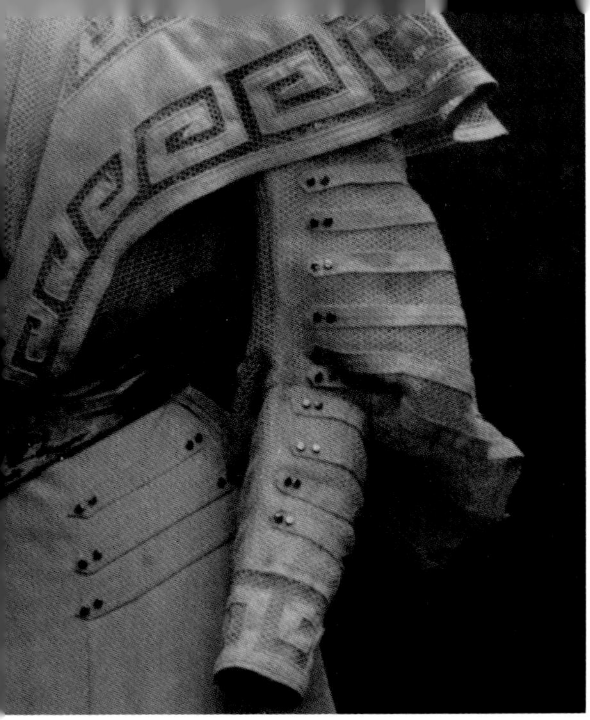
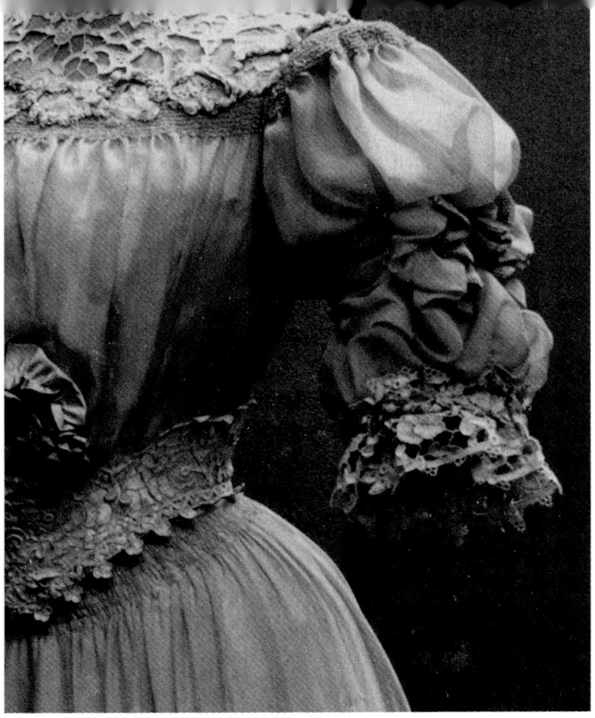
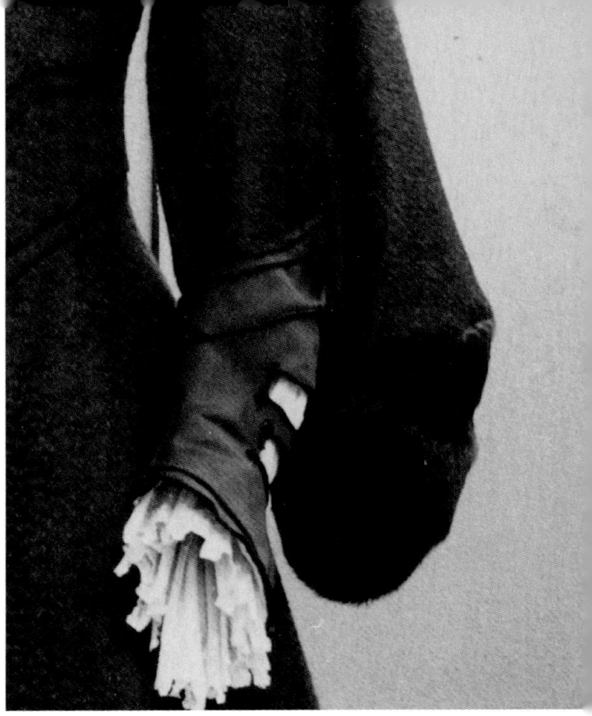
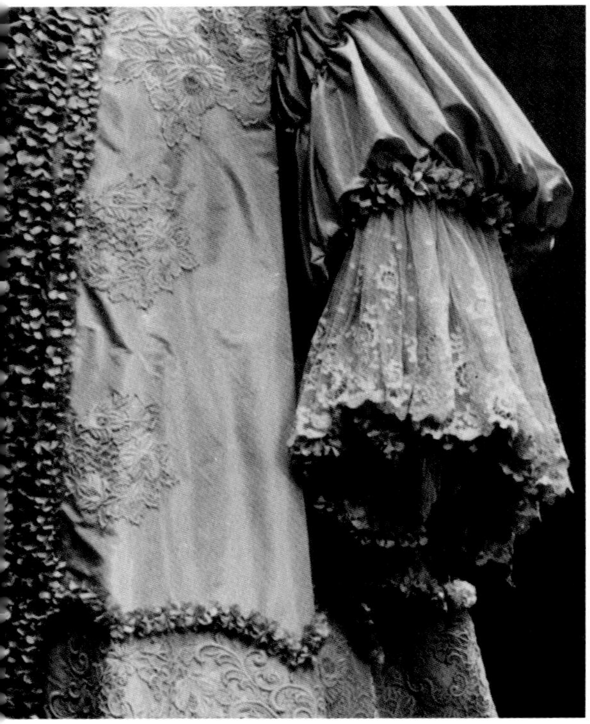
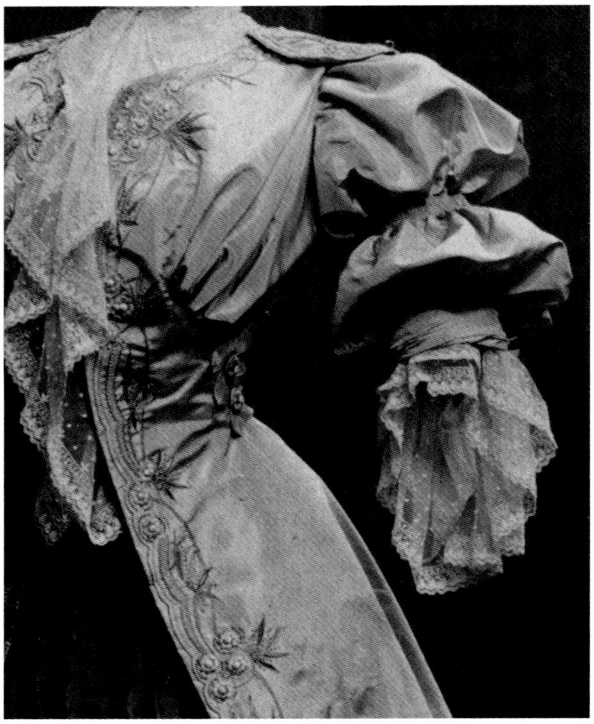
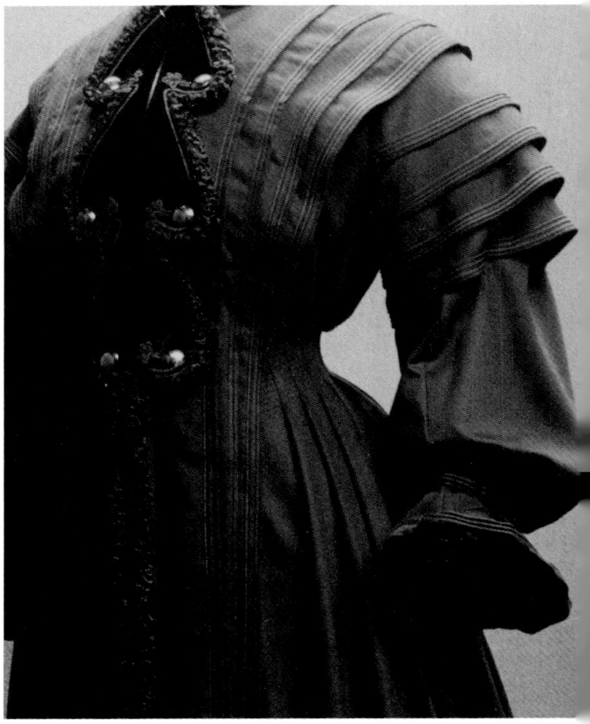
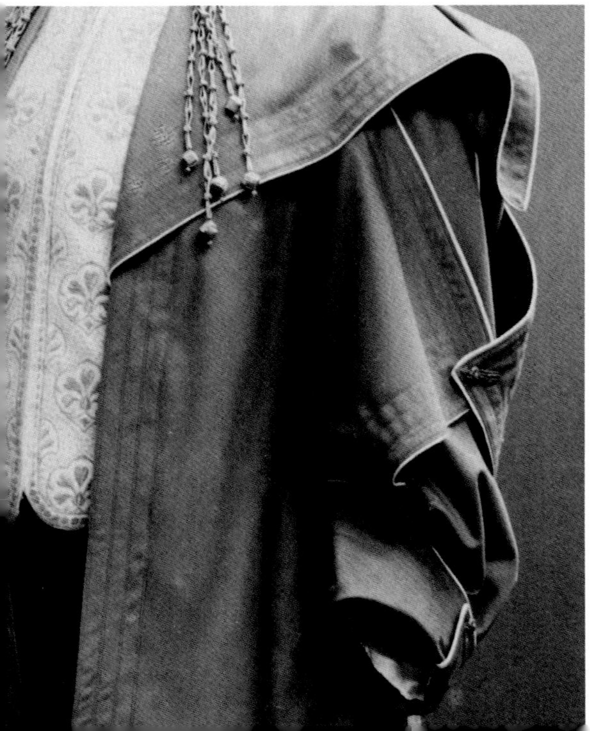
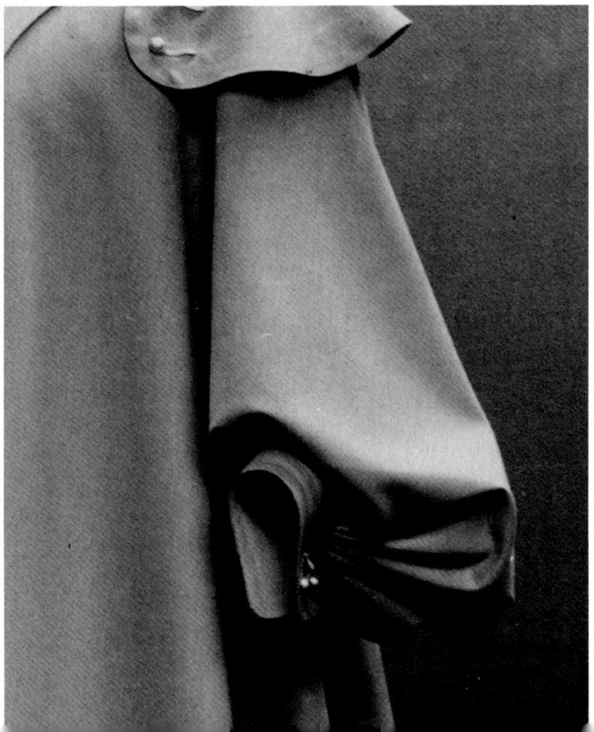
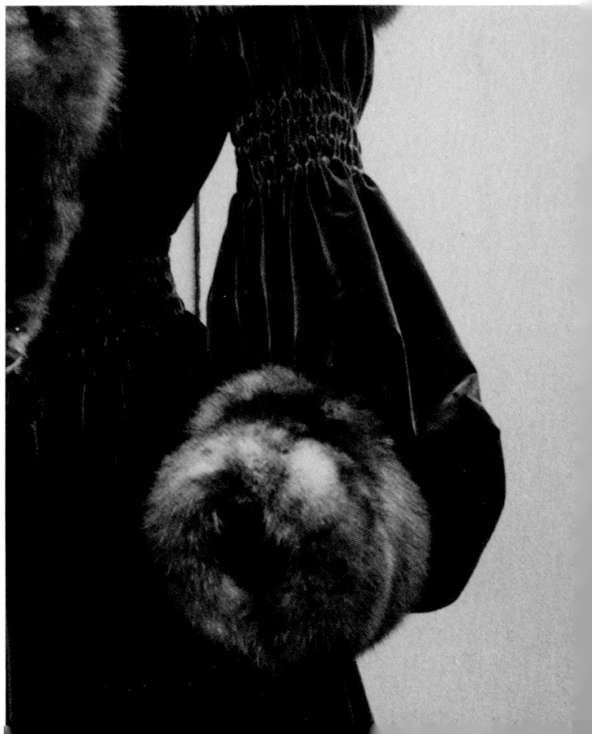

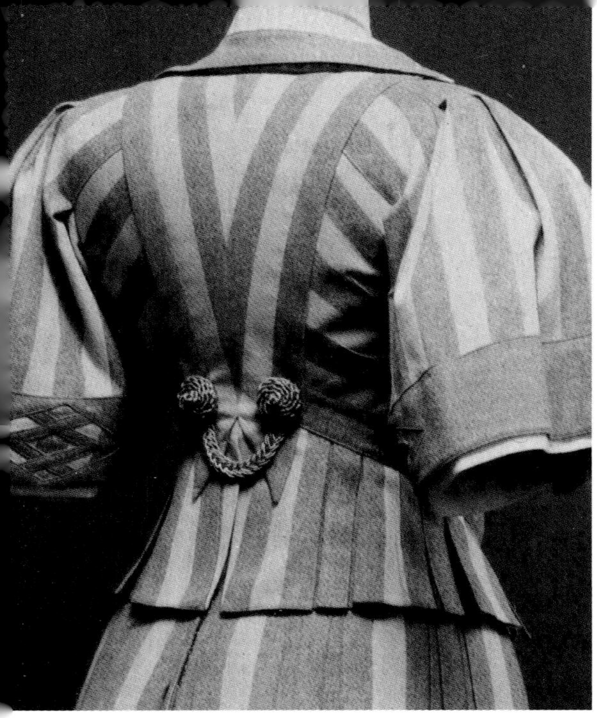
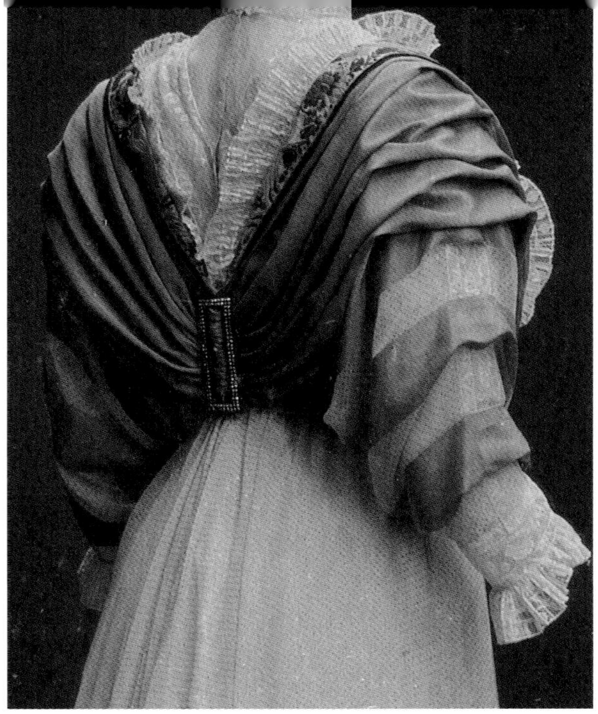
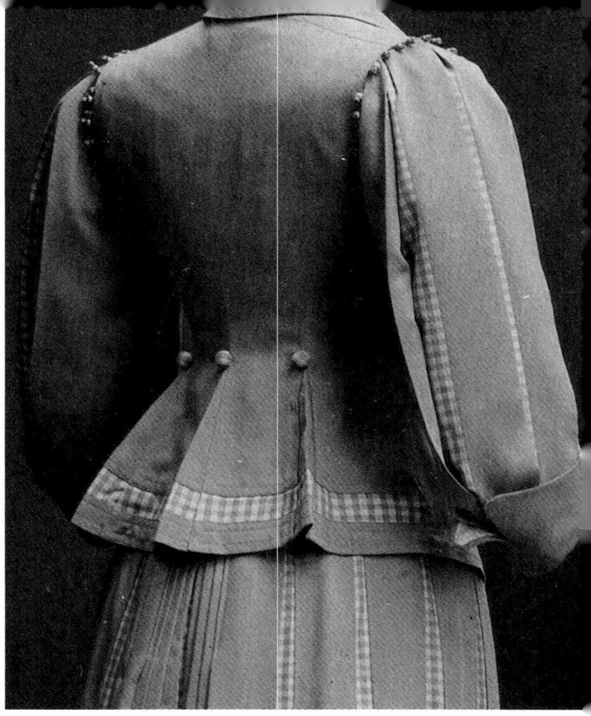
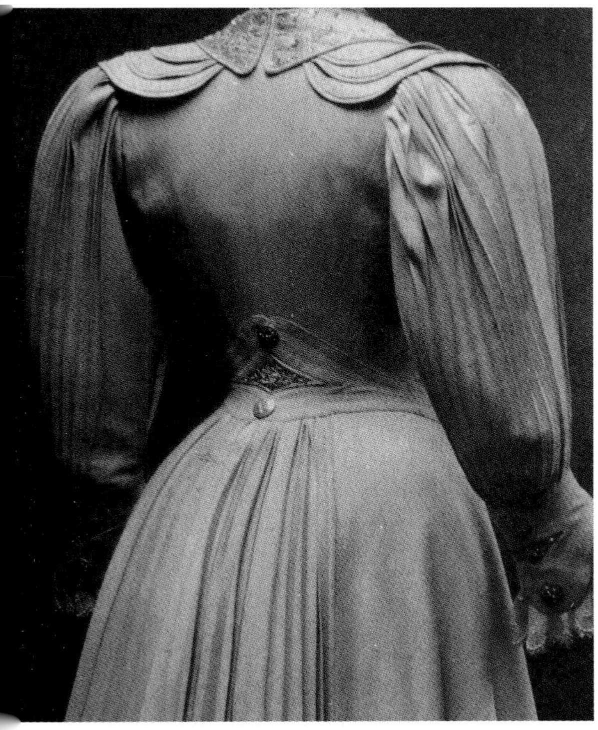
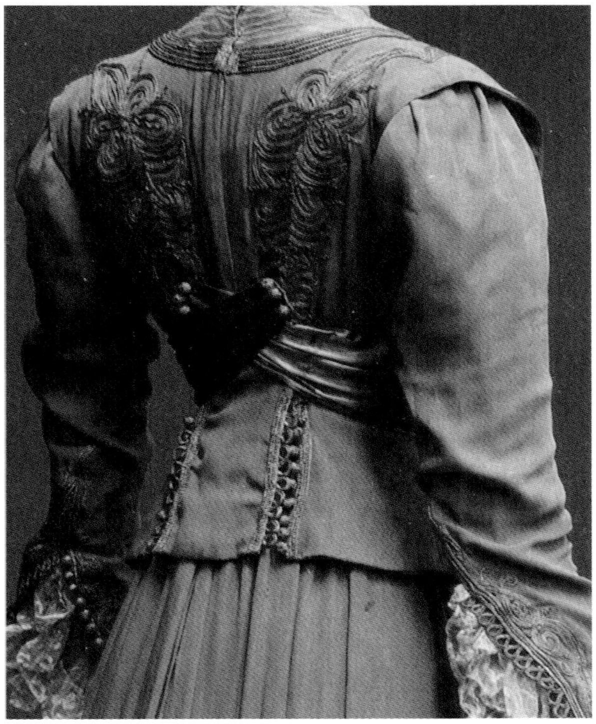
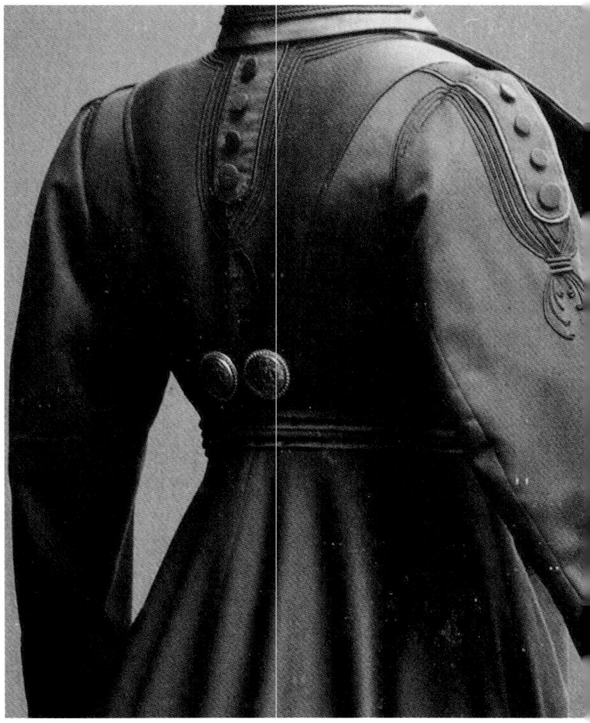
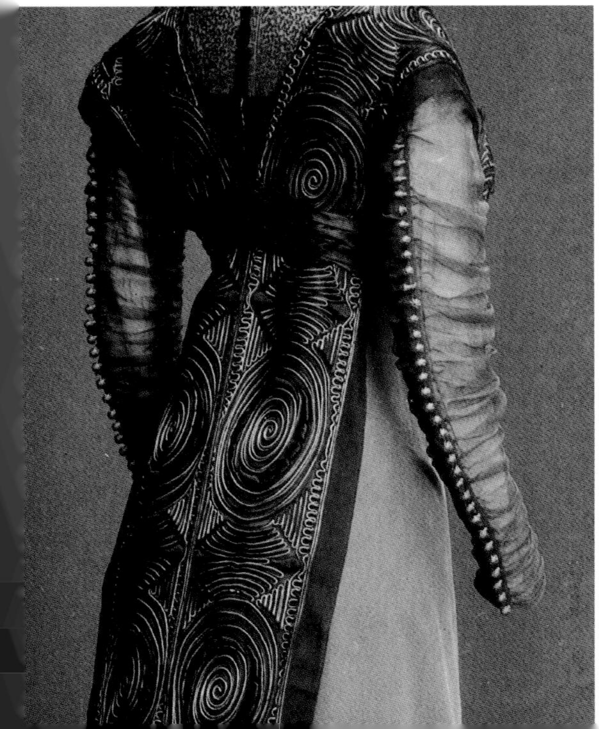
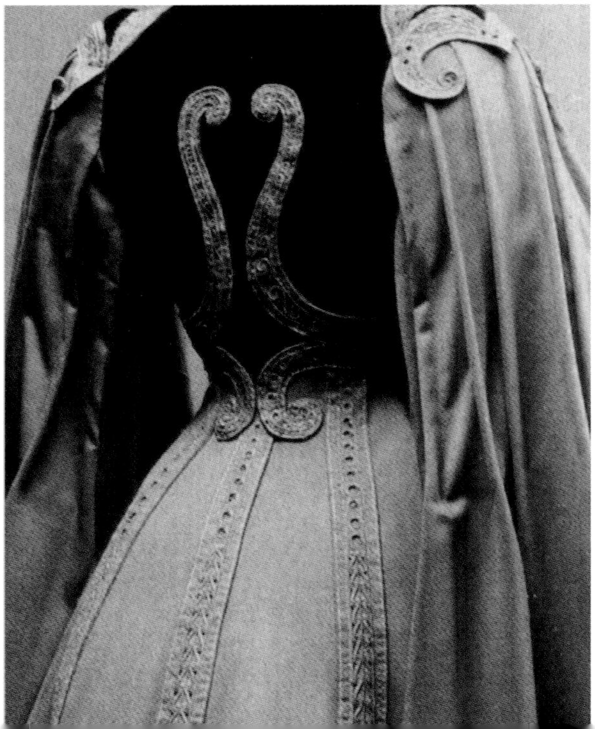
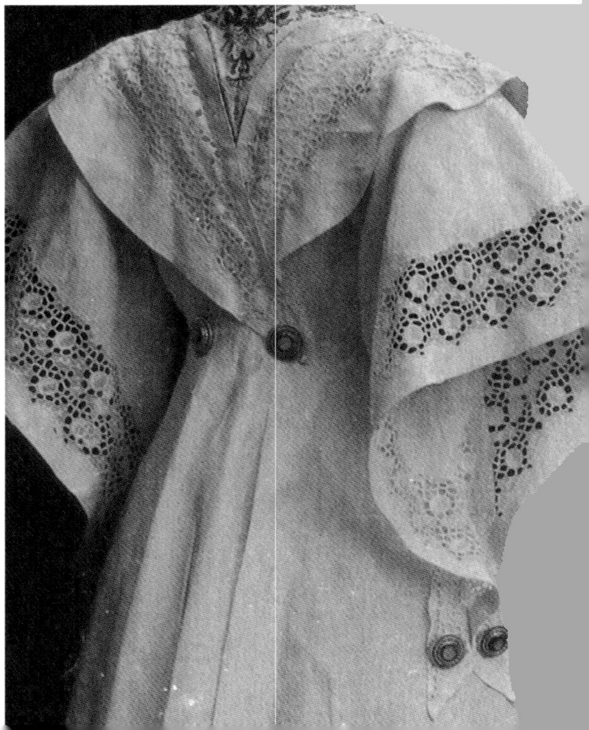

3
TAILORING
VALERIE D. MENDES

The name Worth, synonymous with evening wear in sumptuous fabrics profusely decorated with an array of laces and embroideries, is not immediately associated with the art of tailoring. According to an obituary note in *The Illustrated London News* (23 March 1895), Charles Frederick Worth did not like the 'tailor made', saying that it made ladies look like stable boys.[1] An interview a year later with his son Jean (the company's artistic director) partly explained a continued emphasis on luxurious gowns and frou-frou: 'I firmly believe that the tailor-made gown has gone far to destroy feminine elegance. Perhaps I am somewhat prejudiced: but still, I am the first to admit that when a lady is travelling or taking part in a bona fide mountaineering expedition, or indeed, even when she is driving in a dog cart or on a four-in-hand, it is evident that rough tweeds and serges are much more suitable to the occasion than silks and laces. But you must remember that many women carry this love of the tailor-made very much further than that; they would if they could come down to dinner in a coat and skirt…'.[2] The same interview revealed his antipathy for clothing which he felt to be outlandish or inelegant: 'I need hardly tell you that I myself have never made any cycling costumes; and further, that I entirely approve of the English skirt. Nothing can be more ungraceful and unfeminine than knickerbockers, which make the wearer, when a lady, look like a little dwarf'. In spite of Jean's reservations, the company's archive of photograph albums reveal how Maison Worth satisfied the lucrative and growing demand for elegantly tailored daywear to suit the affluent 'new woman'. They illustrate how Worth married elements from the sphere of dressmaking with those of traditional tailoring, resulting in softly tailored hybrid garments that were both distinctive and sophisticated.

Obviously the crème de la crème did not spend every waking hour draped in flowing 'at home' creations or arrayed flamboyantly to attend balls, court functions or similar grand events. Between the déshabillés of early morning and the tea gowns of late afternoon, women increasingly had commitments and activities that demanded attire of a fairly practical nature in durable fabrics – in fact they needed tailor-mades. The season, time of day and occasion dictated how the beau monde dressed. Women who could afford Worth belonged to this elite group, or to the shadowy but equally well off demi-monde. Tailor-mades were perfect for the not yet obsolete custom of calling, as well as for shopping, travelling and walking. In January 1908, *Harper's Bazar* launched a series of articles titled 'Individuality in Dress' by WORTH OF PARIS in which Jean Worth shamelessly flattered the American readers (potential cash-paying customers), touching on the validity of tailor-mades: 'American women are very delightful to dress. They cultivate a natural *espièglerie*, an alertness, a distinction that causes them to look superb in handsome gowns… their instinct for dress is accurate and penetrating; they are sensible lovers of the beautiful for its own sake, and possess a keen feeling for the exigencies of the "occasion". No one meets a travelling American in chiffon. She voyages in tailor-made tweeds, a picture of appropriate smartness'.[3] While the Worth photographs feature glorious and, at times, outrageous eveningwear, they also depict understated, immaculately made, tailored daywear. Women have always treasured their special occasion clothes, which were frequently passed from generation to generation, while their less ostentatious daywear was frequently discarded. Actual tailor-made couture of the late nineteenth and early twentieth centuries is hardly plentiful though frailer special occasion gowns survive in fair quantities. Fortunately tailoring of the period is abundantly recorded in a wide range of contemporary sources including a plethora of tailoring manuals, fashion magazines, biographies, catalogues, advertisements and, of course, photographs. It could be argued that a photograph from the Worth albums illustrating both front and back of a creation fresh from the tailoring workshop is the next best thing to viewing the actual garment.

'LE STYLE ANGLAIS'

The albums track (somewhat erratically) the house's tailoring output chronologically and season by season. Like other leading Paris couturiers of the time, such as Félix and Laferrière, Worth had the usual complement of ateliers specializing in tailoring, *flou*, bodice and skirt making, furs, lingerie, embroidery etc. Within each atelier a strict hierarchy prevailed from *la première* and *la seconde* to *premières mains* and *les petites mains*. Photographs of Paris couture houses at work reveal that – following tradition – the tailoring workrooms were staffed mainly by men, who cut and assembled, with an occasional female hand to undertake finishing. Men were usually furriers, though the fur ateliers had increasing numbers of female staff. While Paris was still confident in its role as the epicentre of fashion, it was becoming more wary of the competition from London's Savile Row tailors. The London-based firms Redfern and Creed, renowned for their expert tailoring, ran successful Paris branches. Besides menswear, Creed specialized in *costumes d'amazones* (riding habits) for women clients and by the early 1900s it had added tailored fashion to its range. It is recorded that so great was the demand for tailored clothes (especially sportswear) in France that a number of Paris couturiers had to recruit skilled English tailors.[4] Pared down English tailored menswear carried a powerful cachet and had considerable influence on Paris designers. In particular the eighteenth- and early nineteenth-century *style anglais* was much admired. Inspiration was taken from a wide range of sources from portraits of English gentry in their unadorned hunting frock coats to representations of George 'Beau' Brummell in his spotless metropolitan blue-black and white. Worth, along with other Paris couturiers, imposed a feminine chic on its reinventions of menswear classics.

THE ART OF TAILORING

Jean, like his father before him, had a thorough understanding of the textile industries. Together with his fabric buyers, he sourced only the highest quality cloths for the tailoring workrooms. Though the Worths claimed to patronise only French textile manufacturers, it is likely that the then-flourishing weaving industries of Scotland and England provided Maison Worth with some fine wools and tweeds. Lighter weight linens and cottons for late spring and summer costumes probably originated in England, Ireland and Italy as well as France. Silks specified by Jean were woven to order in Lyons – 'the silk looms of Lyons weave my own designs, and the very colors [*sic*] are of my choosing'.[5] Coleman devoted a whole chapter to textiles used by Worth and scrutinized the crucial role played by the house in the

Redingote, lightweight wool
trimmed with astrakhan, c.1900
AAD/1982/1/23

survival of the Lyons weaving industry.⁶ A successful tailored ensemble has always depended on accurate measurement and cut, precise assembly and careful fitting. *The Queen* reported in 1904 that 'The chief feature noticeable in the Parisian tailor-made garments is the exquisite cut.'⁷ Jean was a believer in simplicity and ensured that elegantly tailored lines were not marred by inappropriate decoration. The exact techniques of Worth tailors are not recorded but it is assumed that they followed the time-honoured process of taking a client's accurate measurements and drafting mathematically precise patterns (toiles) usually in muslin. Charles Frederick confirmed this in an unattributed early 1890s interview: 'My models are first of all made in black and white muslin and then copied in the material and colouring which I select…'.⁸ Customarily muslin pattern pieces are assembled, tried on the client, altered for a perfect fit and then taken apart to cut the cloth. Then follows the skilled and complex practice of tailored construction involving interfacings, facings, padding, basting, linings, pressing and finishing – interspersed with regular fittings.

To select clothes for the coming season royalty, aristocrats and a select band of favoured or ultra-rich clients had consultations with the couturier himself at 7 rue de la Paix, while the less privileged were advised by a trusted vendeuse. An extensive work force aided by outworkers enabled Worth to complete orders quickly, even though clothes were made *sur mesure*, followed by the requisite number of fittings. Exceptions were made for customers outside France – their measurements (and sometimes dress forms made to their shape) were kept by the house and clothes made and dispatched to order. In the early 1900s most major couture houses had a *cabine de mannequins* and it was usual for mannequins to parade through the salons wearing the latest collection for customers to consider. Léon Roger-Milès reported that a mannequin's day was utterly exhausting as they passed through the salons time after time, changing regularly into different ensembles. He writes poetically of an infinity of costumes that had to be reinvented endlessly for a long list of occasions: 'ceremonies officielles ou familiales, conferences, receptions à l'Académie, repetitions générale, sermons, séances de musique de chambre diners, concerts, bals, soupers aux cabarets, théâtres, sans oublier les courses, les promenades hors la ville, l'auto, les voyages, les tenues de sleeping et de bateaux, de plage et de montagne et bientôt d'aviation: et beaucoup d'autres que j'oublie.'⁹ After seeing new creations worn by mannequins, customers might possibly have consulted the photographs as supplementary guides, though there is no corroborative evidence.

THE FULL-LENGTH COAT

The photographs indicate that, after 1900, Maison Worth made an increasing number of tailored styles. Jean and his design atelier devised new looks and became adept at composing variations on a theme. The earliest photographs are undated but stylistically sit between 1889 and 1901. They contain a series of imposing full-length coats based upon men's great coats and long frock coats, adapted to meet the desires of fashionable women. The most practical were for wear in inclement weather or, as a *cache poussière* (dust coat) designed to give protection when motoring in open vehicles of the period. A long, streamlined, double-breasted coat of 1900 with slightly puffed sleeves and deep, curved revers is a timeless classic, a forerunner of the iconic Biba maxi-coat of the late 1960s (p.72, left). Of similar length are a group of autumn into winter promenade coats cut *en princesse*, the line that Worth had assiduously promoted since the 1860s. These sweeping coats are described as redingotes, *grand manteaux* or simply *manteaux*. They were fitted close to the body with nipped in waists and invariably had warm linings and fur trimmings. Of course Worth used only the costliest furs, such as astrakhan, ermine and sable. Dating from 1900 a double-breasted coat has a slightly raised waist and, for extra protection, a stand up collar is fitted within wide astrakhan revers. Strong tailored lines are softened by the gleaming fur's curled texture as well as a silk streamer, pulled almost negligently through the front fastening. Four years later Worth rang the changes creating an open fronted coat in

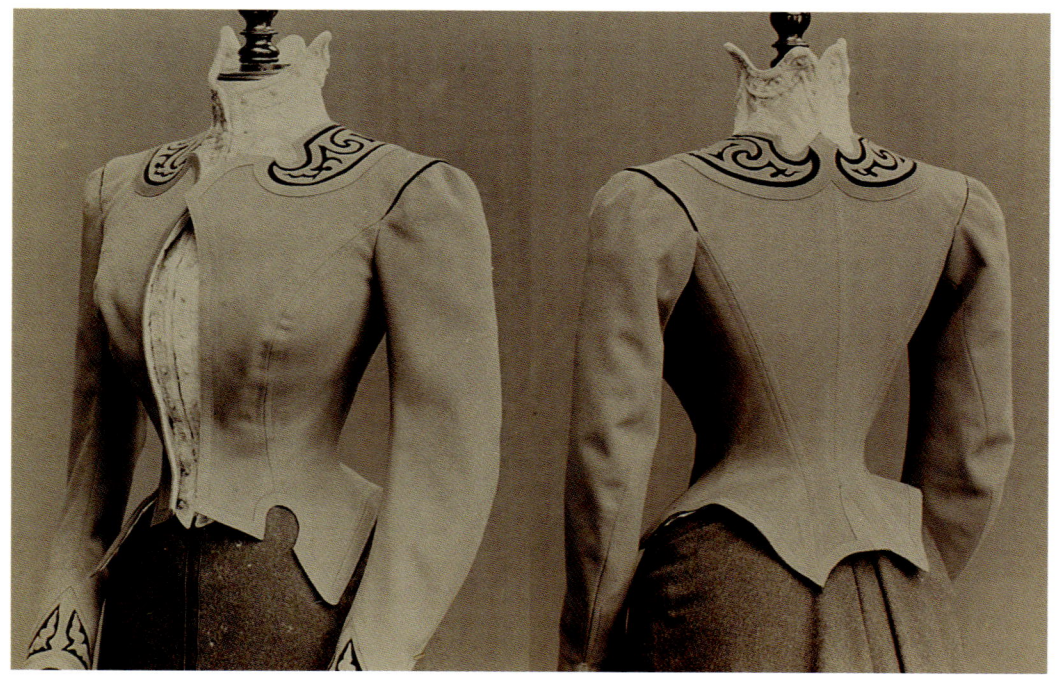

OPPOSITE, LEFT TO RIGHT – Redingote, sky-blue lightweight wool with ecru *entredeux*, c.1904. AAD/1932/1/28

Jacket, mid-green lightweight wool with découpé cuffs and neckline, 1899–1900. AAD/1932/1/21

sky-blue cloth. Capturing an impression of romance and drama he took inspiration from menswear of the Napoleonic era and made reference to the Carrick overcoat with its multi-layered cape. A band of muslin protects the hemline from contact with the floor and stops it gathering any detritus. The year 1904 appears to have been a bumper year for the streamlined redingote. *The Queen's* coverage of the races at Longchamps noted that 'Long, severely-cut, tailor-made cloth redingotes were also eminently popular and looked particularly chic donned by some elegant mondaines'.[10] The same article gives an interesting insight into fashion espionage as the journalist observed dressmakers and girls from well-known couturiers following those 'mondaines' who were wearing the most sensational gowns. Obviously the spies committed new shapes, details and colours to memory, to be sketched and copied as soon as they returned to the workplace.

USE OF FUR

To an elite, far removed from ethical concerns, furs (with a Worth label) were highly desirable and played a key role in the ostentatious display of their wealth. *The Queen* reported in 1902 that the very best furs were sold in London but made up in Paris. It was asserted 'that members of the Imperial Russian family invariably send their sable and fox skins to be worked in Paris… The making up of furs is an art in which the Parisian furrier excels'.[11] Skilled craftsmen in Worth's atelier tailored pelts as if they were fabric – demonstrated by a collection of form-fitting jackets dating from about 1900. Comparable jackets in lightweight wool had bold, linear patterns of applied braid and soutache, and in similar mode silk ribbon was applied in trelliswork with swirls over a moleskin jacket. The Worth furriers perfected a method of shearing fur into three-dimensional patterns; horizontal lines of scallops were popular. Sable and other expensive furs were used to trim garments but most extravagant of all were voluminous floor-length fur winter coats and long ermine evening coats. Fur lovers had been warned in *The Queen* that 'only a sylph-like figure could carry off a sable or ermine Empire coat without looking like a stuffed bear'.[12] Such was the cachet of an exclusive fur that a report in the same magazine went into raptures about a magnificent array of furs by Worth sent over from Paris to be displayed in the London house for a mere three days. 'It was an exceptional privilege to view these exclusive confections, which included regal wraps of chinchilla, broadtail and ermine, while a specially significant stress was laid on some superfine skins of silver fox. A notably magnificent ermine wrap had a broad band of skunk carried in a diagonal line right across the back, another band round the throat forming a natural stole, or if thrown the reverse way revealed a brocade rever, the dominant green note of which was taken up in an emerald-green satin lining… A supreme example of the furrier's art was exhibited in a long chinchilla wrap, the skins of which were worked in delicate mosaic patternings, a panel effect back and front being defined by a bordering of the fur raised in relief, a great rever collar falling about the shoulders. There were also many exquisite stole and muff sets of ermine trimmed with other furs, such as skunk, the deep rich brown of which found an admirable contrast in the purity of the white skins. From every aspect this was to be accounted an altogether unique exhibition, and in the best sense worthy of the great name of Worth'.[13] Numerous garments could be purchased with, or at a lower price without, fur trimmings. At this date, it was most unlikely that this was an option directed by moral aversion to fur. Couture furs signalled wealth and status, and as yet their wearers had not been not persuaded to abandon them by the burgeoning animal rights movement. Members of the Society for the Preservation of Birds (Edward VII sanctioned the prefix 'Royal' in 1904) and America's Audubon Society were often opposed to the fur trade.

THE COSTUME

From the early 1900s to the outbreak of the First World War Worth's tailors excelled in the production of costumes in which long skirts were teamed with a variety of jackets in an array of fabrics with a multitude of subtle decorative touches. Masterpieces of softly tailored construction, they are evidence that Worth, world renowned for glittering evening gowns, could also be relied on for tailoring of immense distinction. Delicate blouses with stand up collars went under the jackets and were made in the finest voiles and silks, often with minute pintucks, lace insertions and intricate embroidery. A whole album is devoted to elaborate blouses, which were displayed on half stands throughout the salons at 7 rue de la Paix. Most have long, white cotton basques to tuck into the skirt and pinned to each garment is a 'Worth Paris' label with model number and description of the blouse.

THE PERFECTLY ALIGNED STRIPE

Jean was a great believer in stripes, entrusting them to clever cutters and fitters to achieve both the symmetry and the carefully calculated asymmetry he found so pleasing. Customers could select from stripes that ranged from the narrowest of pin stripes to immense deck chair stripes. An ensemble (for cold weather wear) with a long fitted jacket over a flared skirt made in striped wool was painstakingly constructed and, as in all high class tailoring, every stripe was perfectly aligned. A variation in blue-and-white striped cotton with crisp white turn-back cuffs and revers was a popular, fresh combination for boating or visits to fashionable coastal resorts. Occasionally caution was abandoned in eye-catching, optically challenging ensembles. In black-and-white linen the softly pleated skirt has unimpeded vertical stripes while its companion jacket is cut to achieve dazzling panels of chevron stripes. This summer seaside ensemble was not for the faint hearted; it required a supremely confident owner and demanded to be worn with panache. For less daring summer spirits, throughout the 1900s Worth made white linen costumes enlivened with discreet striped trimmings, monochrome embroidery or jaunty pleated borders.

NAMING THE DESIGNS

In 1904 Worth made a move towards naming designs when a hooded cape was designated 'Algeriez', but it wasn't until 1909–10 that the house began to assign titles on a regular basis. In 1886 the prolific writer Octave Uzanne asked his readers, in a mocking fashion, if they remembered the *paletot* 'Lydie' or the *pardessus* 'Lalla Roukh' as well as the *sortie de bal* 'Vespertina'?[14] The question of giving garments '*un nom de baptême*' also intrigued and amused Léon Roger-Milès, who duly reflected upon the habit. Reporting back to him (after

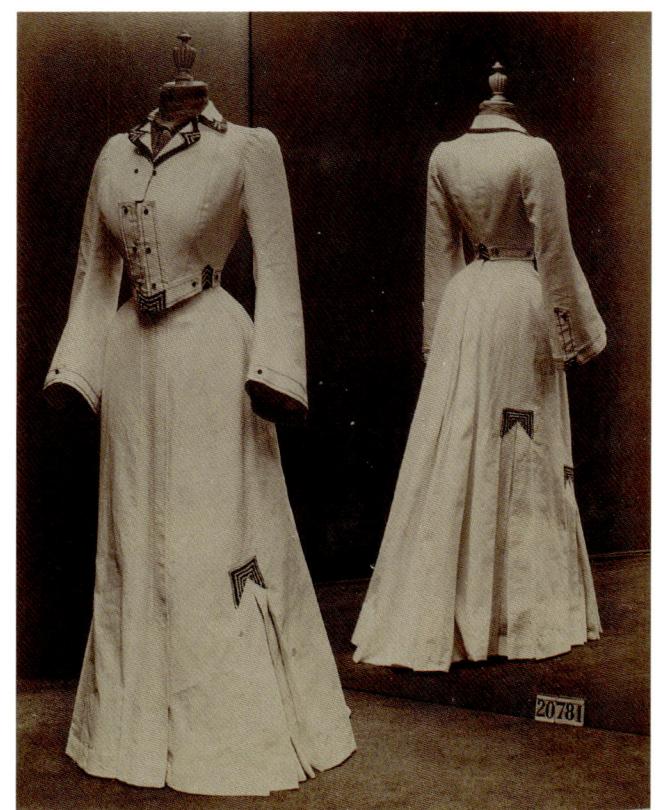

TOP LEFT — Redingote, Canadian mink, 1899–1900. AAD/1982/1/21

TOP RIGHT — Costume, striped wool, 1903. AAD/1982/1/1

BELOW LEFT — Costume, white linen with black stripes and edged with white silk, 1906. AAD/1982/1/8

BELOW RIGHT — Costume, white linen and silk tussore, 1903. AAD/1982/1/1

OPPOSITE — Costume, lightweight sky-blue wool with embroidery and lace, 1905. AAD/1982/1/6

56 — TAILORING

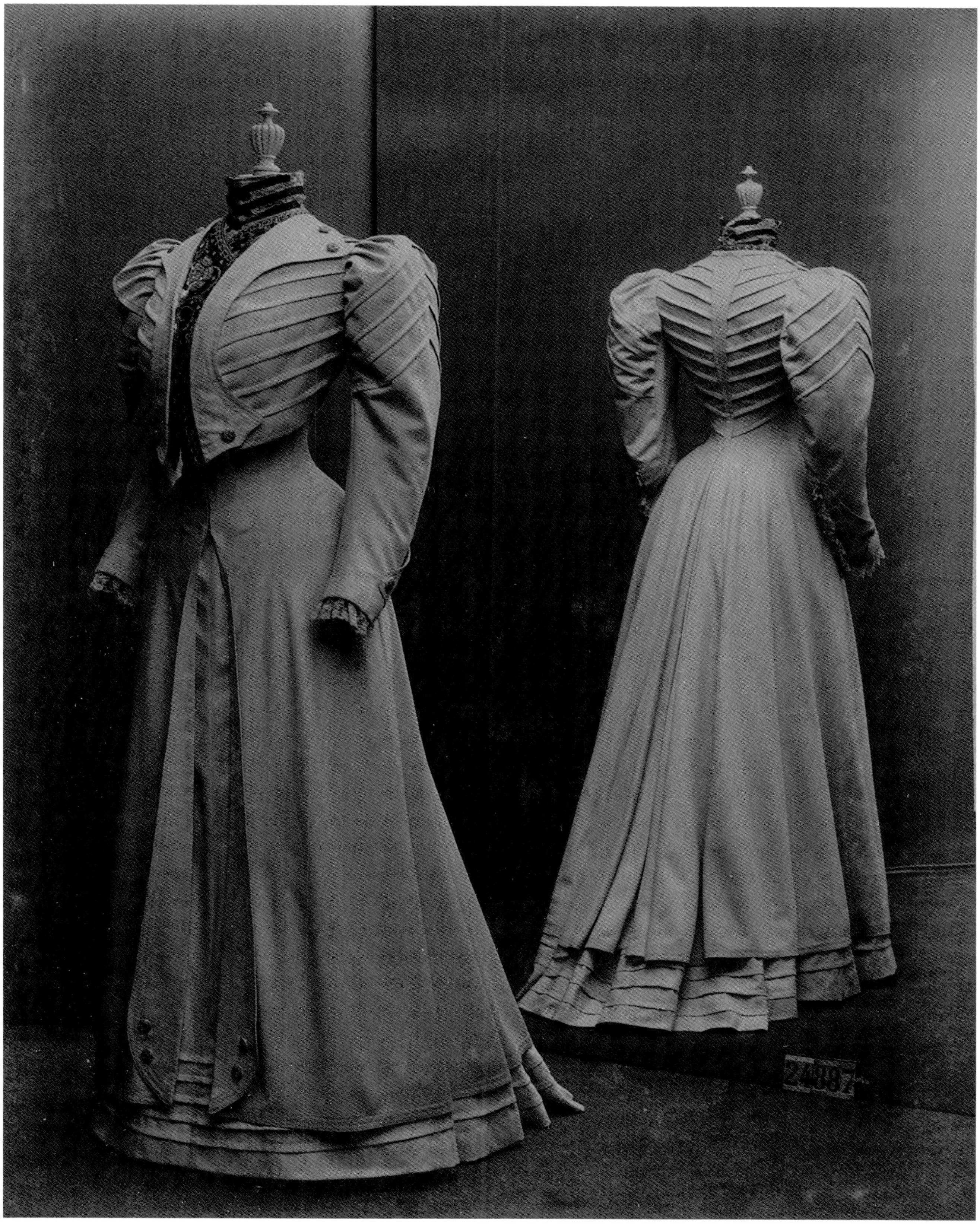
24887

BELOW — Costume, heliotrope velvet, green tussore silk and taffeta with applied braid, 1905. AAD/1982/1/6

OPPOSITE — 'Danton', costume, beige vicuña with striped silk revers and cuffs, 1912-13. AAD/1982/1/18

Danton

5884. Costume en Vigogne beige

Costume seul — 9cr bfg.

Costume avec blouse — 9cr bfg.

62 — TAILORING

OPPOSITE – 'Pégase', costume, lightweight blue wool with striped borders and lower skirt, 1910-11. AAD/1982/1/14

ABOVE AND BELOW – 'Zéa', costume, black velvet with white satin collar, 1912-13. AAD/1982/1/17

Costume, embroidered velvet and 'Liberty' satin, 1908-9. AAD/1982/1/10

ABOVE, LEFT TO RIGHT –
Costume, embroidered green lightweight wool and black satin, 1908-9. AAD/1982/1/10

'Fortunio', costume, lightweight grey wool, 1910-11. AAD/1982/1/14

OPPOSITE – 'Albano', costume tailleur, grey wool trimmed with astrakhan, 1912-13. AAD/1982/1/17

glittering paillettes vie for supremacy'.[16] He advocated harmony and discretion in fashion (hallmarks of classic tailoring), warning against 'a complete mêlée of materials'.[17] In his chapter 'Occasion Should Govern Toilette' for Florence Hull Winterburn, he conceded that 'in the morning we will admit the suitability of a tailor-made gown', adding sanctimoniously, 'worn with a blouse of excessive neatness'.[18] His designs avoided excessively mannish looks by blending dressmaking's soft lines and decorative overlays with tailoring's precision cutting and construction. Jean himself was a dapper dresser (fond of an occasional bohemian flourish) and with ease he reworked the masculine tailored styles that were so familiar to him into high fashion for elegant women clients. He became especially adept at 'feminizing' men's frock coats, tail coats and waistcoats – the latter often made in luxurious pale coloured silks, and cut to fit provocatively tightly around curvaceous (corseted) torsos. Early 1900s fashion journalists were intrigued by such cross-over styling and illustrators such as Adolf Sandoz and E. Gérin liked nothing better than to portray chic Parisiennes promenading in their trimly tailored Worth costumes. Fortunately for the house, Jean's nephew and successor as designer, Jean-Charles, had a complete understanding of the relevance and appeal of the perfectly constructed *tailleur* and continued the fusion tradition established by his uncle.

NOTES

1. Album of Obituaries for Charles Frederick Worth.
2. Jean-Philippe Worth, quoted in Marie A. Belloc, 'La Maison Worth' in *The Lady's Realm*, November 1896.
3. 'Individuality in Dress', *Harper's Bazar*, January 1908.
4. *The Lady's Realm*, June 1900.
5. Winterburn 1914, p.10.
6. Coleman 1989, pp.68-86.
7. *The Queen*, 29 October 1904, p.673.
8. Charles Frederick Worth, quoted in an undated interview with an 'American lady from Paris' and published in Worth's obituary in the *Bulletin*, Philadelphia, 11 March 1895.
9. Léon Roger-Milès, *Les Créateurs de la Mode* (Paris, 1910), p.86: '... official or family occasions, conferences, receptions at the Academy, rehearsals, church services, chamber concerts, dinners, balls, suppers at the cabaret, the theatre, not to forget shopping, country walks, motoring, travelling, nightwear, clothes for boating, the beach, the mountains and, soon to come, for flying: and for many other occasions that I have forgotten.'
10. *The Queen*, 14 October 1904, p.593.
11. *The Queen*, 27 September 1902, p.486.
12. *The Queen*, 28 October 1905, p.730.
13. *The Queen*, 2 December 1911, p.1010.
14. Octave Uzanne, *La Française du Siècle* (Paris, 1886), p.240.
15. Roger-Milès, cited note 9, p.89: literally 'the queen's hair'. A blonde hue that varies from ash to strawberry blonde, named after the colour of Marie Antoinette's hair.
16. Winterburn 1914, p.3.
17. Ibid.
18. Winterburn 1914, p.41.

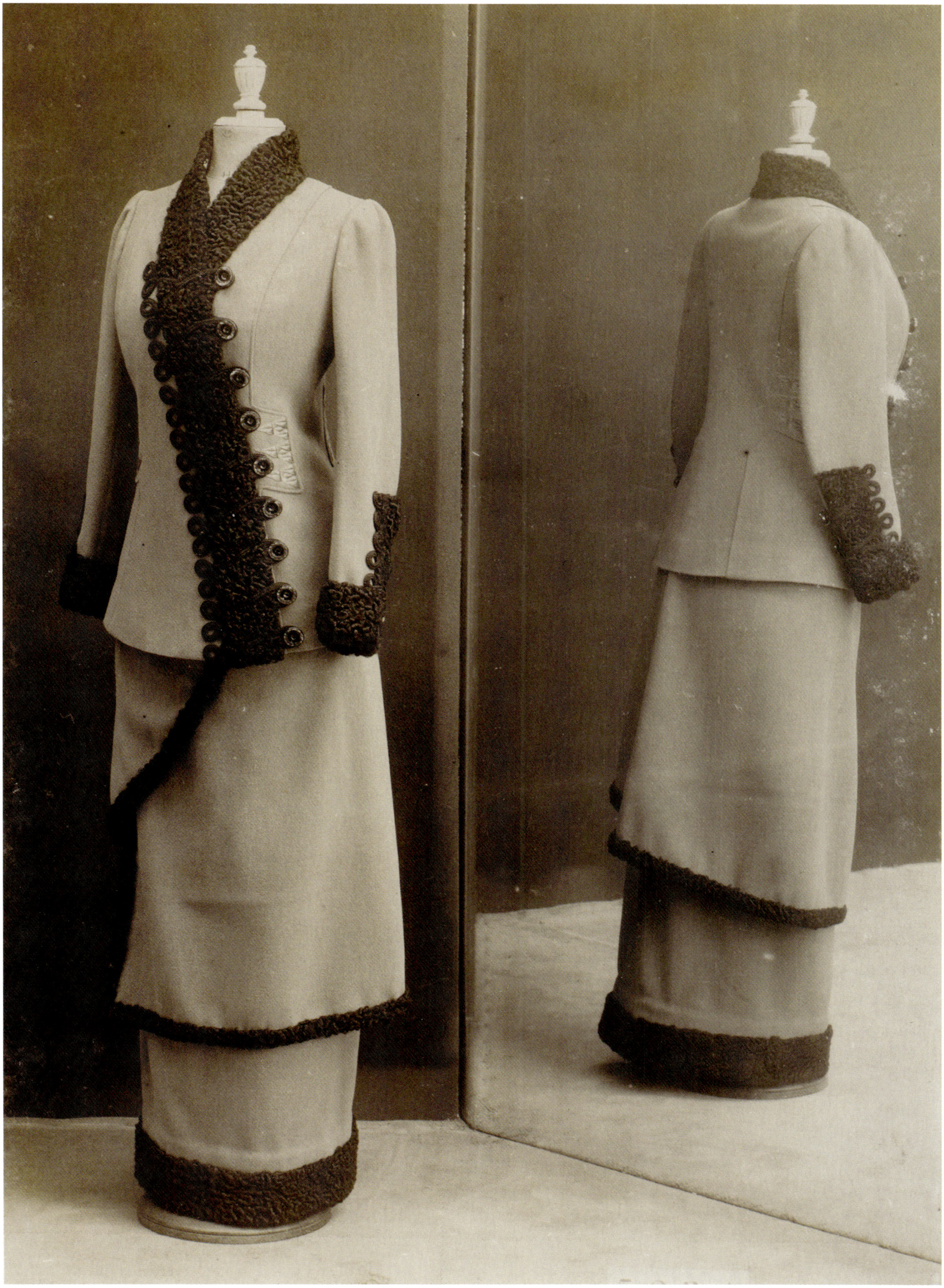

HIVER 1912-13
MODÈLE
1456

HIVER 1911-12
925

ÉTÉ 1913
MODÈLE
1743

ÉTÉ 1909
166

66 — TAILORING

OPPOSITE, TOP LEFT – Costume, embroidered lightweight wool and velvet and white fox collar, Winter 1912-13. AAD/1982/1/75

OPPOSITE, TOP RIGHT – Costume, lightweight wool with deeply scalloped edges with dark binding, Winter 1911-12. AAD/1982/1/73

OPPOSITE, BELOW LEFT – Costume, lightweight wool with embroidered openwork blouse, Summer 1913. AAD/1982/1/76

OPPOSITE, BELOW RIGHT – Dust or travelling coat, top-stitched lightweight wool or heavy cotton, Summer 1909. 1982/1/66

RIGHT – Coat, lightweight wool with large-scale pattern and deep fur hem, cuffs and collar, Winter 1911-12. AAD/1982/1/73

5971 - Costume moire marron

Sans Gêne

Sans fourrure - bcw - mgr

Avec fourrure - cwgr - comg

OPPOSITE – 'Sans Gêne' costume, brown silk moiré with fox stole and cuffs, 1912-13. AAD/1982/1/19

ABOVE – Costume, bronze lightweight wool and blue velvet trimmed with braid, 1907–8. AAD/1982/1/9

BELOW – Costume, bronze striped lightweight wool, green wool serge and satin, 1907–8. AAD/1982/1/9

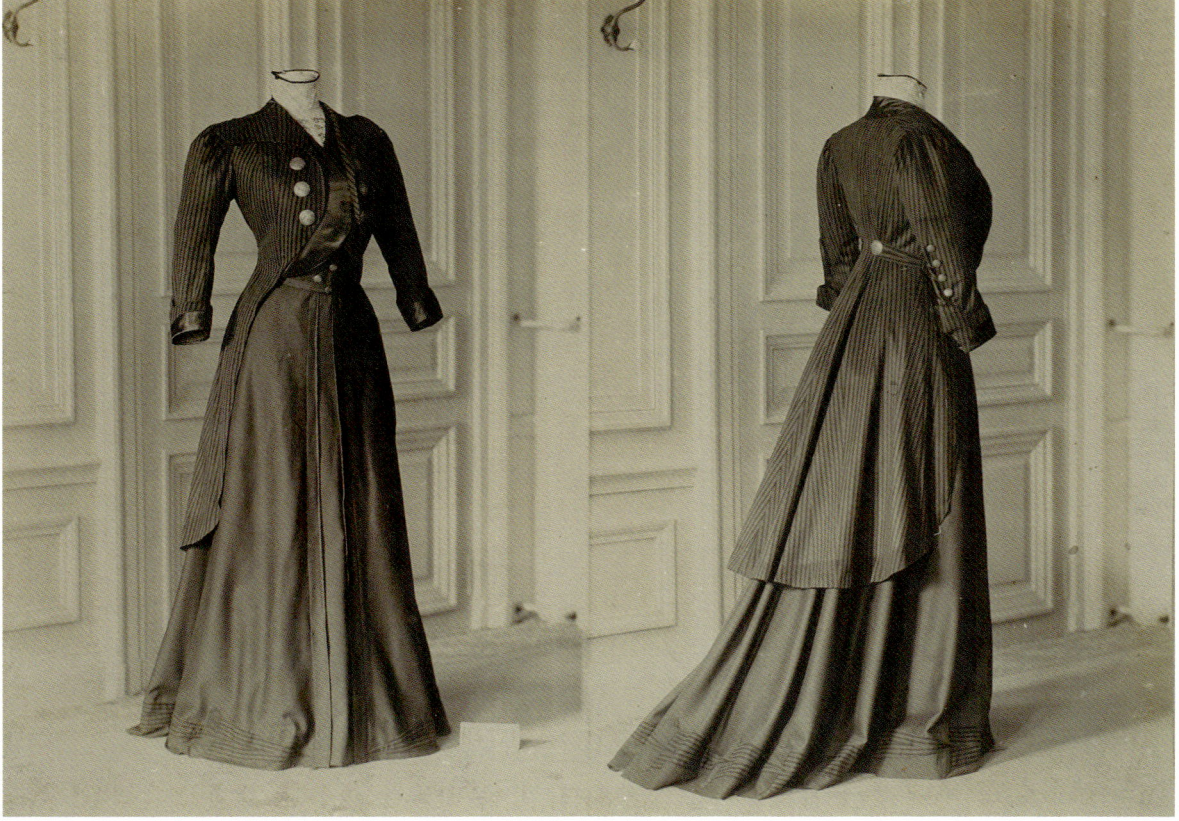

70 — TAILORING

OPPOSITE, TOP LEFT – Costume, blue velvet with applied braid, 1905. AAD/1982/1/6

OPPOSITE, TOP RIGHT – Costume, heliotrope/mauve lightweight wool, violet 'Liberty' silk and black-and-white 'pékin', 1908-9. AAD/1982/1/10

OPPOSITE, BELOW LEFT – Costume, marine blue wool serge, black 'Liberty' silk with cord trimming, lace jabot and cuffs, 1908-9. AAD/1982/1/10

OPPOSITE, BELOW RIGHT – Costume, brown silk ottoman and lightweight wool, satin and velvet, 1908-9. AAD/1982/1/10

LEFT – 'Boule de Neige', costume, white silk damask, 1913-14. AAD/1982/1/19

RIGHT – 'Caprice', costume, marine blue velveteen, 1912-13. AAD/1982/1/17

LEFT TO RIGHT —
Coat, beige wool with topstitching and velvet collar, c.1900. AAD/1982/1/23

Costume, lightweight aubergine and beige wool and black 'Liberty' silk, 1908-9. AAD/1982/1/10

OPPOSITE, LEFT TO RIGHT — Princess gown, lightweight grey wool with striped top and striped rouleau frogging, 1910-11. AAD/1982/1/14

'Chasseur', costume, havanna brown 'velours de laine' with fur trimmings, 1913-14. AAD/1982/1/19

5621

73

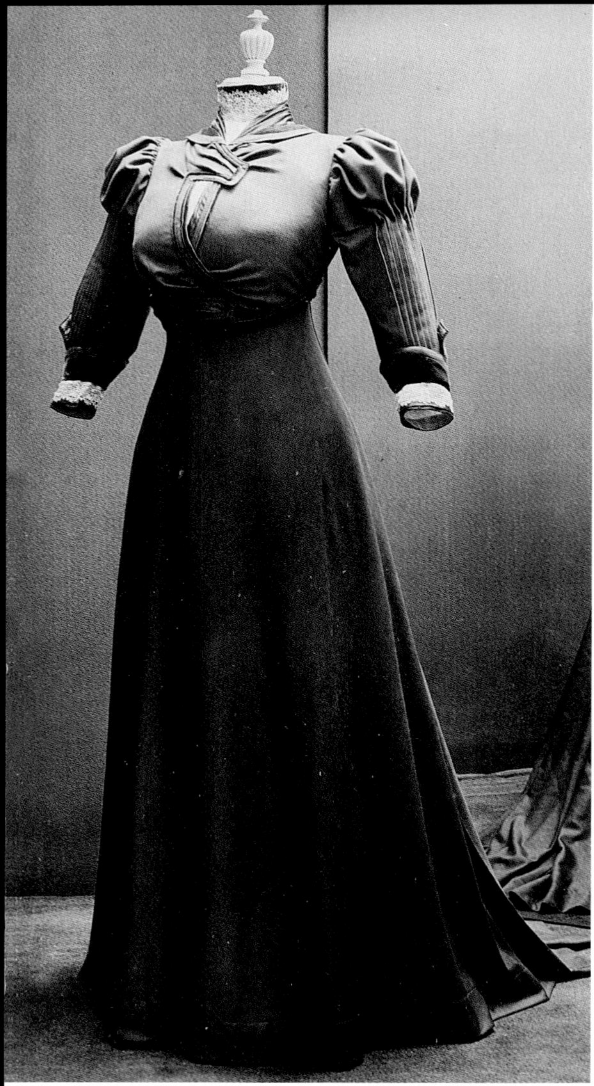
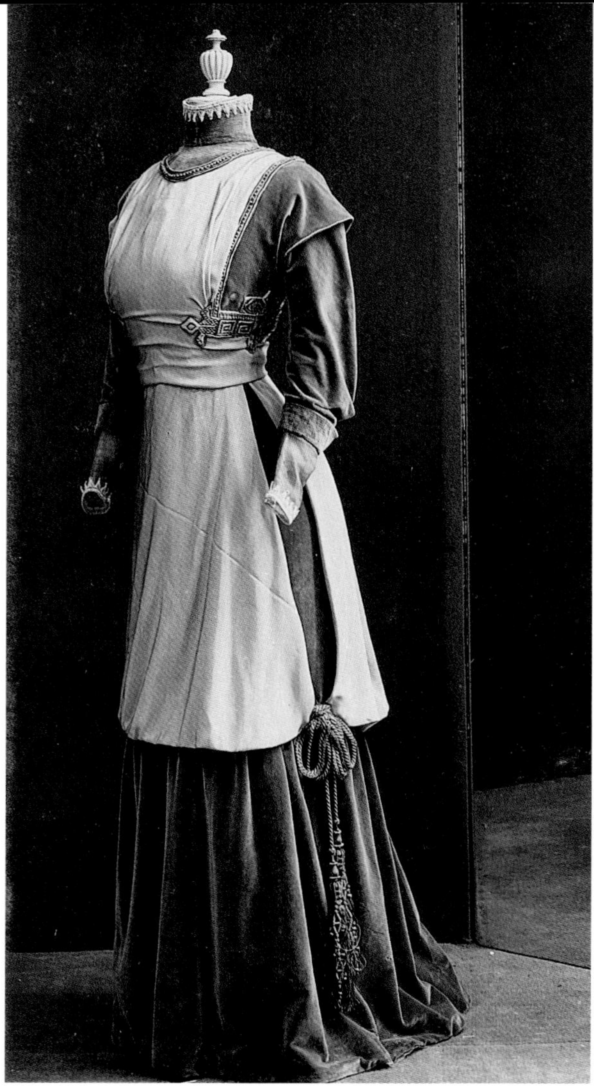
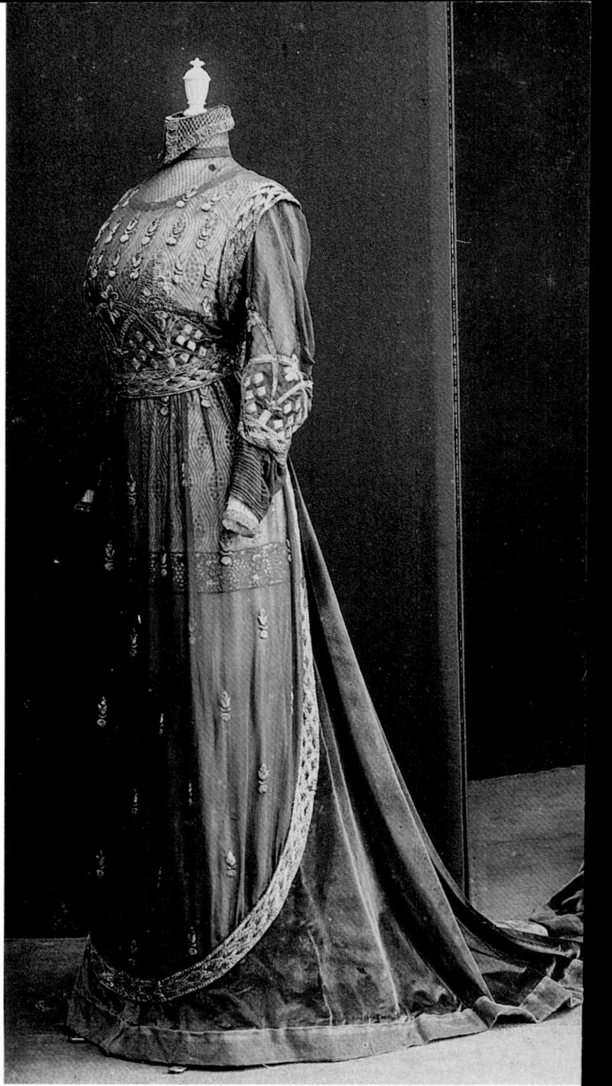
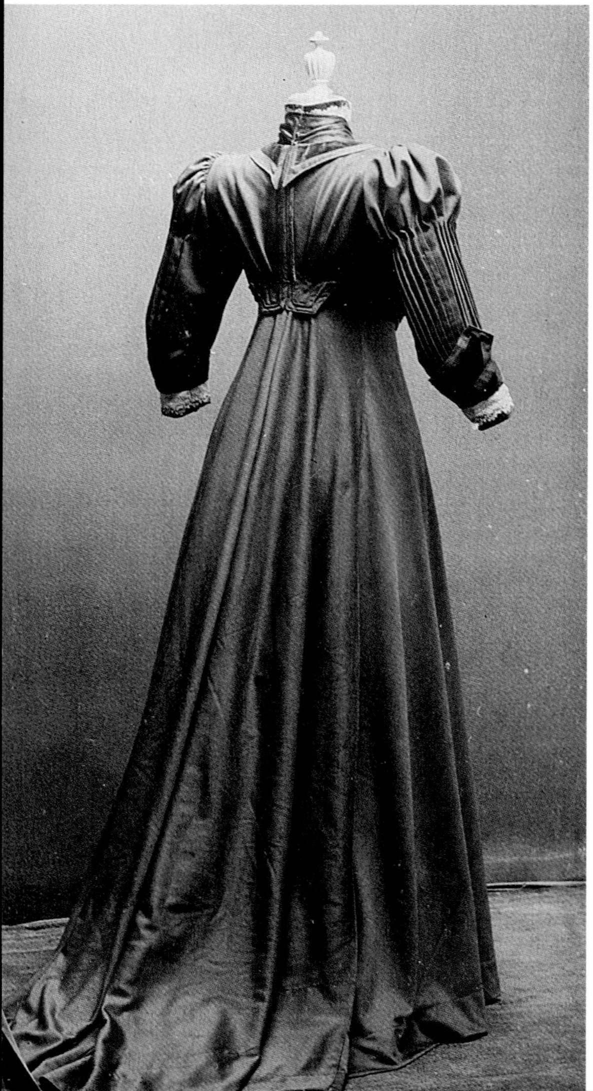
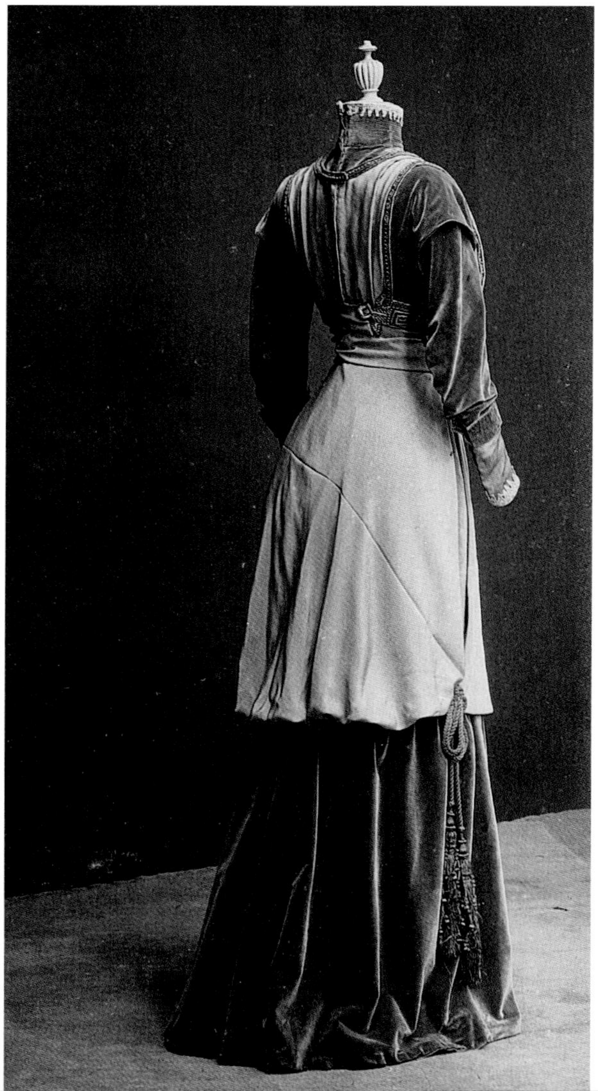
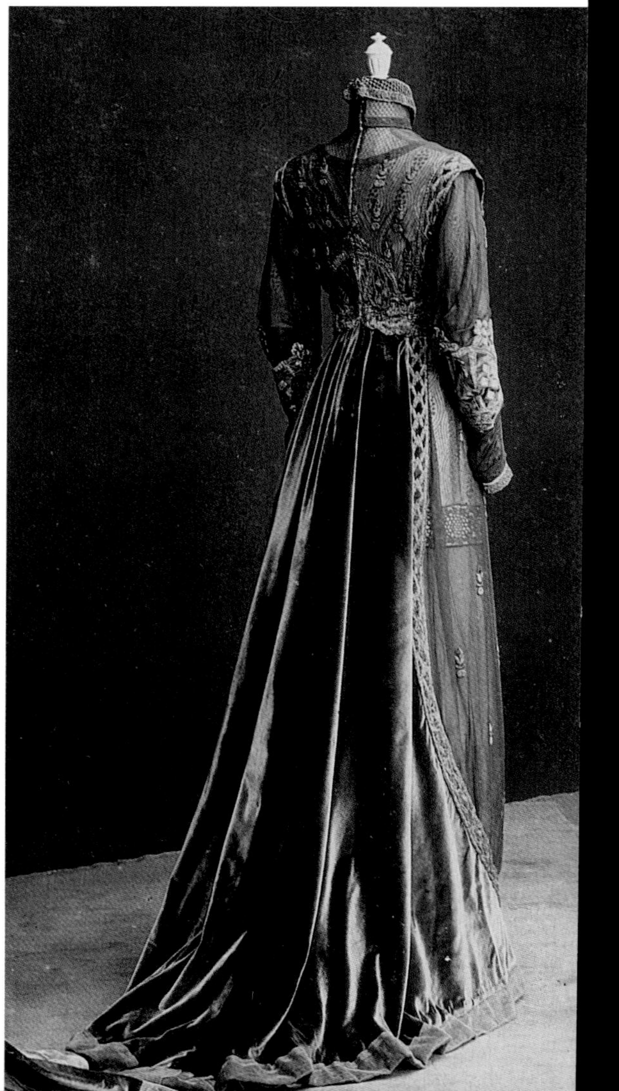

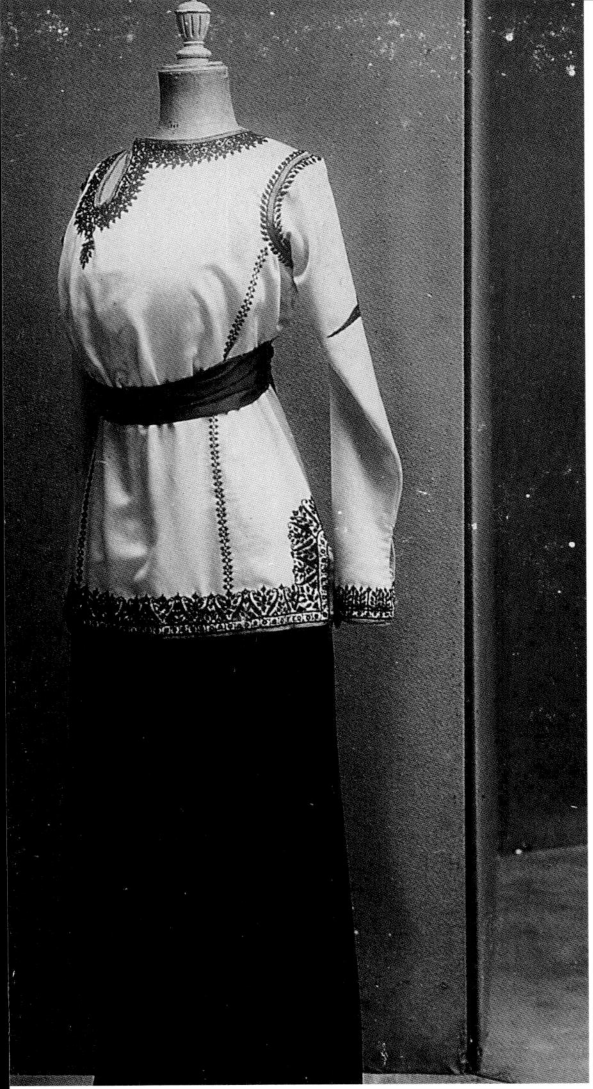
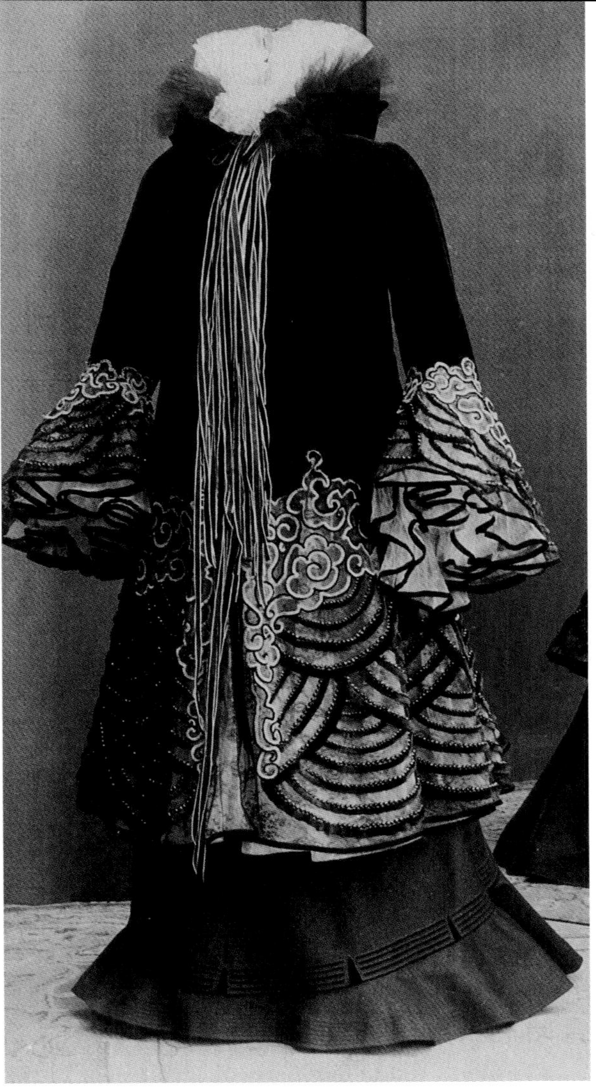
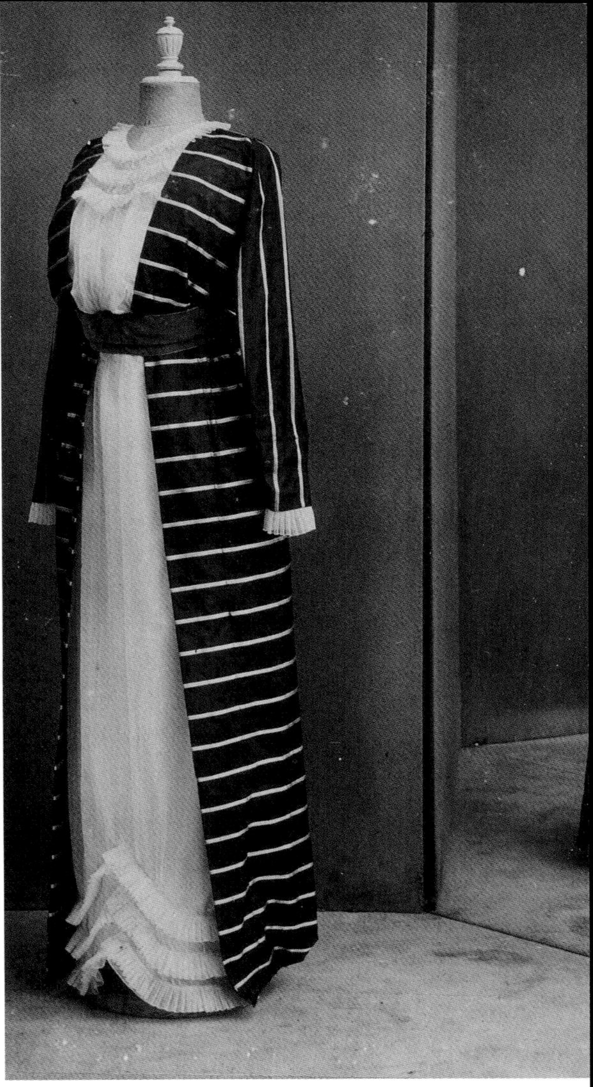
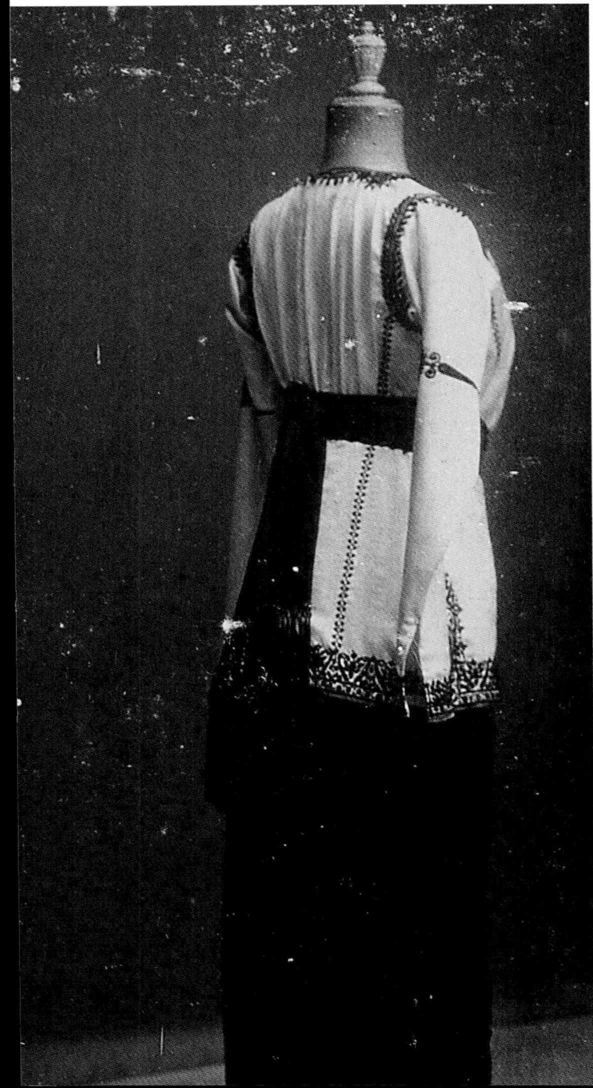
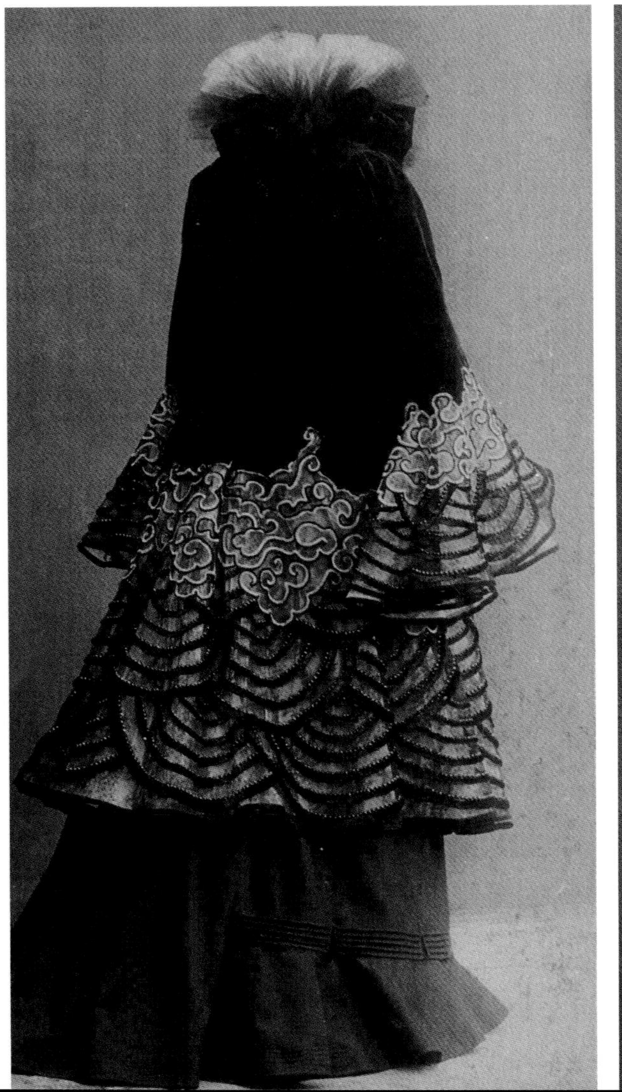
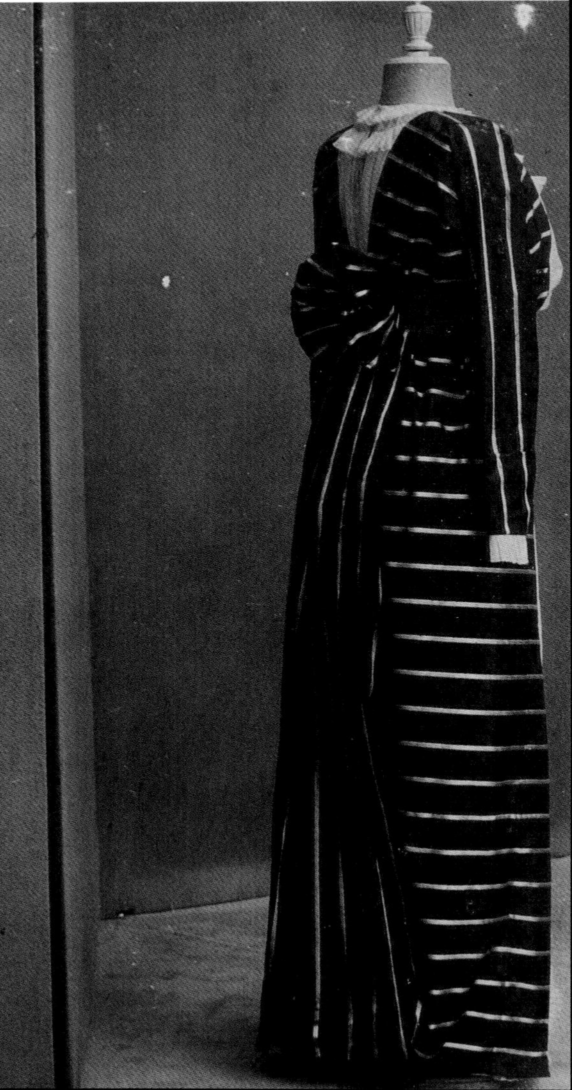

4
DRESSMAKING
AMY DE LA HAYE

n France dressmaking is known as *flou*. With implications of delicate and soft, the term distinguishes day and evening dresses from tailor-made garments; it defines the technique of working with pliant fabrics that are cut to fit, or draped around, the feminine body. Various ateliers were involved in the 'compilation' of day and evening gowns, which, until about 1910, consisted of a bodice or corsage with or without sleeves and a skirt. Dexterous needlewomen dealt separately with the various parts and their decoration before they were brought together. From the outset, it was the glorious fabrics and trimmings rather than the cut of a Worth gown (especially for eveningwear) that provoked rapturous response from clients and journalists alike. In November 1874, in Mallarmé's *La Dernière Mode*, Worth's desirable 'blue-of-dreams' gown was described in minute detail by 'Miss Satin' (probably Mallarmé): 'We have all of us been dreaming of that gown, without knowing it. M. Worth, alone, has the art of creating a *toilette* as elusive as our thoughts. Picture (you can if you try) a long skirt with a rep train, of the most ideal sky-blue silk – that blue so pale, with gleams of opalescence, that one sometimes sees, like a garland, round silvery clouds. The front of the skirt is in *faille*, and furnished with a profusion of pleats; the panels at the sides are decorated, all along their length, with pompoms lined with straw-coloured silk; and from one side to another, under a *grooved* pouff, there passes a serpentine sash in blue and primrose-yellow. The bodice is medieval in style, with straw-coloured slashes; the sleeves are garnished with pompoms. The rich folds of the fichu are in spring-like colours. Here you have a *toilette* for grand occasions such as any young woman should wear, in preference to those red or yolk-of-egg affairs that other great designers are favouring.'[1]

Many skilled hands were required to achieve these elaborate, usually delicate, garments with the speed necessary to fulfil orders from clients anxious to appear in the very latest creations from the House of Worth. In 1884, Gaston Worth told a journalist that they employed 700 workwomen (cutters, fitters, trimmers, embroiderers, skirt makers and sleeve makers), 400 of whom worked on site while the rest were outworkers. In addition to providing statistics of female employees, Gaston's response provides insights into the division of labour involved in the making of an haute couture dress. When he was asked who created the latest trends, he replied, 'M. Worth himself makes our fashions. There are no artists or designers at all – nothing in the shape of design; because if there were designers it would be very often impossible to make in cloth what had been drawn on paper, however beautiful it might be.'[2] Charles Frederick Worth was portrayed as a unique talent, which of course drew status hungry women to his doors. Even in 1892, by which time a number of highly successful haute couture houses had established themselves, *Harper's Bazar* declared Worth, 'The greatest of all the dressmakers of Paris.'[3]

Dresses were designed for – and defined by – the time of day when they were worn: morning, afternoon, teatime and evening. It must have come as a considerable relief to read in *Etiquette for Women* (1902) that while residing in the country it was expected that dresses would be plainer and fewer changes of clothing made.[4] It was acceptable, for instance, for a morning dress to be worn all day. However, its author G.R.M. Devereux had stated emphatically that 'to wear a morning dress in the evening is to commit an outrage on society itself.'[5]

OPPOSITE – Déshabillé, cream figured panne velvet with laurel leaf design, with cream 'Liberty' silk streamers, lace fall and cuffs, c.1900. AAD/1982/1/46

A STATE OF UNDRESS

From the verb 'déshabiller' (to disrobe or undress), the term 'déshabillé' signifies 'undress', that is, a negligee or informal feminine apparel that is worn in private spaces. English-speaking fashion journalists were especially fond of this evocative word and the pages of women's magazines of the early 1900s are sprinkled with the term. A déshabillé, photographed for the Worth album dated 1902–3, is in a figured silk, with a design of laurel leaves; it has a fringed silk necktie, lace hooded fichu and gathered, lace-flounced sleeves. Ten years later – in line with prevailing trends – Jean's designs for déshabillés show influences from world clothing traditions. 'Graziella' is a draped, long-sleeved, gown made in sheer silk, decorated with white embroidered mankolam motifs (Hindu symbols based on the mango). Suspended from each cuff hangs a silken tassel, always a popular decorative device at Worth (p.83, top right). They were used to define edges, to highlight short sleeves or were incorporated into an array of fastenings. In one extraordinary creation they covered the entire garment, making it exceedingly heavy and possibly hazardous. Most effectively they were used to adorn the backs of outfits.

CORSETRY

Throughout the period covered by the albums good corsetry was imperative to achieve the desired silhouette. Jean Worth deplored 'tight lacing, whether for the short, the lean, the young or the old'. He claimed to have safeguarded his own daughter's health and comfort by making straight fronted corsets especially for her. He advocated corsetry 'cut on common sense principles, and with the enlightenment of a knowledge of anatomy'.[6] In 1909 *The Queen* reported, 'The value of a really good reliable corset as the keystone of fashion is a fact uncontested by those who pay serious and knowledgeable tribute to La Mode. The best and most perfectly built gown will never meet with the unqualified success it deserves unless it is accompanied by an immaculate corset, and one, moreover, modelled in accordance with the latest edicts as to silhouette and *forme*…'.[7] By 1913 fashions had changed and the same paper declared, 'Corsets are *démodé* to the last degree, and women who wear them must disguise the fact. As nearly all women do wear them, nevertheless, a clever corset maker is of paramount importance.'[8]

MORNING WEAR

Morning dresses were worn at home or could be teamed with a jacket for walking or shopping. Together with Worth's tailored output, they represent the house at its most utilitarian. Devereux states that, 'Morning dress should always be neat and trim, fashionable, of course, and well cut.'[9] Examples of morning dress, designed for spring and summer, include a box-pleated skirt and short cape bodice with jaunty white collar from 1906 (p.97) and a dashing monochrome-striped ensemble from 1911 (p.100, right). The earliest Worth album, dated 1899, contains photographs of *manteaux* that are closely related to morning gowns in both style and fabric. A draped garment, made in a fine wool with an excessively large tartan repeat design woven in colour-muted tones, has striking (to contemporary eyes) contrasting, vertical striped sleeves (p.80, below). Another coat, executed in a solid colour wool, is garlanded with flowers at the neck and hem, and features prominent spotted sleeves.

THE PRINCESS GOWN

Charles Frederick Worth championed the princess gown. Popularly associated with Princess Alexandra, this was made without a seam around the waist, the bodice and skirt cut and assembled in long panels that swept flatteringly (usually) over the body's contours. Jean continued the house tradition using the style for both day and eveningwear. The albums abound with gowns cut '*en princesse*'. In 1905 *The Queen* reported their pre-eminence: 'One of the leading Parisian houses intends bringing out a model of a most severely cut Princesse gown, with a perfectly tight-fitting sleeve… This mode will be in all probability adopted by many fair Parisiennes who are proud of their *jolie ligne de taille*, and no better style can show to advantage a good figure better than a perfectly cut Princesse robe'.[10] Jean recalled, 'We made dresses for Lady Sykes to wear at Epsom, the biggest race course in England, that to-day would be too gorgeous even for a ball. For instance she had one Princess gown made of alternating breadths of apple green and white embroidered as exquisitely as any Louis XV dress, and with a train two metres long.'[11] Two examples from 1909–10 illustrate the versatility of this style. A fairytale white gown in fine wool has inserts of guipure to match its pointed falling collar and, revolutionary for the time, the back is shaped by long, uncut seams outside the garment (p.109). An understated *robe princesse* in beige wool for daywear is extraordinarily modern in its uncluttered simple lines, which resemble those of the coatdress, that dual-purpose garment in vogue 60 years later (p.107).

THE AFTERNOON GOWN

On returning home from shopping or 'calling', it was customary to change into an afternoon or *après-midi* gown. Devereux states: 'Dress for the afternoon should be a little more elaborate, but here, of course, much depends on what the afternoon's occupation is to be. If a call has to be paid, a pretty, rather dressy gown and hat and blameless gloves should be donned; if it is one's own day for receiving callers a more elaborate style of gown may be adopted.'[12] Worth's designs for ingénue afternoon gowns include a beige lingerie-style frock for 1900 (p.104), a white dress with prominent bow motifs for 1912 (p.98) and another with a design of embroidered flower pots for 1913–14 (p.105). Most understated is a blue voile dress with a draped waistcoat-like top and white voile blouse with a lace fichu. Designed in 1912–13, Jean named it 'Gamine'; it retains its contemporary appeal a century later (p.106). In October 1911 a fashion journalist noted, 'The impression I came away with from Worth's was that he is making everything in black, black and white, violet, or violet and black… The velvet dresses were good, too, both in black and violet, and skunk or chinchilla, with lace, trimmed them all.'[13] Fitting this description, within the 1910–11 album, is a winter *après-midi* gown in a fur-trimmed, violet and black checked silk (p.81). For afternoon wear in 1913–14, Jean designed a dark brown velvet tunic dress (Charles Frederick was said to have initiated the tunic dress as early as 1868) with a crossover fur bodice and sheer, fur-banded, 'oriental' lampshade skirt (p.103, left).

80 — DRESSMAKING

OPPOSITE ABOVE –
Ensemble with bolero in fine wool velvet and satin and jet embroidery, 1891. AAD/1982/1/40

OPPOSITE BELOW –
Day dress, silk tussore, 'écossais' bold check in blue and beige with striped velvet sleeves, 1891. AAD/1982/1/40

RIGHT – 'Miguette', day dress, striped black and violet silk gauze with fur-trimmed high neck and crenellated hemline, 1910–11. AAD/1982/1/13

Soir. Ci-dessus.

OPPOSITE — Tea gown, periwinkle blue 'Liberty' satin and silk chiffon, 1909-10. AAD/1982/1/55

TOP LEFT — Tea gown, blue silk chiffon over white 'Liberty' silk with embroidery and lace, 1907. AAD/1982/1/52

TOP RIGHT — 'Graziella', déshabillé, plum-coloured silk chiffon over white 'Liberty' silk with embroidery, 1912. AAD/1982/1/60

BOTTOM LEFT — Tea gown, white crêpe de Chine, 'gaze pompadour', silk chiffon and lace worn by a house mannequin, c.1902. AAD/1982/1/43

BOTTOM RIGHT — Tea gown (rear view), white satin and taffeta, pink silk chiffon and lace with dark velvet ribbon, c.1902. AAD/1982/1/43

ABOVE LEFT — 'Espéranto', tea gown, crêpe de Chine with gold brocade front panel and trimmed with pearls, 1911-12. AAD/1982/1/57

ABOVE RIGHT — Evening gown (with 'Paisley' border design), embroidered cream 'Liberty' silk with cream and gold lace overlay, 1908. AAD/1982/1/53

OPPOSITE LEFT — *Robe de bal*, white satin and spangled tulle embroidered with sequins and beads in a cloud and shower of rain design, with lace, chiffon, fringes and silk flowers, 1902-3. AAD/1982/1/46

OPPOSITE RIGHT — Evening gown, white silk crêpe de Chine and taffeta with nasturtiums embroidered on green taffeta (matching the corselette), hem and falling sleeves trimmed with ribbons with trailing corsage of artificial nasturtiums, 1901-2. AAD/1982/1/43

DESIGN INSPIRATION

Between 1909 and 1914 – in line with prevailing trends – Worth's collections were influenced by clothes from a wide range of cultures. Charles Frederick and Jean Worth were inspired by the fine arts and illustrations in their excellent fashion library. Confirming this, a reporter (who might have muddled the facts) recounted a conversation with Charles Frederick, who, he said, 'always consulted Jules Breton for his Artois reproductions; he learned a great deal from Felon, a master of Arlesian costume; from Landelle, the painter of costume in the Pyrenees; from Guillemin, Leleux and Fortin, who spent many a long day portraying the strange and poetic costumes of Brittany. Bonnat and Henner he considered as the two best authorities on Italian costume, Hardy and Wells on English matters of dress, Theodore Delamarre on Chinese, Bida on Turkish, and Stevens on Parisian costume.'[14] Jean stated that after attending the 1867 Paris Exposition, his father introduced kimono sleeves into his coat designs.[15] And, in 1869, the couturier was credited with launching the vogue for draping Indian shawls to form a mantle, which was said to be an art that he alone possessed.[16] Later, the decorative motifs and patterning of Indian shawls and the knotted silk fringing that decorates shawls worn in China and Spain were to inspire Jean's designs (p.84, right; p.86, centre). A number of unstructured daywear dresses, from 1910 to 1914, employ the flat-cutting techniques characteristic of various African and Asian cultural clothing traditions. One afternoon dress is made using a textile with a broad decorative border that is shawl-like, while the style bears some resemblance to the North African djellabah (p.102, right). Another, of figured silk with contrasting lining, encircles the upper body and has oriental overtones (p.103, right).

THE TEA GOWN

In *The Cult of Chiffon* (1902) Mrs Eric Pritchard noted, 'At this very moment the perfection of a tea-gown may be realised by a combination of Japanese colouring, Grecian lines and French frivolity. Was there ever a time when fashions of all countries and periods were mingled with such excellent results?'[17] A tea gown was generally a long, flowing, one-piece garment, often cut in a high-waisted style and made in soft materials such as lace, charmeuse or chiffon. Worn at tea-time, it was acceptable for a married woman to receive her female guests thus attired – 'fast' ladies arrayed in tea gowns were known (shockingly) to entertain gentlemen callers. While they were designed to provide comfort, tea gowns were not understated affairs. The same year Mrs Pritchard's book was published, Jean designed a white silk and lace tea gown with a majestic draped back (p.83, below right) and another in white silk crêpe de Chine with voluminous sleeves, which was modelled by a house mannequin (p.83, below left). A filmy garment from 1907 features horizontal embroidered paisley or boteh motifs with coiled tips (p.83, top left), while 'Espéranto' (one who hopes), of 1911–12, with its tabard-like front and beaded pearl trim has medieval overtones (p.84, left).

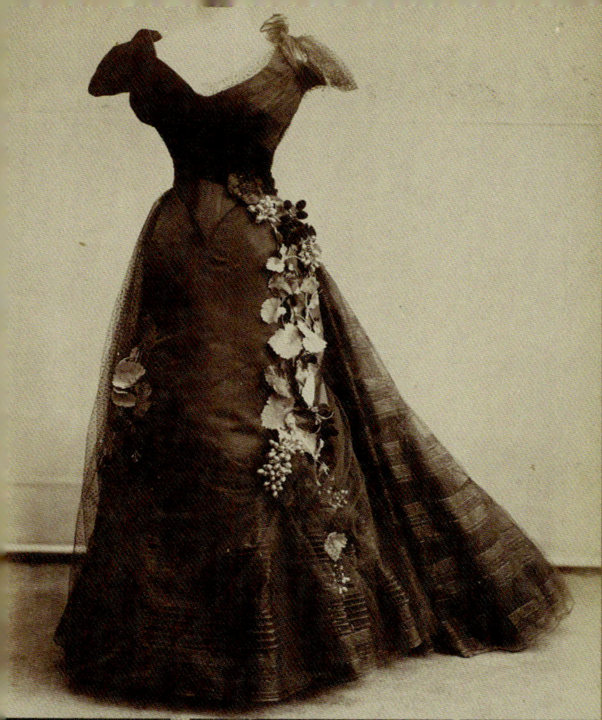
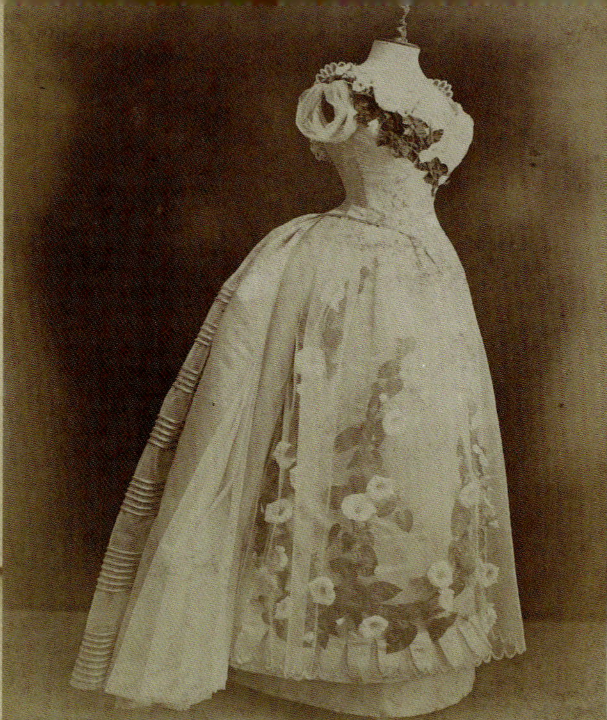
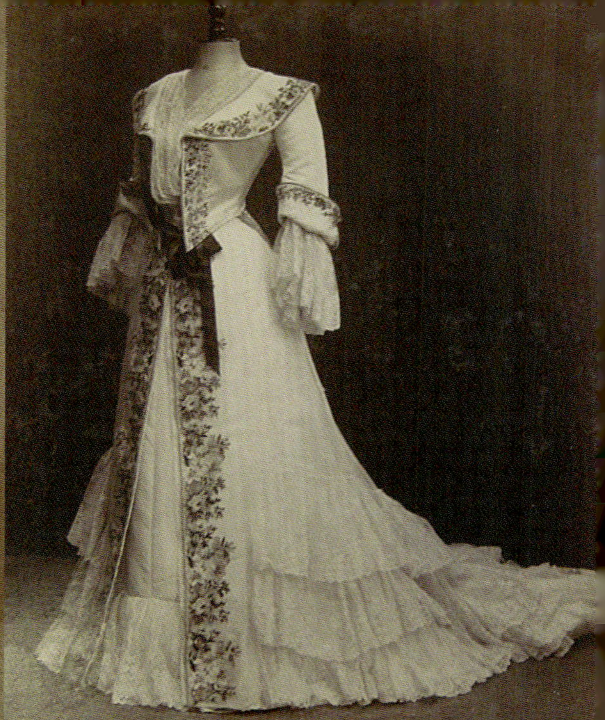
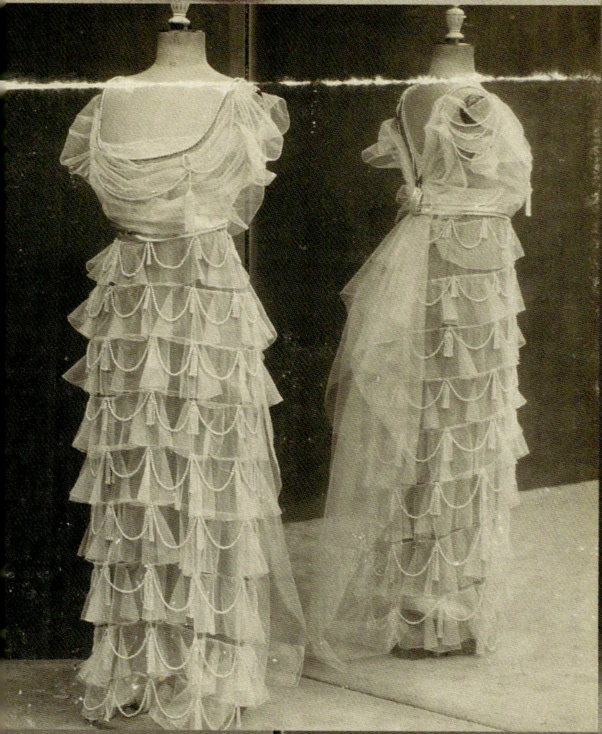
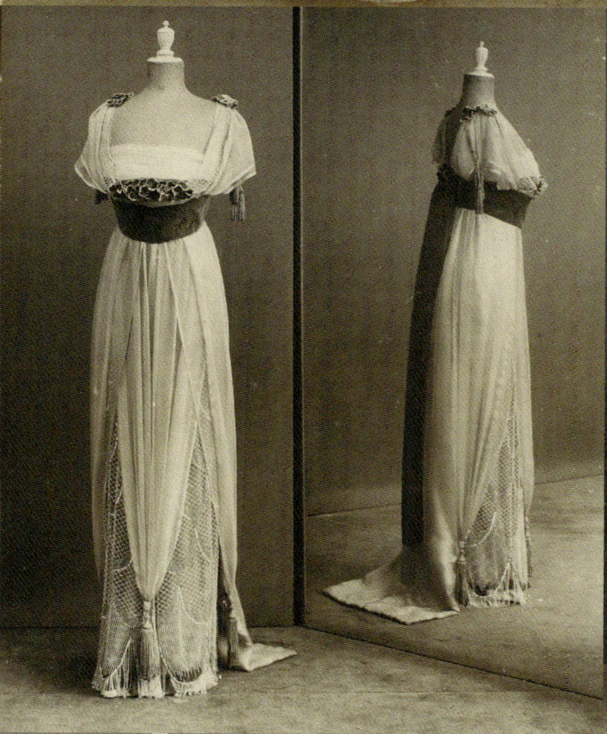
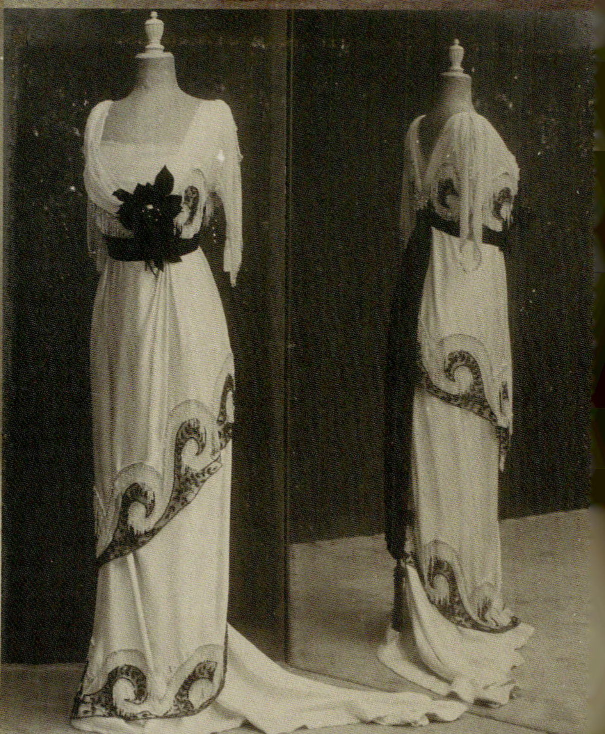
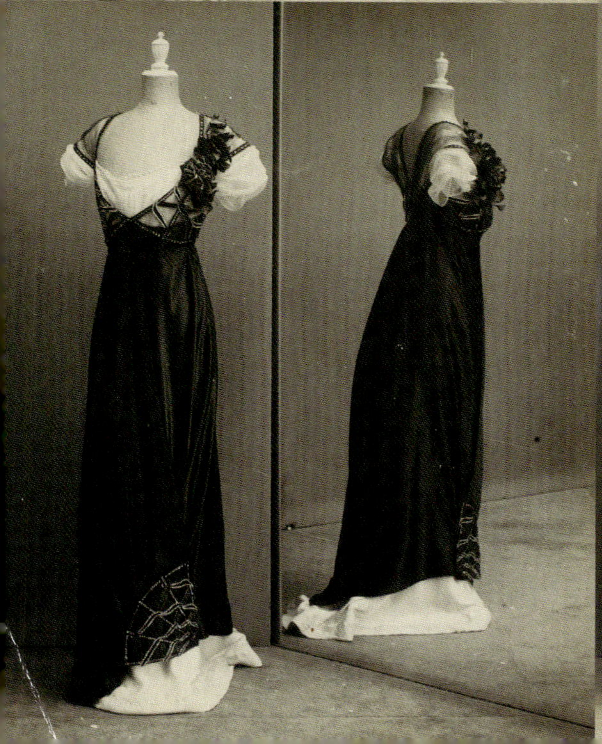
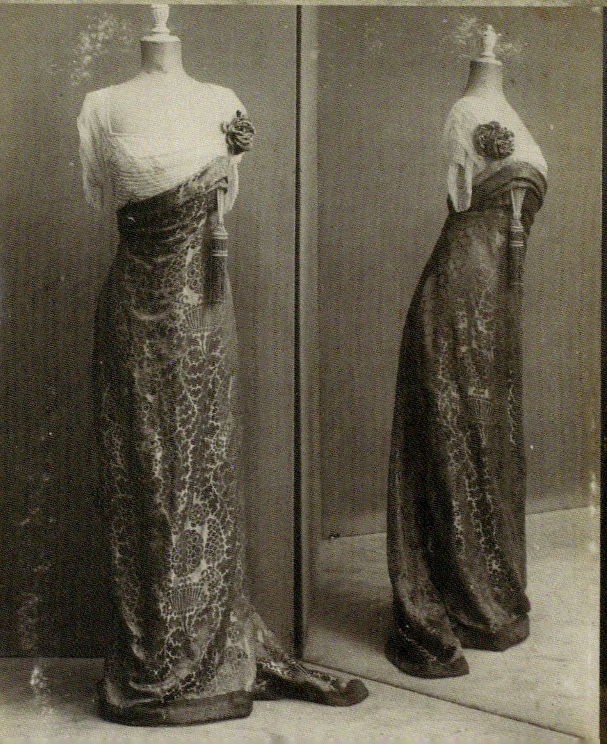
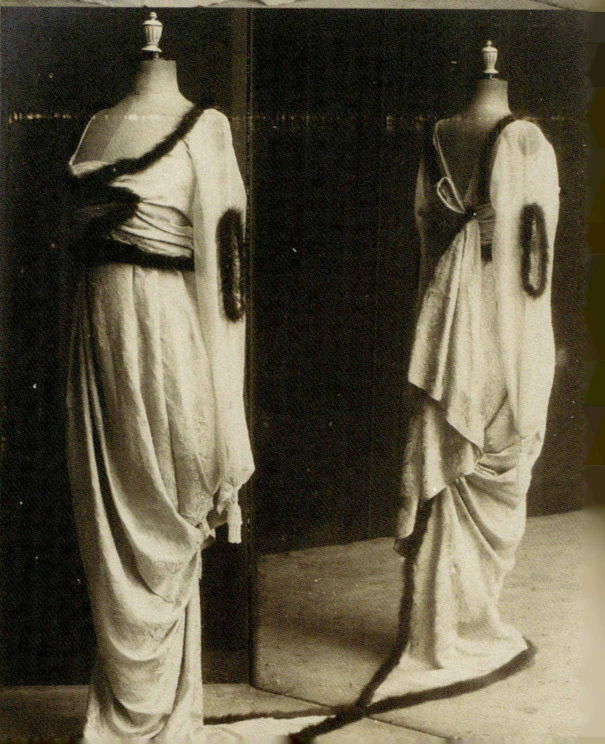

OPPOSITE
TOP ROW, LEFT TO RIGHT – *Robe de bal*, black 'peau de soie' full-skirted gown overlaid with spotted tulle, trimmed with a vine of silk grapes and leaves, 1889. AAD/1982/1/62

Robe de bal, pale green satin with silver embroidery and applied silk garlands of flowering bindweed, overlaid with sheer tulle and with a 'bustle' of silk and tulle, 1889. AAD/1982/1/62

Evening ensemble (taking elements from eighteenth-century dress), 'habit' and skirt in white 'peau de soie' with polychrome embroidered floral borders and flounced lace, 1902-3. AAD/1982/1/43

MIDDLE ROW, LEFT TO RIGHT – 'Paquerette', evening gown, bias cut flounced lemon-coloured chiffon adorned with horizontal looped rows of pearls secured by tassels, 1913-14. AAD/1982/1/61

'Fuchsia', evening gown, violet chiffon and pink tulle over pink 'Liberty' silk, with embroidered scalloped design, velvet sash, applied tassels and velvet pansies, 1909-10. AAD/1982/1/56

'Toscarina', evening gown (with a large floral corsage), layered pale pink crêpe de Chine beaded in black and white with diagonal borders of bold scrollwork, 1911-12. AAD/1982/1/57

BOTTOM ROW, LEFT TO RIGHT – 'Medicis', evening gown, black satin over white chiffon with a cutwork diamanté studded 'spider's web' and silk flowers, c.1912. AAD/1982/1/58

Evening gown, green and gold brocaded silk with asymmetrical neckline over a short-sleeved bodice trimmed with a large tassel and fabric rose, 1911-12. AAD/1982/1/57

'Cupidon', *robe de dîner*, apricot-coloured brocaded silk lamé, with tassel and fur trim, 1913-14. AAD/1982/1/61

RIGHT – Evening gown (rear view), embroidered pintucked eau de Nil satin, with lace and silk flowers, 1902. AAD/1982/1/45

BELOW – Evening gown (rear view), court train suspended from each shoulder, 'Liberty' satin, chiffon and tulle with a deep lace border entwined with white silk roses, c.1902. AAD/1982/1/45

TOP ROW, LEFT TO RIGHT — Evening gown, cream lace over blue satin embroidered in glistening metal threads with hem and bodice trimmed with artificial flowers with long petals, 1907–8. AAD/1982/1/42

Evening gown (rear and side view), pink silk damask and taffeta with embroidery, lace, ribbon, fringes and glittering imitation flowers, 1901. AAD/1982/1/43

BOTTOM ROW, LEFT TO RIGHT — Evening gown (rear view), figured white satin with an overlay embroidered with long stems of wheat and neckline trimmed with silk flowers, 1902. AAD/1992/1/45

Evening ensemble (rear view), black velvet and navy blue satin with an embroidered trompe l'oeil design of swathed and pleated fabric, trimmed with guipure and ribbon, 1902. AAD/1982/1/45

Evening gown (rear view), white chiffon over satin embroidered with interlocked floral ('pompadour') wreaths trimmed with spangled bows and lace, 1902. AAD/1982/1/45

OPPOSITE, TOP LEFT — Princess evening gown (rear view), black velvet and pink satin embroidered with full-length floral garlands, trimmed with lace, c.1900. AAD/1982/1/42

OPPOSITE, BOTTOM LEFT — Evening skirt photographed without a bodice on a Stockman display figure. In white satin and white and yellow chiffon, overlaid with spangled black tulle and lace, 1899–1900. AAD/1982/1/41

OPPOSITE, RIGHT — Evening gown, white satin with an overlay of embroidered blue tulle, 1899–1900. AAD/1982/1/41

92

LEFT TO RIGHT — *Robe de bal*, white satin and taffeta decorated with meandering rows of pleated tulle and sprays of artificial roses and jasmine-like flowers, 1902. AAD/1982/1/45

Evening gown (with detail), strawberry-pink silk velvet and lace embroidered in silks, diamantés and beads with a floral design incorporating bows and tassels, 1904–5. AAD/1982/1/59

THE EVENING GOWN

Evening gowns were ordered in salons flooded with daylight yet were to be worn at night under artificial lights. The House of Worth made an astute decision to provide their clients with a special night-time *salon de vente* with its concomitant lighting. On 30 April 1895 Boston's *Home Journal* reported, 'If an evening frock is desired, the stuff is draped about her in a room lighted either by gas or electricity that she may better judge its effect. If she is tired after her selection, she may return home and an attendant will be sent to take her measurements, and in a few days, if she desires, two fitters with perhaps a third to supervise, will come to her for the trying-on process.' The 'room' became Worth's *salon de lumière*. Originally candle-lit, it enabled the couturier and his clients to evaluate how a dress appeared in artificial light; it is no coincidence that Worth's evening gowns were often praised for their luminescence. Very occasionally the flat nature of light in Worth's photographic studio and salons failed to capture the liveliness of evening tulles and chiffons, or the sparkle of applied sequins and beads. However, two particular photographs suggest how these gowns must have twinkled beautifully under ballroom lights. They have lavishly embroidered sky motifs – favourite decorative emblems for the House of Worth that resulted in some truly magnificent creations. An evening skirt of 1899–1900 (p.89, below left) is spangled with starburst motifs and a *robe de bal* of 1902–3 has a design of glittering clouds and sunrays (p.85, top left). During the design process Worth would take into account the fact that the gown would be accompanied by a set or *parure* of fine, sparkling, jewels.

In 1907 *The Queen* reported that, 'It is in evening dress, there is no doubt, that a woman has the most ample opportunities of displaying her taste in clothes and of appearing at her best. The low-necked corsage is much more becoming than the high-necked one, besides which evening dress allows of a choice in materials and in originality of treatment, the accompaniment of jewellery, and elaborate hairdressing impossible otherwise. On the robe de soirée more thought and money are lavished than on all the rest of the wardrobe put together, and it is most grateful for the attention bestowed on it.'[18] As well as for formal dinners, evening gowns were worn for special occasions – balls, receptions, the opera, the theatre as well as rites of passage. They were undoubtedly the most expensive pieces in a wealthy woman's wardrobe. With personal associations, they tended to be kept and treasured and, in the fullness of time, offered to museums. However, they do not always survive intact. Elizabeth Ann Coleman describes how, 'The extremely ephemeral nature of silk tulle has distorted our ideas of early Worth gowns from the Worth and Bobergh period. After crushing and crumbling like autumn leaves, the often brittle tulle net on these gowns has dissolved almost as quickly. Without the diffusing cover of illusion net, the under gowns of slick satin or taffeta have lost their original meaning.'[19] On a happier note, she explains that the original appearance of these early Worth gowns can be gleaned from paintings, especially by Winterhalter. Fortunately, we also have Worth's photographic albums recording his models fresh from the atelier.

Evening dress was divided into two broad categories: full toilette and demi-toilette. The more informal option, demi-toilette, was permissible for a 'small and friendly dinner',[20] but for an official dinner party and attending the opera or theatre full toilette was *de rigueur*. Devereux states that 'Dinner gowns are usually made of richer and heavier materials than gowns for other social functions. Trains are almost always in fashion for dinner gowns, richness of effect and dignity of style being perhaps more aimed at than the daintiness and prettiness so suitable to a ballroom.'[21] In 1900 *The Queen* described in detail the design of a Worth *robe de dîner*: 'The tight-fitting under skirt and corsage *en Princesse* are of rose satin miroité; over this a slightly loose Empire role of cream gauze is incrusted with floral leaves of painted gauze and black lace motifs. Round the décolletage a tombant of black chantilly lace continues behind in a long Watteau cascaded arrangement, falling over the train in an echarpe. One shoulder has a long, trailing garland of orchids attached to the back. This is a *dernier cri* of an Empire modification, giving all the grace and lengthening effect, with a reflection of the curved lines of a beautiful figure beneath the transparency'.[22] For Winter 1904–5, a trained velvet gown is decorated with a design of bow-tied tassels. For Summer 1911 Worth designed a citron-coloured silk taffeta *robe de dîner* embroidered with a design of flower baskets and monochrome striped under dress that has a Regency feel (p.101). And for Winter 1913–14 an 'oriental', fur-trimmed and hobble-skirted *robe de dîner* is tied at the back in the manner of a Japanese obi (p.86, bottom right).

Evening gowns were often bedecked with a profusion of meticulously crafted fabric flowers. To achieve such exquisite results required a skill that involved a three- to five-year apprenticeship in Paris. In 1900 *The Queen* reported that 'Artificial flowers are immensely used on evening gowns, in bunches, sprays, and garlands, the last-named method being especially favoured, and *la rose* is naturally the queen of flowers.'[23] A Worth *robe de bal* of 1903–4 features a tapering rose garland, entwined with silk that trails down the back of the dress and onto the train. In 1877 a dinner guest made an amusing observation of an eminent Worth client: 'Lady Lytton's dress was so hung with artificial flowers that she made quite a crushing sound whenever she sat down.'[24] Roses are interlaced with twigs of flowering jasmine on a white winter-wonderland *robe de bal* from 1902 (p.90, left). Worth also recognized the decorative potential of more humble garden flowers – fresh looking white daisies were a house favourite in addition to wild flowers and even weeds. One of the earliest photographs of a Worth dress records a white *robe de bal*, which has a trail of bindweed stitched diagonally across the corsage, which creeps down a skirt overlaid with a veil of sheer white silk (p.86, top centre). A 1912 dress made from a printed silk emblazoned with a diagonal design of huge sunflower heads, in (unusually) blue on a pink ground, is unlike any other in Worth's albums (p.100, left).

THE BALL GOWN

The House of Worth is best known for grand and romantic ball gowns. Writing in 1893, the anonymous 'A Member of the Aristocracy' advised readers of *Manners and Rules of Good Society* that 'Balls are given in town and country by society at large and these invitation balls include Hunt Balls, Military and Naval Balls, Militia, Yeomanry, and Volunteer Balls, Bachelor's Balls, etc.'[25] Invitation balls were distinct from balls that required tickets of admission, such as charity balls, which had appointed committee members who vetted prospective attendees. Our anonymous author asserted that the difference between a dance and a ball lay in the number of guests: some 80 to 200 attended the former, while the latter involved 200 to 500 guests. Balls associated with rites of passage – birthdays, 'coming out', engagements and the like – could be lavish affairs. The New York heiress Consuelo Vanderbilt made her debut at a *bal blanc* in Paris, in the spring of 1894: 'A *bal blanc* had to live up to its name of purity and innocence; it could not inspire the mild flirtations of a pink ball where young married women were included. The men who attended them, no doubt with the intention of selecting a future spouse, were expected to behave with circumspection… I wore a white tulle dress made by Worth. It touched the ground with a full skirt, as was the fashion in those days, and it had a tightly laced bodice. My hair was piled high in curls and a narrow ribbon was tied round my long and slender neck. I had no jewels and wore gloves that came almost to my shoulders.'[26] The Worth albums contain an example of an 1899–1900 gown for a *bal blanc*. In her memoir *The Rainbow Comes and Goes* (1958) Lady Diana Cooper recalled that in 1913, the year she was presented as a London debutante, there were as many as three or four *bals blancs* a week.[27]

The rear view of a Worth evening gown is as magnificent as the front. A trained ball gown from 1901 was made in a glistening, rose-coloured, figured silk satin with a floral design that included curvilinear tendrils in the then-modern Art Nouveau style (p.88, top row). More often Worth's designs were generated by historical fashions. In a curiously muddled but telling interview, Charles Frederick Worth told an American reporter, 'Alma Tadema and Gerome are my favourites for costumes of antiquity, which these wonderful artists have studied in all their details. The fifteenth and sixteenth centuries are, in my humble opinion, best shown in the works of Roybet, Tissot, G. Jacquet, Edward Ward and Pauwels. I always consult Meissonier and Gerome for the best illustrations of the seventeenth and eighteenth centuries. And as for those of the nineteenth, I have seen the most famous with my own eyes.'[28] Jean followed in his father's footsteps. He was obviously a perfectionist, pointing out that 'zealous attention to detail is observed throughout the whole composition of a robe, for whose mere sleeves the art galleries of Europe will be canvassed for ideas…'.[29] In a chapter written for Florence Hull Winterburn's *Principles of Correct Dress* (1914), Jean stated: 'The world's great picture-galleries, where the priceless portraits painted by the old masters are hung, are the most inspiring sources to which a designer of modes can repair. Such great painters as Nattier, Madame Lebrun, Romney, Lawrence, and Gainsborough serve again and again as aids to the costumier in colour, design, and trimming.'[30] Jean made overt references to the cut and floral embroidery style of a man's eighteenth-century tailored coat in a design of 1901–2, while the wide box pleats, suspended from the shoulder down the centre back bodice of an eighteenth-century sack-back dress, inspired a gown of 1902–3.

The albums show that the House of Worth came into its own with that genre of protective eveningwear known as *sortie de bal*. These highly elaborate, often full-length and sometimes hooded evening cloaks (p.94, above left), mantles or sleeved coats were the ultimate in frou-frou, made in all manner of figured silks, organzas, chiffons and velvets with the requisite embroideries and trimmings. These eye-catching, ornate and ephemeral garments were worn over ball gowns to offer protection for the few steps women took from carriages or motor vehicles to make their spectacular entrance. Worth's *sortie de bal* are particularly elaborate confections – the ultimate 'look at me' garments – and would have generated quite a stir. A model of 1899–1900 is made from a jacquard silk with a woven foliate design, decorated with pom-pom like floral forms resembling hydrangea or alium flowers (p.94, bottom right). Ruched silk flounces are gathered together to form a high collar to draw attention to the wearer's face. Another, altogether fanciful, silk garment from 1901 is designed with cloud and star motifs, which recur in Worth's collections. Because of their inherent fragility few summer *sortie de bal* survive today; a rare example by Worth dated 1897–1900, in the V&A's collection, reveals that hidden among the frou-frou curved steel supports were attached to the lining at the shoulders to strengthen and emphasize the sweeping lines of the garment (V&A: T.86-1991). For winter wear, a *sortie de bal* was necessarily more substantial and frequently supplied with a warm quilted lining. A design of 1899–1900 is made in velvet, patterned with a design of buddleia stems. It retains the

ABOVE LEFT – Wedding gown, plain white satin with a piecrust pleated hem (concealed on the left side is a trail of artificial bridal flowers), 1899-1900. AAD/1982/1/62

ABOVE RIGHT – Court gown and train (rear view), silver gauze, tulle and chiffon, 1903-4. AAD/1982/1/47

OPPOSITE – Wedding gown, white satin and taffeta, white and cream tulle with lace and trimmed at shoulders and waist with traditional sprays of wax orange blossom, 1903-4. AAD/1982/1/47

airy, gathered silk frill that characterizes the summer models and has a lower skirt made of silk with a seasonal holly design (p.94, below left). A winter model, of *c*.1901, is made from a berry-and-foliate patterned silk and has ermine collar and cuffs (p.95, above).

THE WEDDING GOWN

Though the five albums devoted entirely to wedding gowns, or *robe de mariée*, were transferred to Bath's Fashion Museum, the V&A's albums also contain photographs of several wedding gowns. They appear, at random, amid *robes de bal*. A trained *robe de mariée* of 1899–1900, executed in plain white silk satin, is powerful in its simplicity; though the inscription mentions 'fleurs', there are none to be seen in the photograph. The dress is unadorned apart from a self-fabric pie-crust frill around the hem (see above). Mlle de Greffuhle's satin wedding gown (of 1904) by Worth was similarly understated. As the daughter of the eminent Comte and Comtesse de Greffuhle, her marriage to the Duc de Guiche was fully reported in fashion and society columns.

The Queen's reporter painted a lyrical picture of the scene but was clearly taken aback at such a stark wedding gown: 'Within the sacred edifice a veritable fairy scene was *en evidence* where high banked exotic plants and flowers were lighted by twinkling candles… This together with the rich and multi-coloured toilettes of the distinguished guests was strange in contrast with the simplicity of the youthful bride whose silvery-white satin robe, although a creation of Worth, was marked by plain severity. The corsage draped slightly towards one side in Louis XVI fashion, terminated above a high corselet, and finished with tulle, illusion rosettes and a garland of orange blossom, which fell to the base of the plain skirt'.[31] The bride's mother, said to have inspired Proust's Princess de Guermantes, was a regular Worth client and indeed wore an 'exquisite Worth gown' to the wedding, 'luxuriously embroidered in gold and silver', according to *The Queen*. 'The long Princesse simplicity of the robe was embellished by Byzantine embroidery on tulle nacré, which effected a toilette of the style in vogue in the Middle Ages'.[32] This magnificent gown survives in the Palais Galliera collection in Paris.

CEREMONIAL COURT DRESS

The specific design criteria for ceremonial robes were dictated by each nation's court. Lillie de Hegermann-Lindencrone was wife of the Danish Minister stationed in Rome and made her first official appearance in 1881 at the Corps Diplomatique, which started at 2pm. She wrote to her mother that this was 'a rather trying time to be *décolletée* and look your best. In my letter from Paris I told you about my dress made by Worth. It really is quite lovely – white brocade, with the tulle front – all embroidered with iridescent beads and pearls. The *manteaux de cour* is of white satin, trimmed with Valencienne lace and ruches of chiffon. I wore my diamond tiara, my pearls on my neck, and everything I owned in the way of jewelry pinned on me somewhere.'[33] She continued, 'In crossing this *salon* one lets one's train drag on the floor and proceeds, peacock-like, toward the ball room. It seems that this is the proper thing to do as it is expected of you to allow all beholders to admire your train and to verify its length. It must be four and a half yards long… On entering the ballroom you pick up your train and go to your place – for every lady has her place according to her *ancienneté*.'[34] The Worth albums contain one particularly splendid, flower decorated silk court robe with a long train, dated 1902–3 (p.87, below). In order to fulfill his fashion aesthetic Worth did not always adhere to court regulations as diligently as he might. By 1903 the couple were resident in Berlin. Lillie noted that 'The ladies of the *Corps Diplomatique* are not always as observant of court rules as they ought to be, and their *décolletage* is not always impeccable. If Worth sends a corsage with the fashionable cut – what can they do? They manage, when they stand on their platform *en vue*, to slip their shoulders out, thereby leaving a tell-tale mark, only to slip the shoulders in place when royalty has its back turned.'[35]

Paul Poiret evokes memorably the excitement caused by an extremely important ceremonial commission: 'One day the House was filled with red velvet, and no other word was heard but Crimson. It was the colour of the cloaks of State at the Court of England, and the forthcoming coronation of Edward VII had been announced. M. Jean Worth proudly showed me a notice received from the English Court, describing the etiquette. All the nobility wore, according to their titles and precedence, longer or shorter trains, and more or less numerous ermine borders. For three months we made nothing but Court mantles. They were distributed throughout every room in the House, for one could not think of working on tables these fragile velvets, woven according to secular tradition – they would have been ruined if they had been pulled about. They were therefore placed over wooden mannequins, and their trains pinned to the floor; swarms of workwomen circled them, working at pressure but meticulously, like arch-deacons around some holy relic. M. Worth showed everyone these hieratic masterpieces, which to him seemed to represent the superlative beauty. He exulted. I must avow, with shame, that I never understood what he found admirable about them. I compared these conventional get-ups with the red, gold-fringed draperies held high by the Maison Belloir over important marriages, or distributions of prizes, in municipal ceremonies.'[36]

NOTES
1. P.N. Furbank and A.M. Cain, *Mallarmé on Fashion: A translation of the fashion magazine La Dernière Mode with commentary* (Oxford, 2004), pp.124–5.
2. Gaston Worth, quoted in the *Pall Mall Gazette* and the *New York Times*, both 21 June 1884.
3. *Harper's Bazar*, 23 January 1892, p.67.
4. Devereux 1902, p.16.
5. Devereux 1902, p.14.
6. J-P. Worth 1908, Part 1, n.p.
7. *The Queen*, 1 May 1909, p.745.
8. *The Queen*, 1 March 1913, p.372.
9. Devereux 1902, p.15.
10. *The Queen*, July 1905.
11. J-P. Worth 1928, p.100–1.
12. Devereux 1902, p.6.
13. *The Queen*, 14 October 1911, p.677.
14. *Herald*, Rochester, NY, 10 April 1895.
15. J-P. Worth 1928, p.154.
16. Picken 1924, p.197.
17. Pritchard 1902, p.24.
18. *The Queen*, 9 February 1907, p.235.
19. Coleman 1989, p.44.
20. Devereux 1902, p.15.
21. Devereux 1902, p.41.
22. *The Queen*, 31 March 1900, p.519.
23. 'The Mode of March', *The Queen*, March 1900, p.366.
24. Laura Ponsonby, 'Marianne North in India', *Saalg Newsletter 1*, p.10.
25. Anon. ['A Member of the Aristocracy'], *Manners and Rules of Good Society*, 1893, p.83.
26. Consuelo Vanderbilt Balsan, *The Glitter and the Gold* (first published London, 1953; Maidstone, Kent, 1973)
27. Lady Diana Cooper, *The Rainbow Comes and Goes* (London, 1958), p.85.
28. *Herald*, Rochester, NY, 10 April 1895.
29. J-P. Worth 1908, Part 1.
30. Winterburn 1914, p.50.
31. *The Queen*, 26 November 1904, p.835.
32. *The Queen*, 26 November 1904, p.835.
33. Hegermann-Lindencrone 1914, p.93.
34. Hegermann-Lindencrone 1914, pp.93–4.
35. Hegermann-Lindencrone 1912, p.292.
36. Poiret 1931, pp.63–4.

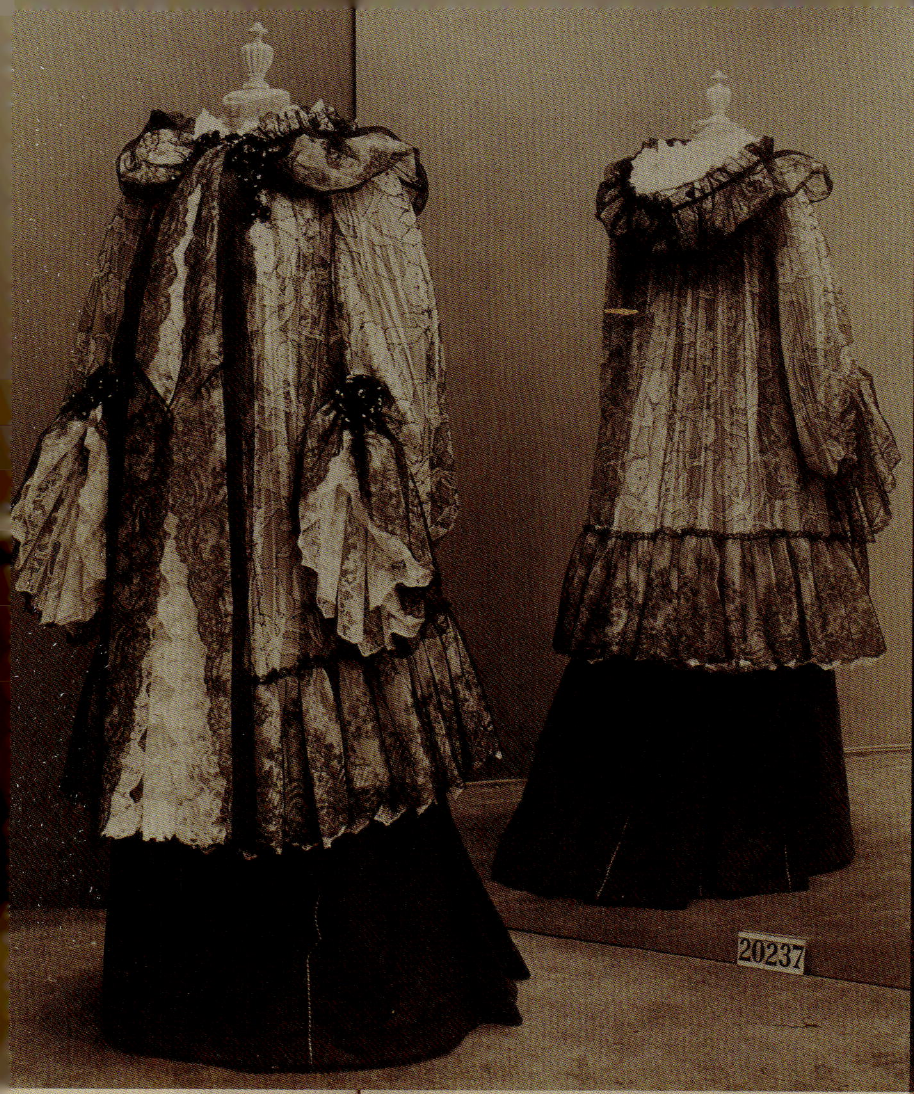
20237

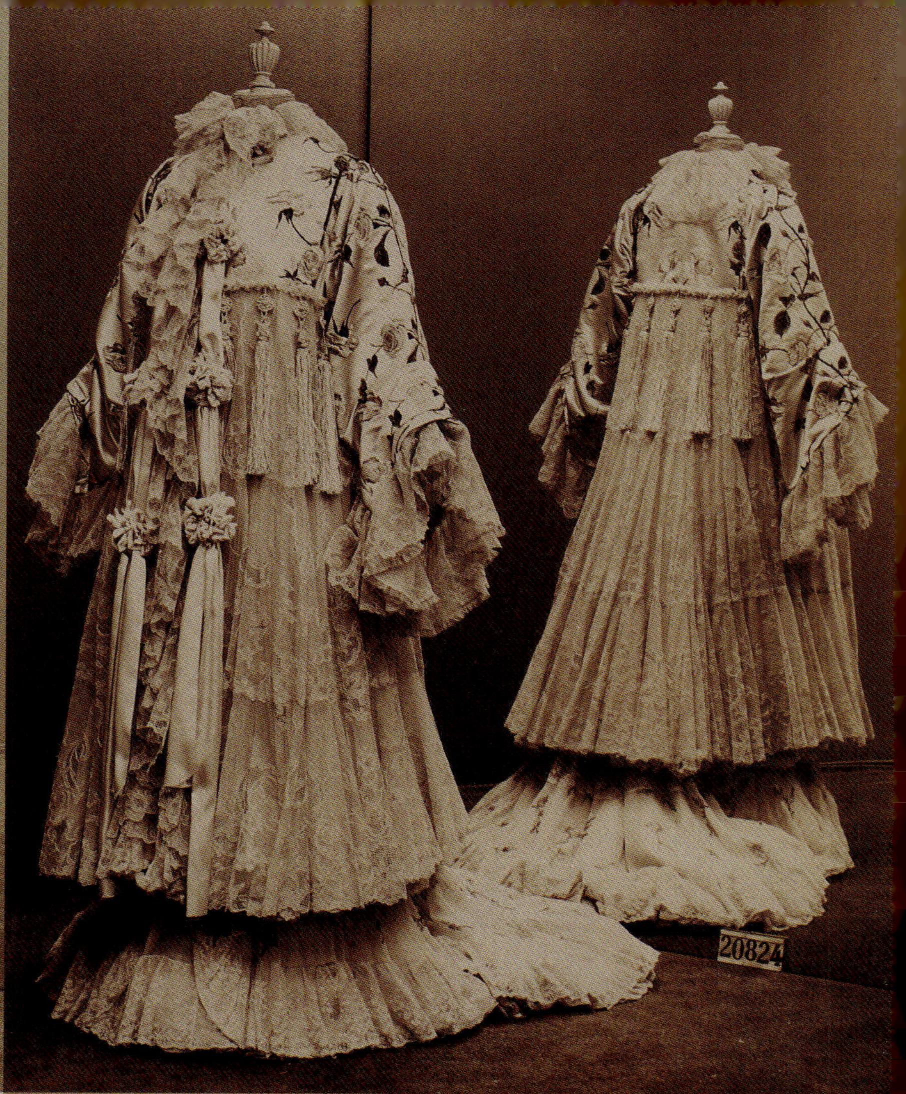
20824

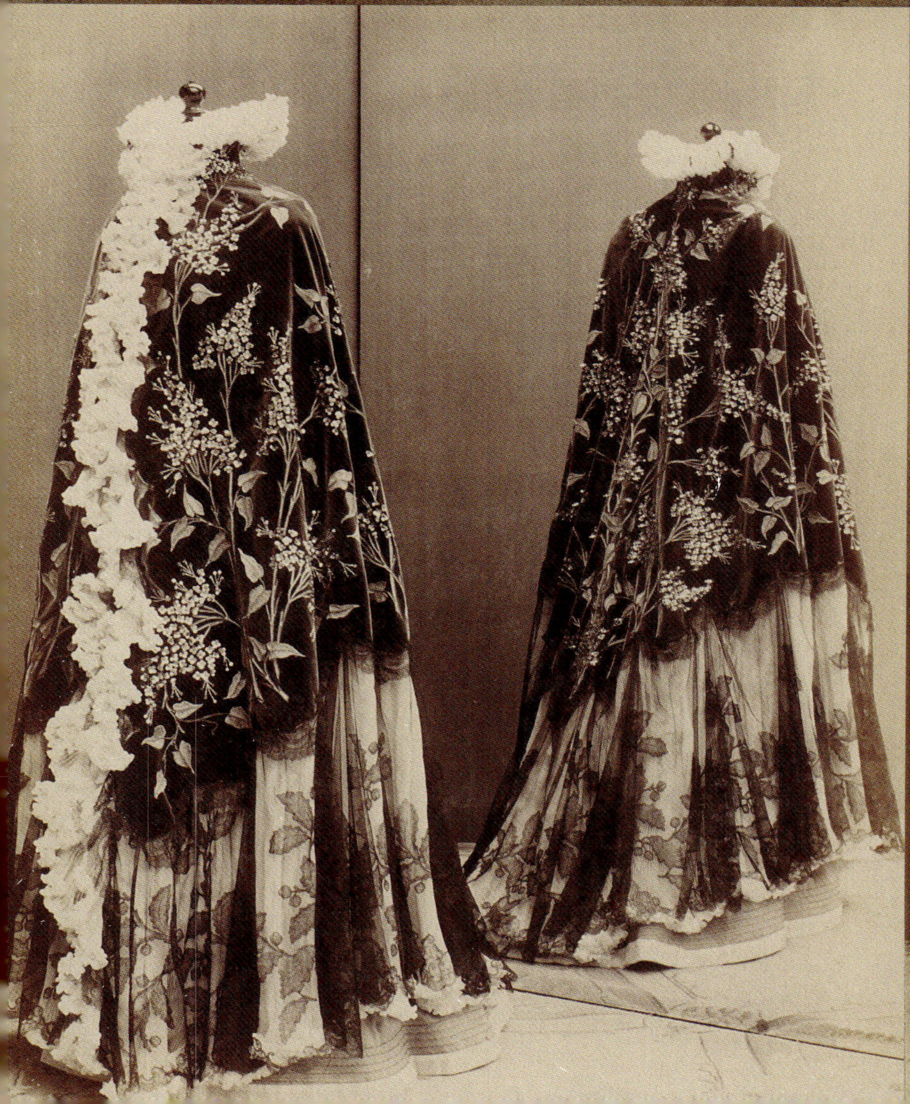

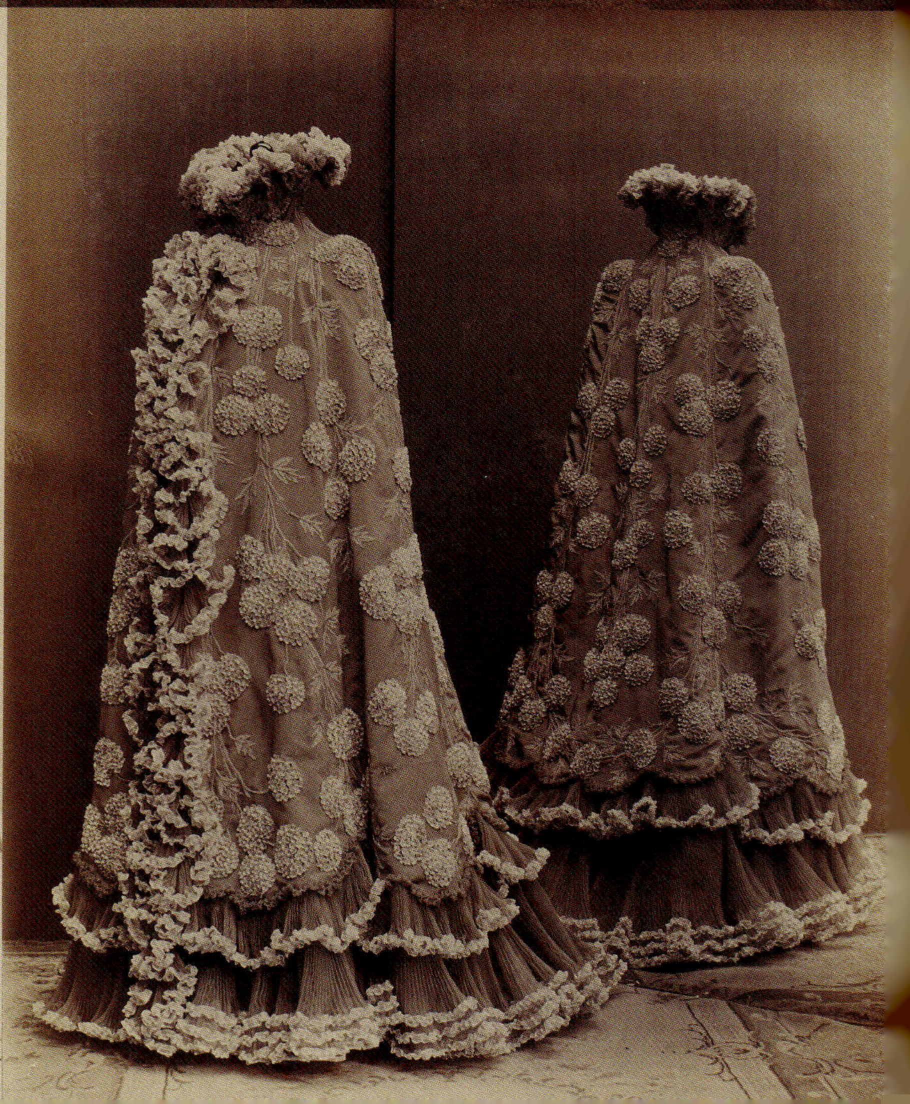

OPPOSITE, ABOVE LEFT – *Sortie de bal* (with a wide hood), figured silk and lace over white silk and lace, embroidered with jet and with jet rosettes, 1902-3. AAD/1982/1/25

OPPOSITE, ABOVE RIGHT – *Sortie de bal*, blue satin brocaded with polychrome rose tendrils with lace, sky-blue chiffon, long silk tassels and streamers, 1902-3. AAD/1982/1/25

OPPOSITE, BELOW LEFT – *Sortie de bal*, silk velvet with design of buddleia stems and deep lace border trimmed with pleated and ruched chiffon, 1899-1900. AAD/1982/1/21

OPPOSITE, BELOW RIGHT – *Sortie de bal*, yellow silk faille embroidered with 'boules de neige' and embellished with ruched silk chiffon, 1899-1900. AAD/1982/1/21

ABOVE – *Sortie de bal*, panne velvet embroidered with jet and diamanté with ermine cape and flared ermine cuffs, trimmed with lace, ribbon and ruched silk chiffon, c.1901. AAD/1982/1/24

BELOW – *Sortie de bal*, satin embroidered with stars and clouds and starred, spangled, pleated and ruched chiffon with streamers, bows and fringes, c.1901. AAD/1982/1/24

BELOW — Mantle, pale green crêpe de Chine with lavender Liberty silk, 1912-13.
AAD/1982/1/37

OPPOSITE — Day ensemble, caped top and pleated skirt in yellow-green lightweight wool with neat collar and a high-necked chemisette, 1906.
AAD/1982/1/8

1979. Robe lainage réséda plissé
Jupe plissé CW.
Satinette f
Dessus vert 9   ffr - fbg
Taffetas blanc 6 (autant)

ABOVE — 'Calipso', afternoon dress, white taffeta and black Chantilly lace with embroidered bows and sash with long streamer at back, 1912. AAD/1982/1/17

OPPOSITE — Day dress, gold-coloured fine wools, and 'Liberty' silk and black-and-gold lace with an apron back, decorated with soutache swirls, 1908-9. AAD/1982/1/10

99

ABOVE, LEFT TO RIGHT – 'Chanteler', evening gown, printed silk mousseline, in blue on a pink ground with skirt composed of diagonal bands of striped silk alternating with bands printed with huge sunflower heads with lace bodice, paste buckle and long satin sash, 1912. AAD/1982/1/58

'Postillion', striped silk gown, with cropped black silk and lace jacket, 1911. AAD/1982/1/15

OPPOSITE – 'Glameuse', *robe de dîner*, lemon taffeta embroidered with a design of floral baskets and ruched silk borders with black and white silk under dress and lace trimmings, 1911. AAD/1982/1/16

4024 Robe de dîner,
Glaneuse   pékin blanc à noir,
               garni taffetas citron

BELOW, LEFT TO RIGHT —
'Monique', afternoon dress (sari like), with layered or 'wrapped' skirt with wide borders and collar with deep revers in navy blue satin, 1910–11. AAD/1982/1/34

'Vicletta', high waisted *robe de dîner*, centre front and borders of brocaded silk trimmed with fur, 1910–11. AAD/1982/1/14

OPPOSITE, LEFT TO RIGHT — 'Frileuse', high waisted afternoon dress, brown silk velvet with tiered skirt; bodice with cross-over straps and layered pale silk top with embroidered central medallion, 1913–14. AAD/1982/1/19

Mantle, in beaded figured silk with contrasting coloured lining, 1910–11. AAD/1982/1/34

103

BELOW – 'Tripoli', afternoon dress, very fine wool with a pleated overskirt and embroidered borders of geometric cutwork, 1900. AAD/1982/1/16

OPPOSITE – 'Ostende', day ensemble (tunic and skirt), cream and white linen with velvet sash, lace and embroidered flowerpot motifs, 1913-14. AAD/1982/1/19

4772. Robe en toile crème
Ostende — toile blanche avec broderie

wbo ogr

BELOW – 'Gamine', afternoon ensemble; blue voile with white voile and lace blouse, beaded belt and tassels, 1912-13.
AAD/1982/1/18

OPPOSITE – Princess line day gown, beige wool with a faux divided front and waistcoat worked in soutache, 1909-10.
AAD/1982/1/12

5441. Robe princesse en lainage beige
Lainage beige a.gr
Merveilleux blanc o.gr.
Broderie ma

BELOW – Afternoon gown, figured silk over grey satin with lace jabot, trimmed with fur (including a collar with pair of paws), 1909-10. AAD/1982/1/12

OPPOSITE – Princess line afternoon gown, lightweight wool with flared turned back cuffs, lace trimming and deep fur hem, 1909. AAD/1982/1/11

2867. Robe Satin sestale gris.
Satin sestale gris srf
Toile de Soie   cr Exter- cqmg (sans fourrure)
Broderie   gr
Fourrure   gaa   a f g (Sans fourrure)

2851 Robe drap blanc garnie ?...?

Drap blanc ca avec fourrure
Manc bl.
broderie bl cw99 cbfg
fourrure bwr

5

FANCY DRESS

AMY DE LA HAYE

BELOW, LEFT TO RIGHT —
Evening gown (possibly fancy dress), yellow voided silk velvet with meandering pattern based on a Venetian fifteenth-century velvet, 1902–3. AAD/1982/1/46

Henri III style fancy dress, designed for a bal blanc, c.1889. AAD/1982/1/62

A sixteenth-century style gown worn over a farthingale, designed by Worth for a calico ball, 1913–14. AAD/1982/1/42

OPPOSITE, LEFT TO RIGHT — Lady Paget, dressed by Worth as Cleopatra for the Devonshire House Ball, 1897. Her headdress was made from real jewels from her own collection. Photograph by Lafayette Studios

Louisa, Duchess of Devonshire, dressed by Worth as Zenobia, Queen of Palmyra, for the Devonshire House Ball, 1897. Photograph by Lafayette Studios

The Duke of Marlborough, dressed by Worth as the French Ambassador at the Court of Catherine of Russia, for the Devonshire House Ball, 1897. Photograph by Lafayette Studios © Devonshire Collection, Chatsworth. Reproduced by permission of Chatsworth Settlement Trustees.

117

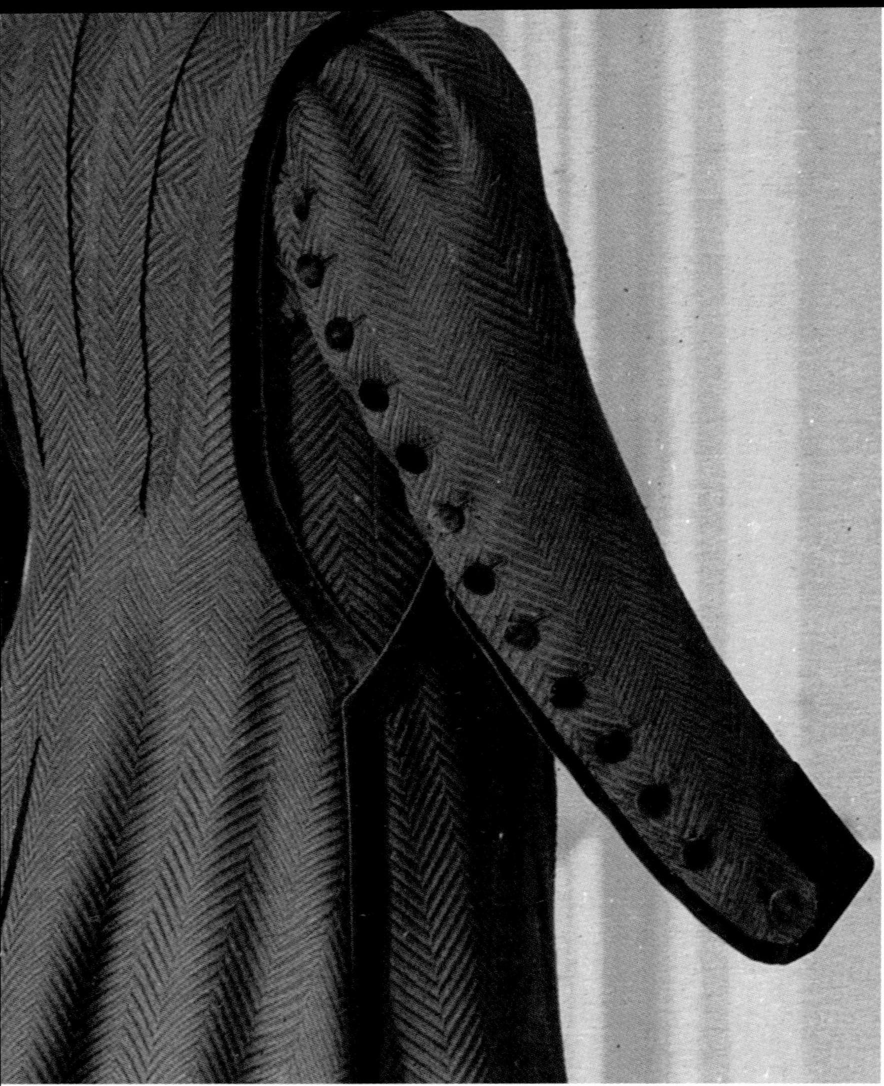
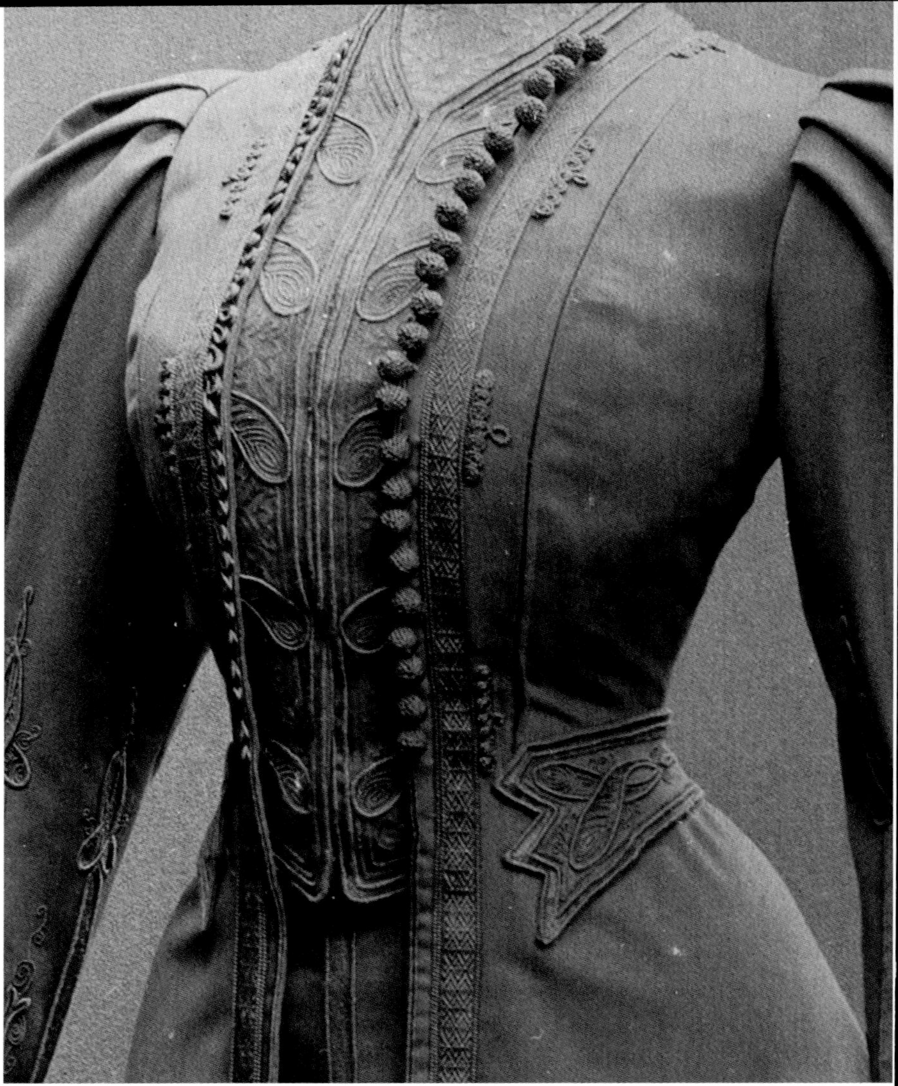
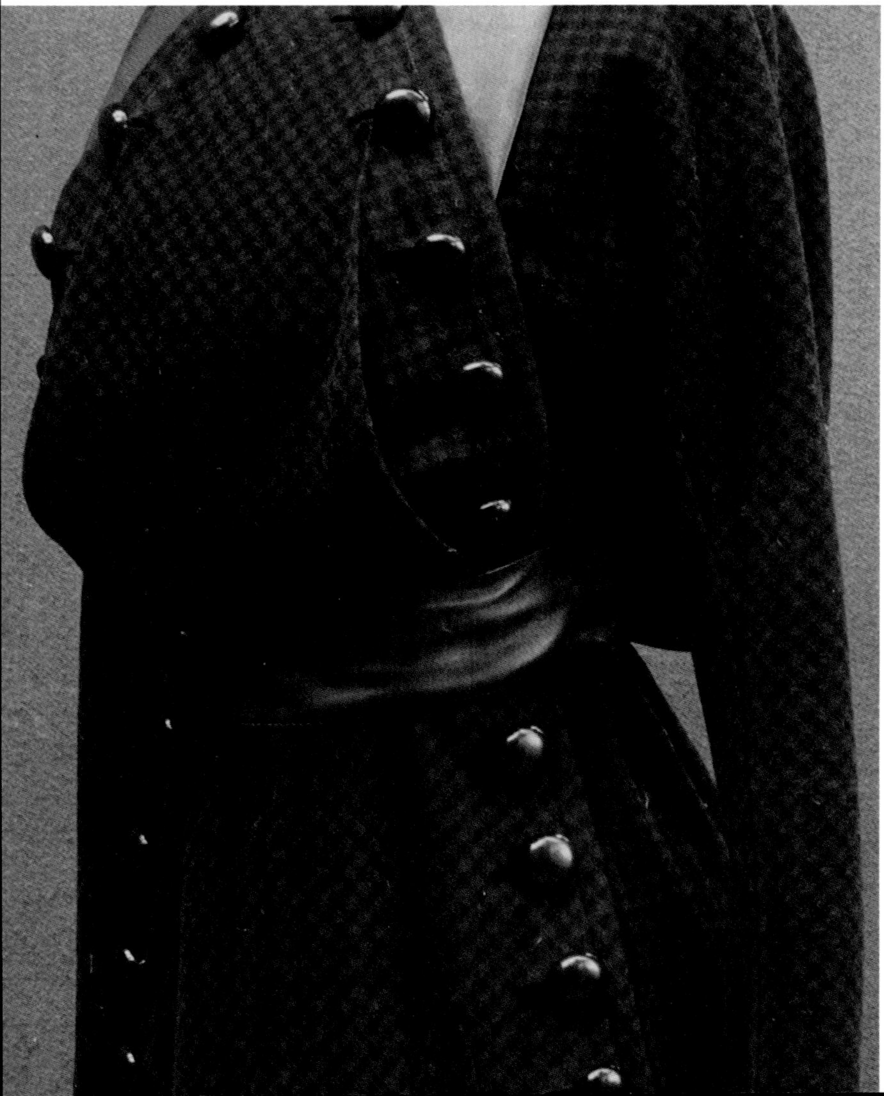
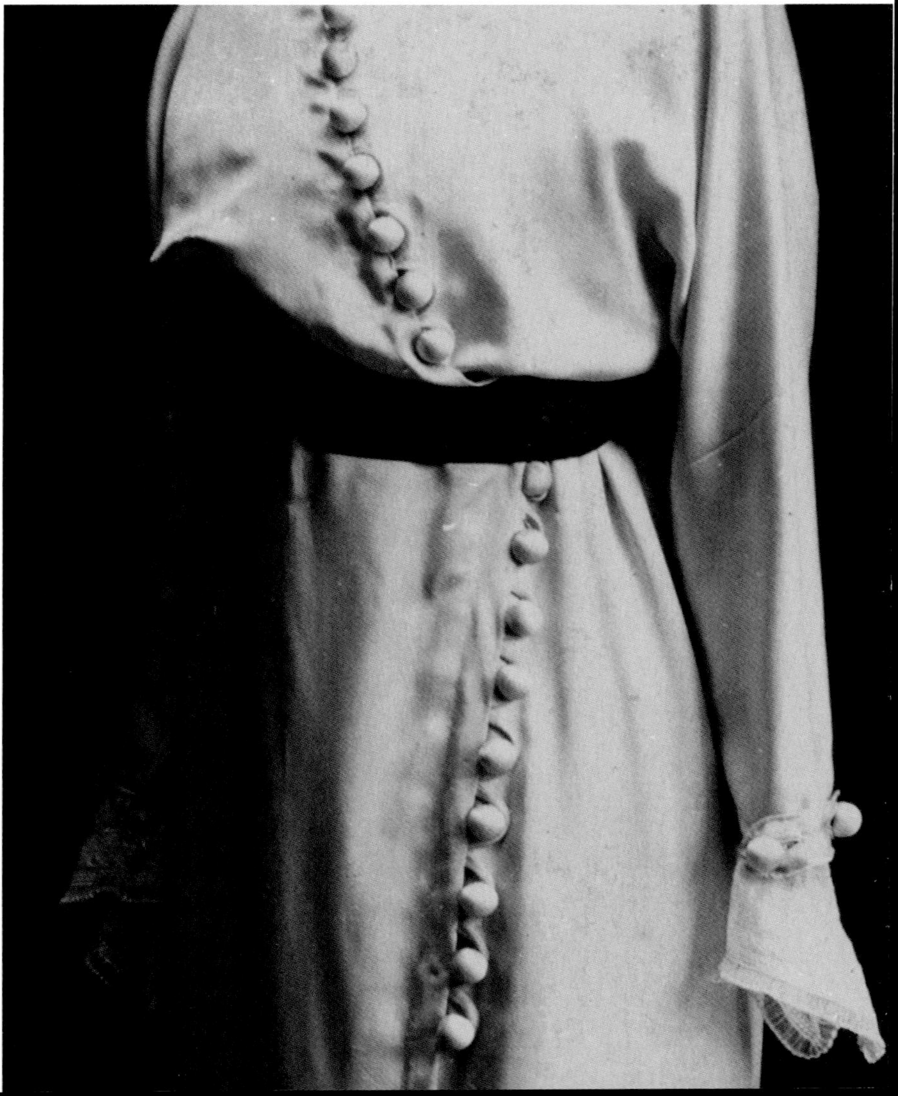

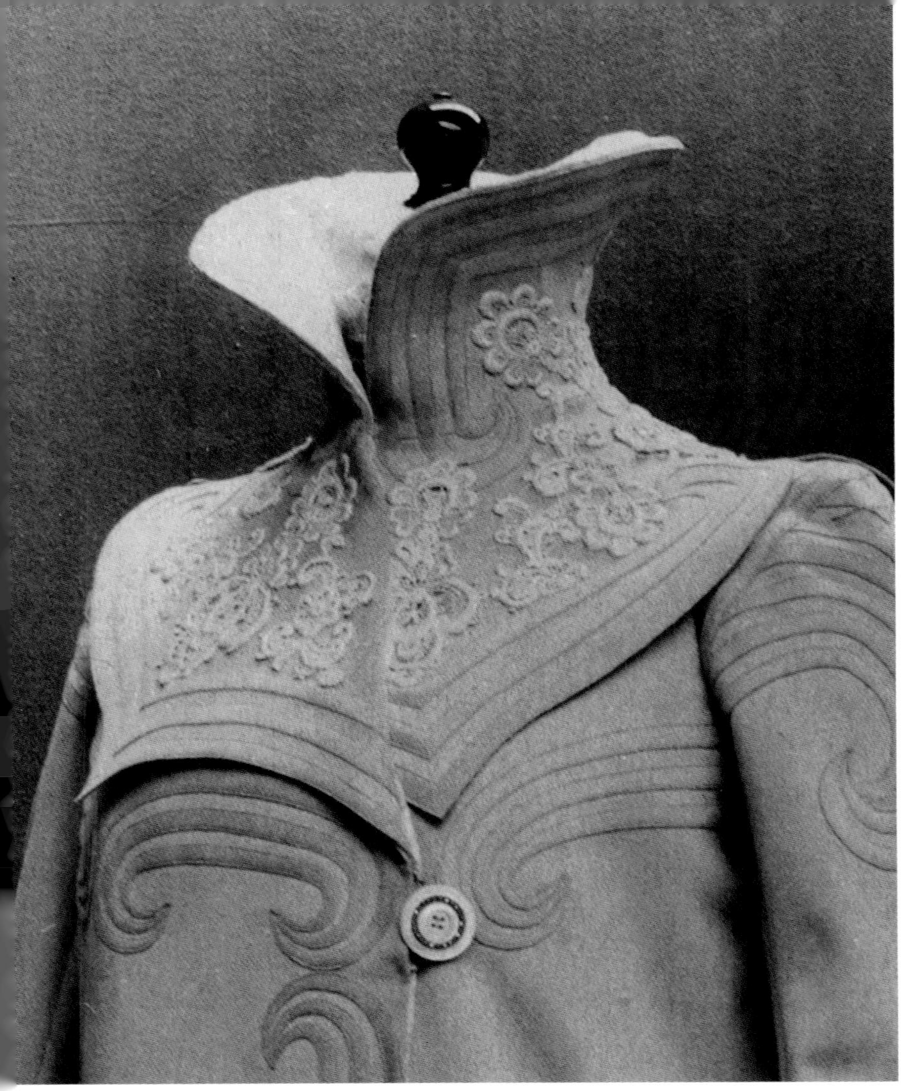
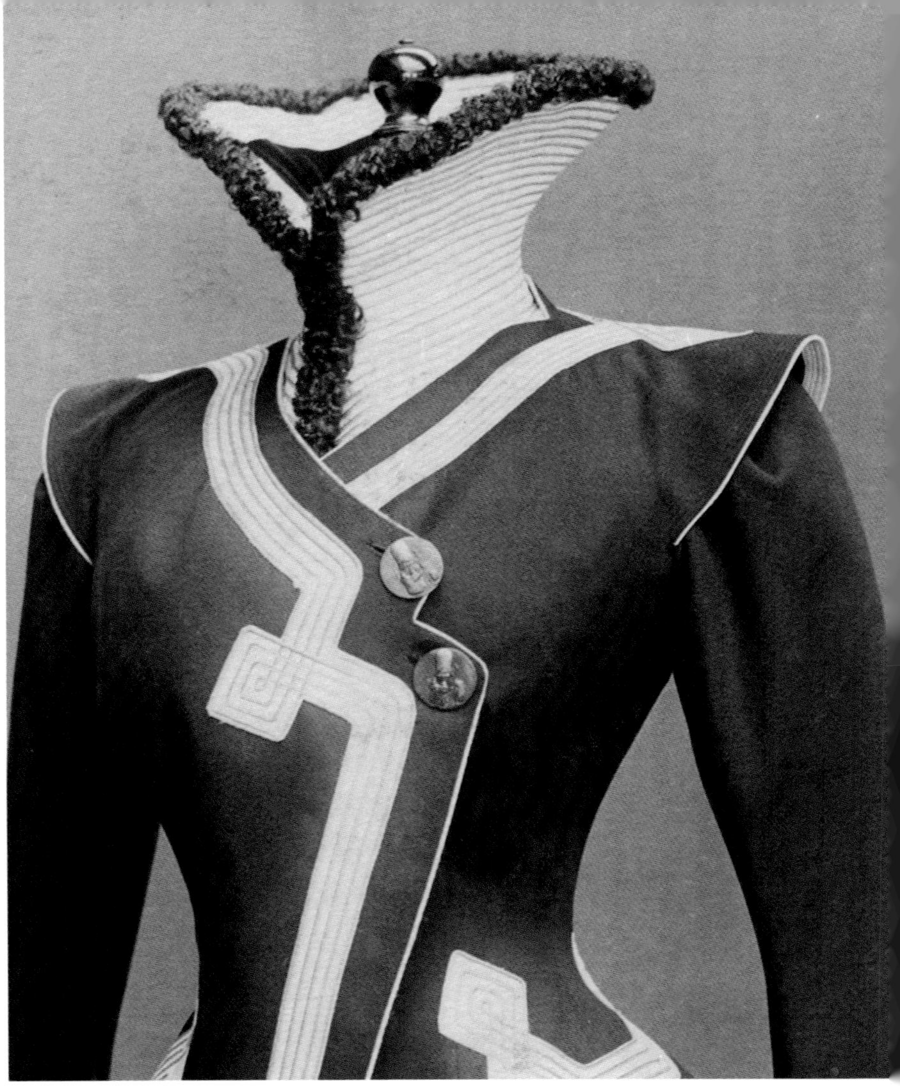
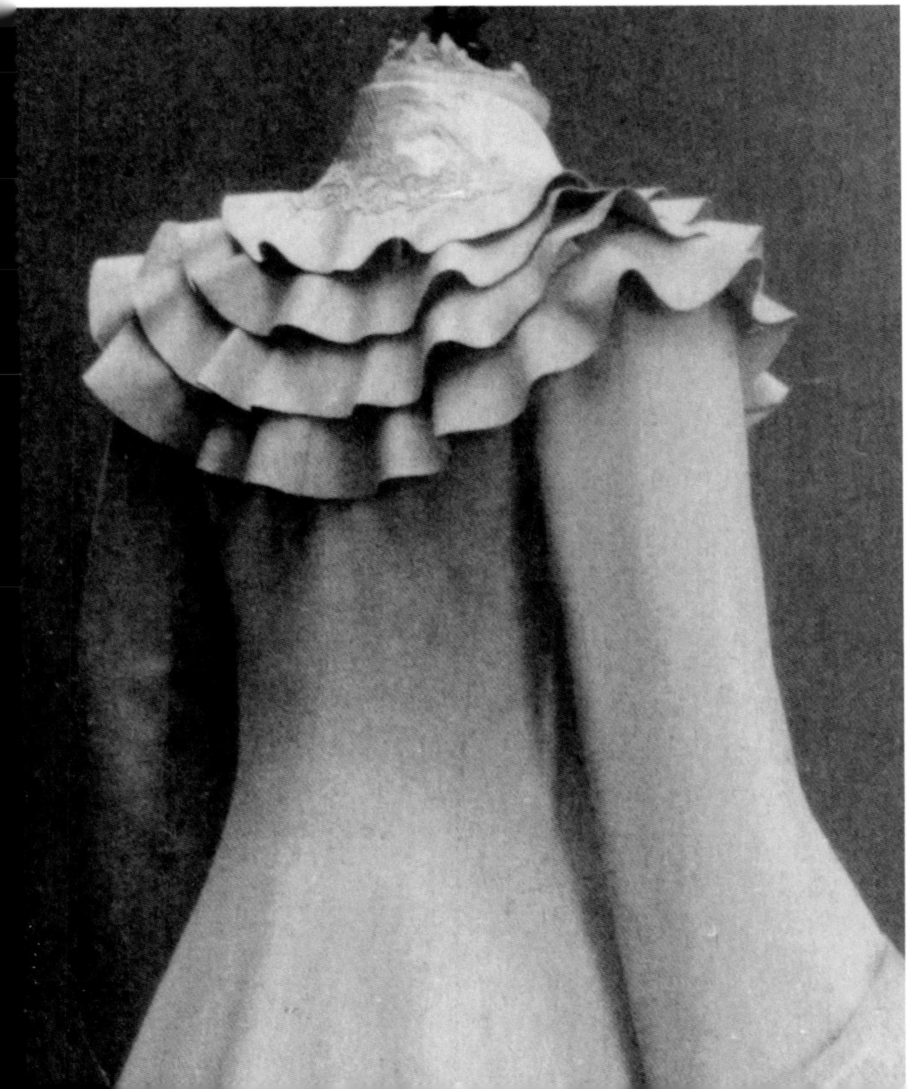
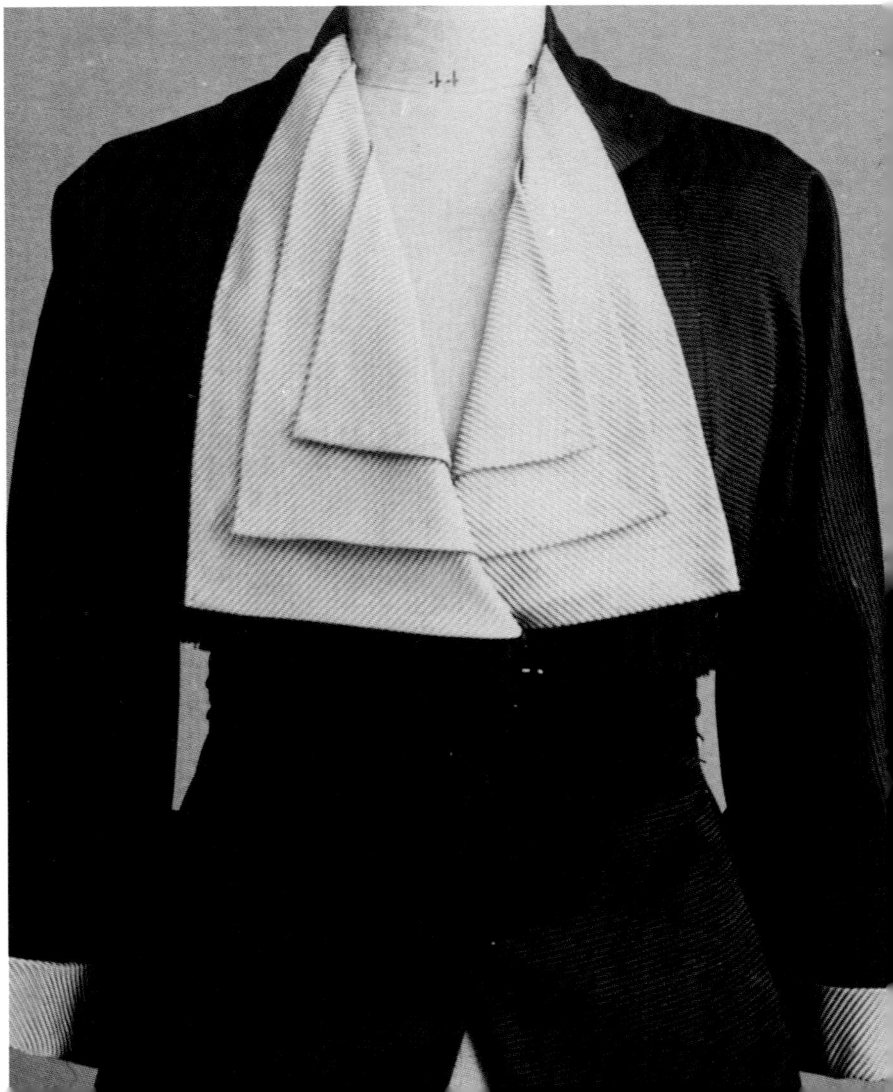

6

CLIENTS

AMY DE LA HAYE

ABOVE – Frances ('Daisy'), Countess of Warwick, cabinet card studio photograph by Herbert Rose Barraud, 1889. National Portrait Gallery, London

Lindencrone, Danish Minister to the United States and subsequently his country's representative for Stockholm, Rome, Paris, Washington and Berlin. She continued to shop at Worth.

COUTURE COURTESANS

Worth's clients necessarily had access to wealth, but not all were socially illustrious. France's Second Empire gave rise to the ascent of a coterie of high-class courtesans, popularly known as *demi-mondaine*s or *grande cocottes* (the former derived from Alexandre Dumas' play *Le Demi Monde*, staged in 1855). Cecil Beaton described this group of 'déclassé women' as, 'exotic blooms, who were nurtured in the hothouse of all that money could buy, [and who] thrived in an easy atmosphere that created a tacitly agreed place for them in the social scene.'[7]

The more daring members of the *demi-monde* made themselves highly visible and occupied a high-profile place in society's 'half-world'. Jean Worth recalled the spectacle as they circled around Paris in their luxury carriages: 'No modern beauty pageant ever equalled their stately parade. It was the day when fashionable fast women were veritable queens.'[8] The actress Cora Pearl, born Emma Elizabeth Crouch in England, rose from poverty to become one of Paris's most famous courtesans. Her resplendent carriage was attended by footmen uniformed – defiantly – in the same shade of bright yellow as those engaged by Princess Pauline de Metternich. Author W.H. Holden researched her attendance at all the major balls, 'which she attended either smothered in diamonds or dressed in – as nearly as possible – nothing at all. At a fancy dress ball in 1866 she arrived as a scantily clad "Eve" whereas sister *grande horizontale* Giulia Beneni (known as La Barucci) came as a peacock in a dress by Worth.'[9] Julian Osgood Field remembers Cora Pearl at Baden Baden, 'gracefully sailing into the Kursaal, all dressed in white satin and white lace, covered in diamonds and pearls…'.[10]

Cora Pearl claimed to be one of the first women to stop wearing the crinoline in 1859. 'I believe that I did as much as anyone else to end its predominance, drawing my dresses up over a petticoat and underskirts made of new stuffs and colours – a white dress over a lilac and black petticoat, for instance.'[11] The image on p.129 (right) shows her wearing the successor to the crinoline, with the fullness of the skirt swept round to the back.

The author of *The Elegant Woman* (1923) noted that, 'All the *cocottes* of any reputation dressed at Worth's.'[12] Duchesses and *demi-mondaines* might have been dressed by the same couturier, but it was the responsibility of the house to ensure their paths never crossed. Jean Worth made light of the fact that Cora Pearl 'occasionally' shopped at Worth; of the *grande cocottes* in general he pointed out that, 'Few… came to the shop in the rue de la Paix: and when they did, it was not because we sought them out.'[13] However, their business was far too lucrative to shun.

STARS OF THE STAGE

Early in his career Charles Frederick Worth became aware that fashionable stage attire did much to attract female audiences and, once reviewed and illustrated in magazines and newspapers, fuelled the fashion choices made by countless women. Worth costumed many international stars of the stage, even though actresses were still tarnished with a reputation for dubious morals. As early as 1865, for instance, he dressed Jeanne Sylvanie Arnould-Plessy – 'Madame Plessy' – for her leading role in Edmond de Goncourt's *Henriette Maréchal* at the Comedie Française. Before a major row, he also dressed the famous French actress Sarah Bernhardt, an influential style leader who seemingly caused chaos when she visited the rue de la Paix to order her clothes. One newspaper reported that, 'She has many a time revolutionised, by her fancies, the fashion of women's attire. The house that costumes her humbly obeys her behests. When she goes there it is a big event, a fête which turns the whole establishment topsy turvy from roof to basement… she is truly the queen, the fairy that commands and transforms, as if by magic, silk and velvet into ideal costumes. She has twenty or thirty pieces of stuff rolled out before her to compare their shades. They are wound round her, heaped up in a pile, and form a fantastical frame-work for her… She becomes more and more amused, asks for other tints and shades, compares, objects, makes grimaces, twists her pocket-handkerchief as if she were on the stage, changes her mind, eats cakes, drinks a little champagne out of an ancient silver-bound goblet, and, in short, tires every one out. And the mighty man-milliner submits to all that, because it comes from Sarah…'.[14]

In 1896 *Vogue* reported that, 'Critics at first night performances of a play give close attention to details of costume. A famous actress is famous for her dresses as well as for her acting.'[15] It was not only the choice of gown, but also the manner in which an actress wore it that could render it so desirable. As Jean Worth realized, 'an actress of elegance can contribute to an ordinary idea something upon which its originator has not counted. By her personal charm, and above all if her talent is so attuned, she gives to the detail of her costume which constitutes the idea such emphasis that women who admire her seek immediately to imitate it – thinking that this artifice of the *toilette* they will each gain her gracious allure!'[16]

In London, the actress Mary Moore, who with her husband Sir Charles Wyndham established the Wyndham Theatre in 1899, wore Worth both on stage and off. She regularly ordered dresses from Paris and recalled how, 'as they had my pattern over there, [they] arrived ready to put on, without all the trouble of fitting. How delightful it was to receive such lovely gowns at a special prix d'artiste. In those days, one could afford to dress well!'[17]

One of Jean Worth's favourite clients and a life-long friend was the Italian actress Eleanor Duse, about whom he declared, 'To my mind, the greatest aristocrat was not of noble birth, but of royal soul, Eleanor Duse.'[18] Eleanor relied on Worth for advice on her clothes, make-up and coiffure, both on and off stage (p.123, right). In the biography *Eleonora Duse: The Story of her Life* (1924), Jeanne Bordeux stated that according to Duse he 'knew more about dressing a woman than anyone else in the world.' In his article 'Individuality in Dress' for *Harper's Bazar* (February 1908), Jean Worth described dressing Eleanor, who suffered from ill health: 'To give her gowns that would increase the impression of physical frailty would not be right, however beautiful they might be in themselves'. And concerning her personal fashion tastes, he continued: 'Her vogue in dress is usually *fourreau*, or princesse, and her main choice is white…'.[19]

Mrs James Brown-Potter, the famous auburn-haired actress, was a regular client at Worth for both stage and non-performance gowns. In 1899, Mrs Aria eulogized in *The Queen* about the glorious gowns that Worth had designed for the actress to wear in *The Physician: An Original Play in Four Acts* written by Henry Arthur Jones, at London's Majesty Theatre. 'They hail from Worth in Paris and do credit to their author, who must really feel very pleased to see his gowns so well worn. Mrs Potter does know how to put on her clothes, and they lack no possible grace under her adjustment.'[20] There followed detailed descriptions of various gowns, including one made of white satin with a design of irises in palest tints of green, pink and mauve, decorated with pearls and brilliants, with a fichu of mousseline and lace, accessorized with a belt of gold braid clasped with bronze, studded with matching coloured jewels. According to an obituary for Charles Frederick Worth in 1895, a visitor had once asked him, '[What is] your favourite figure to design for?', to which he responded, 'One of my ideals is Mrs Brown-Potter's. I consider her one of the most beautiful women I have ever seen'.[21]

Nellie Melba, born Helen Porter Mitchell, was Australia's famous operatic soprano. She, too, was dressed by Worth. In 1891 Jean created a much applauded 'cloak of angels' in cloth of gold, hand-painted and sewn with jewels, for her to wear in her role as Elsa in Wagner's *Lohengrin*. (In 1978 her granddaughter donated it to the Performing Arts Collection in Melbourne). Thereafter, Nellie Melba became a loyal customer, repeatedly returning to Paris for collections of new clothes. Her letter of commiseration to Marie Worth on the death of Charles Frederick is mounted in an album of condolences compiled by the family (see Appendix 05).

WORTH IN LITERATURE

Not only did Worth's desirable gowns clothe many a literary celebrity, they also entered the realm of fiction, where the world of couture combined with the pomp and grandeur of Charles Frederick's constructed artistic persona to provide particularly rich pickings for novelists from the 1870s onwards. While fictional heroines also became part of the Worth clientele, dress and the language of fashion became a means of building character and informing narrative.

The eccentric and extravagant novelist Maria Louise Ramé, known as 'Ouida', was a devoted if irritating Worth client. She was not a beauty but was unduly proud of certain features, instructing Worth that her opulent gowns should not be too long as she wished to display her dainty feet and sleeves should not hide her delicate wrists. While writing *Pascaral* (1873), a tale about Tuscan peasants, to suit the mood of the story she abandoned her costly silks and attired herself in the style of a village maiden. Her biographer describes how 'The exotic silks and velvets she usually took such pride wearing hung neglected in her wardrobe and Mr Worth made – to her own design – a number of simple white muslin frocks. In these rather musical comedy versions of peasant garb, Ramé presented a curious picture, because her vanity would not allow her to discard her expensive satin slippers and she could not resist adding decorations such as ruffles of real lace.'[22] While this practice has overtones of fancy dress, Maria Louise wore these especially commissioned clothes as part of her daily life. Her penchant for spectacle and riotous social gatherings was the stuff of novels. Around 1869 she greeted her guests thus: 'Against a rioting background of orchids, lilies, roses and white lilac she stood, an incongruous small figure in a pale coloured satin gown made specially for the occasion by Worth to receive her guests.' One gentleman guest, a seasoned traveller, exclaimed that he expected to see monkeys and parakeets appear at any moment![23]

Maria Louise (until financially bereft) patronized top Paris couturiers and was familiar with the world of fashion and its language, which pervaded her written work. A descriptive passage in chapter III of her short story *A House Party* (1887) captures an *élégante* of the period with precision: 'Mrs Faversham, the prettiest brunette in the universe, for whom Worth is supposed to make marvellous combinations of rose and gold, of amber and violet, of deep orange and black, and of a wondrous yellow like that of a daffodil, which no one dares to wear but herself'.

In *La Curée* (1872) Emile Zola's waywardly profligate Renée ordered her clothes at 'Worms' (Worth). Zola's multi-sensorial and emotive descriptions are especially evocative, using the language of fashion as a vehicle for setting the scene for his characters and describing their psychological state of mind.[24] When Renée's gentleman admirer accompanies her to Worms, Zola reflects that, 'Dresses, undoubtedly, have a perfume of their own; silk, satin, velvet, and lace had mingled their faint aromas with those of hair and of amber-scented shoulders; and the atmosphere in the room had the sweet smelling warmth, the fragrance of flesh and luxury, that transformed the apartment into a chapel consecrated to some secret divinity.' Zola even captures the sound of fashionable dress and entwines the noise made by long trained gowns with anxiety: 'Renée felt restless and nervous there; her silk skirts glided with snakelike hisses over the thick carpets…'.[25]

Novelist Edith Wharton, born in New York, was part of the privileged society whose lives she chronicled. She knew from experience how it felt to be dressed by Worth. Her mother had worn Parisian haute couture and the writer recalled, in her autobiography *A Backward Glance* (1934), how in childhood, 'I shared the excitement caused by the annual arrival of the "trunk from Paris", and the enchantment of seeing one resplendent dress after another shaken out of its tissue-paper.' In March 1896 *Vogue* noted that fortunate women were having their spring visiting gowns sent over, 'from the great maker Worth. The seas have treated them most tenderly, to judge by appearances, for they look as if they had been carried in some footman's arms, in their box-wrappings, not more than a square or two. You would not give them an hour from the atelier at most.'[26] The packing of export orders was a skill undertaken in-house, and also by specialist companies, and was especially critical for their export trade.

Writing in the aftermath of the First World War, a recurrent theme in Wharton's work was the erosion of elite social hierarchies within American society. *The Age of Innocence* (1920) is a sentimental tale set in the 1870s about May Welland, a fictitious client of the House of Worth, and her fiancé Newland Archer, who nearly succumbs to the charms of the Europeanized Ellen Olanska. Wharton exploits the colour associations of fashion to reveal the nature of the would-be seductress who dons a cloak of scarlet (harlot) red. Newland ultimately bows to convention and marries May whose white (with its associations of purity, but also coldness and deathliness) wedding dress comes from Worth. While on their three-month 'wedding tour', the couple are invited to a London dinner party and May expresses uncertainty about which of her new gowns she should wear. Newland proposes her wedding gown (which

BELOW – Mrs James Brown-Potter in theatrical dress, c.1880. AAD/1990/4/243

many brides had altered and wore in their first year of wedlock), but May bemoans, '"Oh, dearest! If I only had it here! But it's gone back to Paris to be made over for next winter, and Worth hasn't sent it back!"'[27]

Couture clients regularly returned garments to the fashion houses to be altered to accommodate changing trends, shifting body silhouettes or different requirements. The exhibition *Eight Chicago Women and their Fashions 1860–1929* included clothing belonging to Mrs Cyrus Hall McCormick (née Fowler), who was a thrifty haute couture consumer. Her surviving gowns from Worth revealed evidence of extended wear as a result of alterations. Amongst her collection was a mid-1860s Worth evening bodice. The luxurious silk from the voluminous matching skirt had been made into a dress by an American dressmaker named Maison Savarre (to give it a French cachet).

Wharton describes alterations undertaken by American dressmakers in terms of the prejudices of 'old' American families about wearing the very latest fashions from Paris. Miss Jackson, a secondary character in *The Age of Innocence*, is taken to the first night at the opera and reports to Newland's mother what a fellow attendee wore: '"Jane Merry's dress was the only one I recognised from last year; and even that had had the front panel changed. Yet I know she got it out from Worth only two years ago, because my seamstress always goes in to make over her Paris dresses before she wears them."' '"Ah, Jane Merry is one of us," said Mrs Archer sighing, as if it were not such an enviable thing to be in an age when ladies were beginning to flaunt abroad their Paris dresses as soon as they were out of the Custom House instead of letting them mellow under lock and key, in the manner of Mrs Archer's contemporaries.'[28]

Mrs Archer then cites the case of a Mrs Baxter Pennilow, who had a standing order with Worth for her seasonal gowns. After enduring a two-year illness she died, whence her daughters found 48 dresses from Worth, still in their original packing. When they came out of mourning, they were able to wear them to '"the Symphony Concerts without looking out of fashion."'[29]

CONSPICUOUS CONSUMPTION

By the turn of the century haute couture and its consumers were attracting the attention of social commentators. In his seminal text, *The Theory of the Leisure Class* (1899), the economist and cultural theorist Thorstein Veblen reported that it was women's 'conspicuous consumption' that served to demonstrate a family's wealth and social status. A biting critique of materialistic American culture, Veblen's views, in many respects, still ring true today. In the chapter 'Dress as an Expression of the Pecuniary Culture', he wrote: 'Dress must not only be conspicuously expensive and inconvenient; it must at the same time be up to date.'[30] Veblen argued that it was by wearing conspicuously expensive and impractical corseted fashions that women, as wives and daughters, demonstrated the economic wealth of the family unit. Veblen championed women but any personal pleasures and/or reassurance they might derive from fashion practices eluded him entirely. He condemned fashion as a wasteful, narcissistic activity that was driven by a desire for admiration and envy.

The shopping habits of America's Morgan banking dynasty, whose business, as stated by Jean Worth, 'meant everything to the Maison Worth', supports Veblen's thesis.[31] Patriarch Junius Spencer Morgan chose the models his wife was to wear. 'In 1900 a dress that had been made more for the Exposition than to be worn, caught his fancy and he immediately had it duplicated for his wife at the cost of about eight thousand francs, which would be well over fifty thousand francs today. She wore it, I believe, only once.'[32] In turn, his son, John Piermont, ordered the clothes his daughter wore. On one occasion Jean showed John a piece of precious *point de Venise* handmade lace, which cost a staggering $22,000, quickly followed by the suggestion that he might prefer a cheaper machine-made lace. When Mr Morgan enquired about the difference, Jean drew an analogy with a real and an imitation pearl. Without hesitation, Mr Morgan proclaimed, '"then we'll have the real one. Take the imitation away."'[33]

Writing in 1904, American sociologist Georg Simmel interpreted the function of fashion quite differently. He considered it a useful social tool that could help women create an individual appearance within the parameters of established fashion trends. In other words, fashionable dress could be interpreted as evidence of both individual distinction and commonality. Like Veblen, he depicted fashion as a device that made explicit class differentiation: once the social elite had disseminated a new style, they swiftly moved on to something new in order retain their distinction.

DOLLAR PRINCESSES

In the late nineteenth century a number of wealthy American women married relatively impoverished British aristocrats. The contract between each family was explicit: the bride's family provided much needed revenue in exchange for the status that a prestigious title conferred. The experiences of the young American heiress Consuelo Vanderbilt Balsan might well have formed another of Veblen's case studies. In the early 1890s the 17-year-old Consuelo was launched, by her mother's friend Lady Mary ('Minnie') Paget, into London society for the purpose of securing a 'good' marriage. Lady Paget, born Mary Stevens in New York, was Consuelo's godmother. Along with the Duchess of Manchester, Lady Randolph Churchill and Mrs Cavendish-Bentinck, she numbered among the American contingent of London's fun-loving 'Prince of Wales set'.

Consuelo Vanderbilt's autobiography, *The Glitter and the Gold* (1953), is – for this period – unusually candid. She recalled Lady Paget giving her a long, hard stare and then declaring imperiously to her mother that, '"If I am to bring her out, she must be able to compare at least as far as clothes are concerned with far better-looking girls."'[34] Deciding that Consuelo was devoid of taste, her mother took her to Worth and determined which designs she would wear. By the end of the season Consuelo was engaged to Charles Spencer-Churchill, 9th Duke of Marlborough, who then accompanied both women to Worth. Consuelo rued, 'Unfortunately, his taste appeared to be dictated by a desire for magnificence rather than by any wish to enhance my looks. I remember particularly one evening dress of sea-blue satin with a long train, whose whole length was trimmed with white ostrich feathers. Another creation was a rich pink velvet with sables. Jean Worth himself directed the fittings of these beautiful dresses, which she and my husband considered suitable, but which I would willingly have exchanged for the tulle and organdie that girls of my age were wearing.'[35]

LEFT TO RIGHT – *Consuelo Vanderbilt, Duchess of Marlborough and her Son, Lord Ivor Spencer-Churchill*, by Giovanni Boldini, 1906. © 2012 The Metropolitan Museum of Art/Art Resource/Scala, Florence

Cora Pearl wearing a Worth riding habit, 1860s. Photograph by A.A.E. Disdéri. National Portrait Gallery, London

BY ROYAL APPOINTMENT

During the late nineteenth century and the early years of the twentieth, Queen Victoria's son Edward and his wife Alexandra were the leaders of aristocratic life in Britain, which revolved around the court and the seasonal calendar of social events. As prince and king, Edward was fastidious about dress and sartorial etiquette; paradoxically, he was instrumental in relaxing rigid traditions and social conventions.

Though Worth dressed international royalty, Jean claimed he did not receive direct orders from the royal household of his country of birth. Queen Victoria and, as princess and queen, Alexandra patriotically championed London's court dressmakers. However, Jean claims that they each – unwittingly – wore designs that originated at Worth, although they were made and purchased in London. With reference to Queen Victoria he wrote, 'In spite of her rabid allegiance to goods of British manufacture, we made many a dress to her measurements, sold it to her through English dressmakers and had the joy of watching her complacently wearing it, believing it untainted by alien handiwork.' Similarly, of Alexandra he noted, 'She was loyal to England and would only buy from British modistes. However, as these stocked our models for retail purposes, Alexandra wore many a Worth model unawares.'[36] However, as Diana de Marly reveals, using photographic evidence, Alexandra sometimes ordered and wore simultaneously, the same Worth model as her sister, which made a bold statement that was inextricably associated with Worth.[37]

As prince and king, Edward mixed socially with a racy, fun-loving international group amongst whom extra-marital affairs were common. He conducted relationships with three beautiful, strong-minded women: Lillie Langtry; Frances Evelyn Greville (née Maynard), Countess of Warwick; and The Hon. Mrs Alice Keppel. All three women shopped at Worth.

Lillie Langtry was born Emilie Charlotte le Breton in St Helier, Jersey, Channel Islands; her father was the Dean of Jersey. In 1874 she married an Irish landowner, Edward Langtry. The couple rented premises in London's exclusive Belgravia, where in May 1877 they were invited to a supper party hosted by the explorer Sir Allen Young and attended by the Prince of Wales. Young's lively, bohemian gatherings were precisely the sort of event the Prince enjoyed best. During the course of the evening, Edward became entranced by Lillie, who succumbed to his attentions. From this point, the young woman became highly aware of the transformative potential of fashion. In her autobiography *Days I Knew* (1925) Lillie recalled, 'I shuddered when I remembered that two morning costumes and one evening gown had seemed ample in my unsophisticated days, and that when I was suddenly, so to speak, assimilated by London society I was quite unaware of the fact that dress mattered at all. Now I required a new outfit for every occasion, and my husband aiding and abetting me by his approval, I became more and more reckless, allowing insidious saleswomen to line negligees with ermine or border gowns with silver fox without inquiring the cost, until the Christmas bills poured in, laying bear [*sic*] my colossal extravagance… Constantly mingling with bejewelled and beautifully clad women, who changed their gowns as a kaleidoscope changes its patterns, created in me a growing desire to do likewise. For the first time in my life I became intoxicated with the idea of arraying myself as gorgeously as the Queen of Sheba…'.[38]

Lillie became, as described at the time, a 'professional beauty' (as distinct from a 'lady of quality'), whose likeness was painted by the leading artists of the day: James McNeill Whistler, Sir John Everett Millais, Edward Poynter, George Frederick Watts and Edward Burne-Jones. Lillie's beauty exemplified the fashionable ideal; her relationship with the Prince of Wales became public knowledge and her photographic likeness travelled around the globe in postcard format.

In 1878 the Prince secured Lillie's entrance into the upper echelons of British society by arranging for her to be presented at court. All the time Lillie was associated with

BELOW — Lillie Langtry languishing in a Worth evening gown, 1899. V&A: LAF.2193D

OPPOSITE, LEFT TO RIGHT — Lillie Langtry dressed by Worth for *The Degenerates*, 1899. V&A Theatre Collection

Lady de Grey, the photograph inscribed 'á Monsieur Jean Worth. Gladys de Grey/89'. AAD/1990/4/239

Edward, she enjoyed extended credit from her suppliers, who charmed her and encouraged her extravagances. She describes how, at an after-theatre supper party, her butler, 'swaying under the combined influence of champagne and women Americaine', spilt the contents of a dish into the lap of her new blue Worth gown. 'There was nothing to be done but to excuse myself, and to change from top to toe. Whenever a gown suited me extra well Worth used to say, "Ave 'alf a dozen in different colours," so that when I returned in ten minutes in the facsimile in pink it created some amusement.'[39] In January 1880 Lillie was feted; by October that year, when her relationship with the Prince ended, her creditors had closed in and she was forced to sell everything she possessed of any financial value. Lillie was beautiful, accomplished and self-assured; she was also resilient and tenacious.

Over 20 years later she was still shopping at Worth, for her private and – having become a professional actress – public wardrobe of modern and historical-style dress. The dress she wears in the photograph on p.130 (opposite), made in velvet-patterned silk satin, has been identified as a Worth gown[40] but does not appear in Worth's photographic albums for 1899. However, the fabric design bears some similarity to the large-scale woven designs used for historical-style fancy dress costumes (see p.116, right) and evening gowns presented in the Worth photograph album labelled 'Robes de Bal', c.1900. Worth designed the costumes Lillie wore in *The Degenerates*, a comedy by Sydney Grundy that opened at London's Haymarket Theatre in August 1899 before touring to America, where it opened at the Garden Theatre, New York, in January 1900. Worth paid great attention to the design and ornamentation of the back, as well as the front, view of garments. A trained evening gown featured a pendant of faux flowers that trailed diagonally down Langtry's back, a feature she exploited to full advantage in the publicity images taken for the show. While Lillie's gowns in the production were gorgeous, audiences were shocked by what they perceived as the low moral tone set by the actress, who had agreed to play the role of an abandoned society woman whose biography was said to echo her own.

In 1901 Lillie Langtry appeared as Marie Antoinette in *A Royal Necklace* (see p.40) by Pierre and Claude Breton. *The Queen* praised Worth for his 'authentic reproduction of the old-time toilettes'.[41] This was one of several costumes, based on those worn by Marie Antoinette, which the house had produced since its inception. The first was for the Empress Eugénie, who wore it to a masquerade ball in 1866.

Edward continued to support Lillie by attending her theatre performances and he also arranged for her daughter to be presented at court. He invited Lady de Grey (later Marchioness of Ripon), a dominant figure in London society, to mentor her passage into elite social circles. Tall, elegant and influential, Lady de Grey was an important Worth client. Jean Worth states that when she wore a diamond horseshoe in her hair, she took the world by storm (below, right).[42]

The Prince embarked on his next great love affair in about 1889. This time it was with an aristocrat and heiress – Frances, Countess of Warwick, affectionately nicknamed 'Daisy'. Daisy was presented at court in spring 1880; later that year the press announced her engagement to Lord Brooke. He became the 5th Earl of Warwick and – like others – was compelled to 'turn a blind eye' to the liaison that finished in 1898. It is reported that the Prince of Wales accompanied Daisy to Paris so as to order her clothes at Doucet and Worth.[43] Reflecting on this period in her life, she wrote: 'A Worth frock was, of course, very costly. I never had one for which the bill was less than a hundred guineas, and often his gowns were half as much again. But against this, I always set two facts, that they were the creations of a man of genius, and that the materials would never wear out. If it had not been for the fire at Easton [Easton was the family estate], I could have remained an exquisitely dressed woman for the rest of my life, without any expense other than would be incurred by changing the style of a frock. Curiously enough, I always used to say that nothing but fire could destroy Worth fabric'.[44]

Daisy was painted by another celebrated society portrait artist of the Edwardian era, the American painter John Singer Sargent. Known for his flattering depictions, Sargent captured the spirit of the age with his atmospheric lighting, complimentary portrayal of the female form (often elongating limbs and necks) and dramatic compositions. The plate opposite shows the Countess wearing an elaborate evening gown in the setting of her grand country estate. Against all odds, she went on to become a socialist; she stood as a Labour MP, supported wartime conscientious objection (belatedly) and championed animal rights. In her first autobiography *Life's Ebb and Flow* (1929), Daisy barely mentions the costly fashionable dresses she wore, privileging her social and political endeavours. Jean Worth wrote that, upon entering politics, she 'put away such feminine things as a delight in dress'.[45] In her less earnest autobiographical sequel, *Afterthoughts* (1932), Daisy included a chapter called 'Mainly Feminine', in which she recorded her earlier forays into fashion. After stating that 'the Mecca of the woman of fashion was Paris, and Worth her prophet',[46] she records, 'Twice I consulted Jean Worth regarding a costume for a fancy-dress ball, when he dressed me as Semiramis for a big affair in Paris, and as Marie Antoinette for the fancy-dress ball at Warwick Castle – the ball which was responsible for awakening me to the activities of Labour, since it aroused the wrath of the *Clarion* and brought me into contact with Robert Blatchford.'[47] It was her meeting with this socialist editor that alerted Daisy to the huge inequalities that existed within society. She subsequently dedicated much of her life to changing the broader culture, while maintaining her own lifestyle. In 1898 her relationship with Edward, who was now King, came to a close and the same year he embarked upon his next relationship.

The Hon. Mrs Alice Keppel – a beautiful and popular society hostess – was the King's last, and perhaps, greatest love. Her biographer Diana Souhami records that, 'Dressed in gowns by Worth, with collars of diamonds and ropes of pearls, Mrs Keppel was there at the King's left hand for racing at Ascot, sailing at Cowes, grouse shooting at Sandringham, sea air and casinos at Biarritz and Monte Carlo. She dazzled and seduced.'[48] Alice did not write an autobiography, but her two daughters Sonia and Violet did. Sonia records her mother's magnificent clothes but does not provide explicit references to Worth, while Violet describes visiting the House of Worth with her mother when she was about 11 years old: 'I have vivid memories of the first time I accompanied my mother to the dressmaker, where she was received like a goddess, Monsieur Jean (Worth) supervising her fitting in person, the *vendeuses* quite shamelessly forsaking their other clients to vie with each other in flattering epithets… My mother was everything that could most appeal to them, lovely, vivacious, fêted, fashionable, with a kind word for each of the anonymous old crones who had been for years in the establishment.'[49] Mrs Keppel remained intimate with the King for the rest of his life.

NOTES
1. *Courier Journal*, Louisville, 15 March 1895.
2. J-P. Worth 1928, p.140.
3. J-P. Worth 1928, pp.140-1.
4. At the time, this was considered correct etiquette but more recently has been interpreted within the discipline of post-colonial studies as the inappropriate re-presentation of the cultural symbols of a subjugated people.
5. Hegermann-Lindencrone 1912, p.96.
6. Hegermann-Lindencrone 1912, p.100.
7. Cecil Beaton, *The Glass of Fashion* (London, 1954), p.48.
8. J-P. Worth 1928, p.101.
9. W.H. Holden 1950, p.83.
10. Julian Osgood Field, *Uncensored Recollections* (London, 1924), p.57.
11. Cora Pearl 1886, p.95.
12. G. Aretz, *The Elegant Woman* (London, 1932), p.257.
13. J-P. Worth 1928, p.101.
14. *Manchester Evening News*, 20 March 1895.
15. *Vogue*, 18 March 1896, pp.iv-v.
16. J-P. Worth 1928, p.6.
17. Mary Moore quoted in Christopher Breward, *Fashion and Modernity* (Oxford, 2005), p.116.
18. J-P. Worth 1928, p.215.
19. J-P. Worth 1908, pp.0-4.
20. Mrs Aria, *The Queen*, 15 April, 1899.
21. Obituary, for Charles Frederick Worth, published in *The Sun*, New York, 11 March 1895.
22. Bigland 1950, p.100.
23. Bigland 1950, p.53.
24. In *Sensory History* (2007) Mark M. Smith explores depictions of the sensate in terms of history and gender construction. He writes that while nineteenth-century man was perceived as a champion of the new industrialist, capitalist and 'visualist order', 'women, conversely, were custodians of smells, especially domestic ones, and particularly smells that were accorded with their supposedly more emotional and intuitive nature' (p.66).
25. Emile Zola, *La Curée* (Paris, 1872), pp.90-1.
26. *Vogue*, 15 March 1896, p.206.
27. Wharton 1920, p.122.
28. Wharton 1920, p.162.
29. Wharton 1920, p.163.
30. Veblen 1899, p.106.
31. J-P. Worth 1928, p.222.
32. J-P. Worth 1928, pp.223-4.
33. J-P. Worth 1928, p.234.
34. Vanderbilt Balsan 1953, p.30.
35. Vanderbilt Balsan 1953, p.54.
36. J-P. Worth 1928, pp.116-17.
37. De Marly 1980, p.131.
38. Langtry 1925, p.137.
39. Ibid.
40. Coleman 1989, p.106.
41. *The Queen*, 27 April 1901.
42. J-P. Worth 1928, p.95.
43. Aronson 1988, p.176.
44. Warwick 1929, p.160.
45. J-P. Worth 1928, p.191.
46. Warwick 1929, p.160.
47. Ibid.
48. Souhami 1996, p.7.
49. Trefusis 1952, p.44.

BELOW LEFT TO RIGHT – *The Countess of Warwick and Her Son*, by John Singer Sargent, 1904–5. Worcester Art Museum, Worcester, Massachusetts Bridgeman

Alice, the Hon. Mrs George Keppel, with her daughter Violet Trefusis, 1899. National Portrait Gallery, London

7

THE HOUSE OF WORTH
1914–1956

AMY DE LA HAYE

LEFT TO RIGHT, TOP TO BOTTOM –
'The House of Worth has a good shop front decorated with dainty material, lace, and furs. Inside can be bought all the necessaries of the boudoir: lingerie, fancy belts, handbags, umbrellas, scents, fans etc., in fact, all the paraphernalia of modern woman'. (Picken)[7]

A doorman was stationed at the entrance of the house. When a client entered she was met by the chief saleswoman (a *vendeuse*), or her assistants.

'On a visit to the House of Worth, after taking the elevator, we reach a wide gallery in front of which is the dress showroom, which, though small, is cozily furnished and delicately lighted. On each side of the chimney are glass cases in which lingerie is exposed to view. Passing into the lingerie showroom, we notice, on two of the walls, glass show-cases filled with delicate underwear, and on the table bottles of scent bearing the name of Worth; cushions are nearly everywhere'. (Picken)[8]

This photograph shows house mannequins being fitted. Nystrom stated that the couture houses each employed between two and twelve house mannequins depending upon the size of the business. (Nystrom)[9] 'During the last few years it has come to be recognized by practically all of the leading Parisian dressmaking establishments that the manikins [*sic*] are much more important in effecting sales than was formerly the case, so that much more attention is now given in the selection and training of manikins than heretofore. Some of the houses go so far as to pay them a commission on the sales which are made as a result of their exhibition of the garments'. (Nystrom)[10] A client can be seen trying on a fur-trimmed coat.

LEFT TO RIGHT, TOP TO BOTTOM –
'A dressmaking stockroom may contain thousands of dollars' worth of goods with practically no investment whatsoever on the part of the dressmaking establishment. From the goods that are left with the dressmaker the latter prepares his models, and settlements are effected with the manufacturers of the fabrics and other materials for goods used four times a year, or at the end of each season. This system was unique to Paris and is an important contributory factor to the business success of their fashion houses'. (Nystrom)[11] It is probably Jean-Charles Worth modelling cloth onto the mannequin's body, with a seamstress assisting him.

Whereas most commentators focused upon the creativity of the house and its designer, Nystrom reported that 'Jacques Worth, the business manager, is well educated, an artist, a connoisseur eye, a sportsman, a famous and witty orator, as well as the capable manager of the business'. (Nystrom)[12] Behind him, positioned centrally on the wall, is a framed portrait of his grandfather, company co-founder Charles Frederick Worth.

'Other employees take care of the accounting and other office work, the messenger service, door tenders, cleaners, watchmen, etc.' (Nystrom)[13] Three young women undertake their administrative roles, overlooked by a male manager. There is also a portrait of C.F. Worth on the wall in this office.

'A room is set apart for the women designers. The editors of dressmaking patterns often call Monsieur Worth for new designs, which are not necessarily executed by the firm. Also, some clients ask for new designs or modifications of existing ones. In this case, special designs are then made and submitted with samples of suitable materials'. (Picken)[14]

140 — THE HOUSE OF WORTH 1914-1956

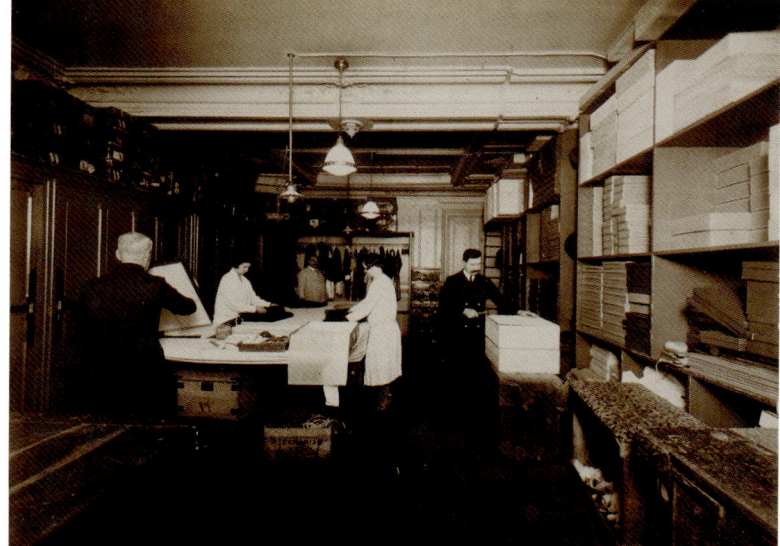

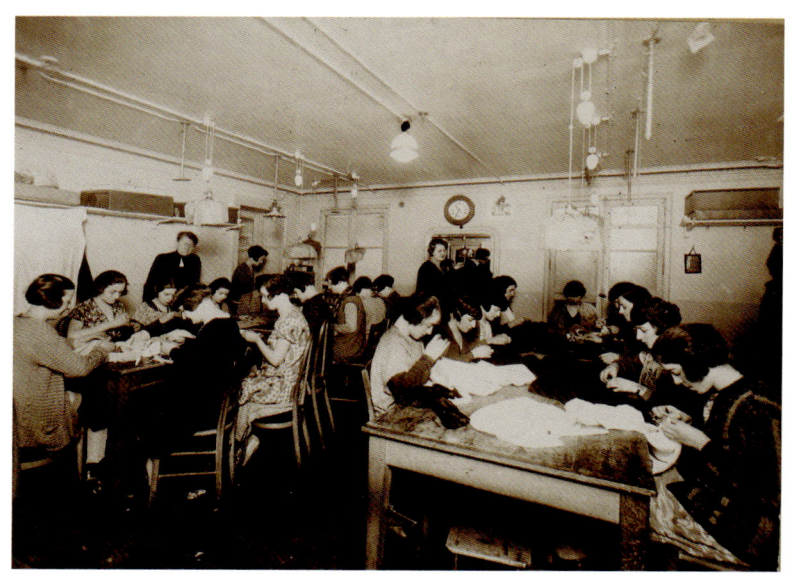

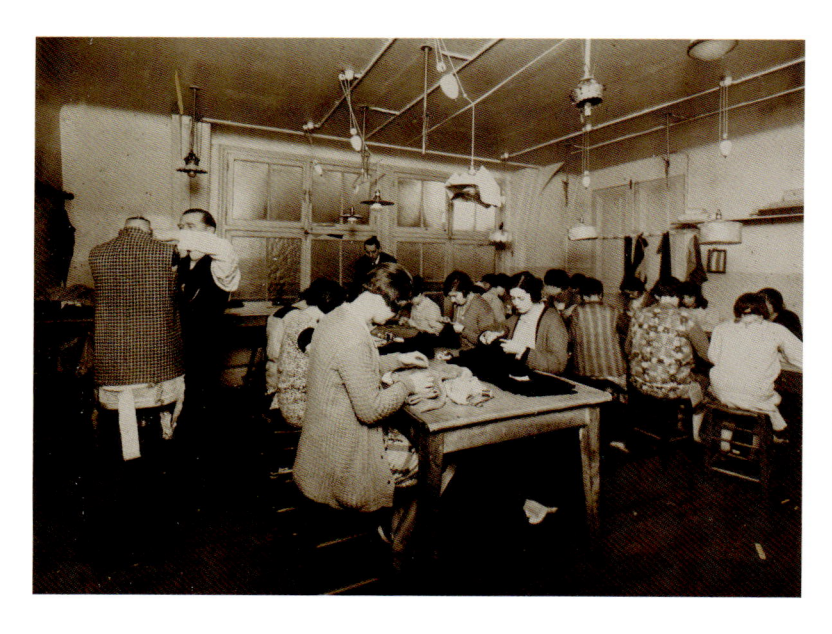

OPPOSITE, LEFT TO RIGHT, TOP TO BOTTOM — The Furriers Workshop: fur remained an important part of the Worth business, for coats, collars and trimmings. On 15 January 1926, American *Vogue* showed a 'Coat of dull green crêpe Elizabeth, over bois-de-rose Rodier homespun with baby fox trimming' and a cape coat in black broadcloth, lined with natural coloured kasha, with a large collar of beige Asian fox fur.

Once clients' orders were ready, they were sent to the packing room to be meticulously packaged. Picken noted that finishing touches might include 'sprinkling a drop of delicate toilet water or perfume on the tissue paper...'. (Picken)[15] The couture houses also engaged specialist companies to undertake this work, which was essential, especially for shipped export orders, to ensure garments arrived fresh, immaculate and ready to wear.

Worth's large female workforce, dressed in the latest *garçonne* fashions with cloche hats, arriving for work at the staff entrance.

The Dressmaking Atelier: the head of each department was called a *première*. 'These are skilful dressmakers who know the arts of cutting and sewing and of reproducing the work of the designing department of the establishment'. (Nystrom)[16] They were assisted by *secondes*, while less experienced *petites mains* undertook routine work.

The Tailoring Workroom: tailoring was an industry traditionally dominated by men, who also often headed up the tailoring workshops. Heavy woollen fabrics, which were difficult to handle, were used to make winter-weight coats and suits designed for country wear. Here the tailor, assisted by women workers, is making a checked woollen jacket.

In this large attic workshop, women workers are undertaking handstitching on leather handbags. On 1 September 1926 American *Vogue* described 'A gorgeous evening bag designed by Worth... of gold-and-rose brocade banded with gold leather with a ruby and diamond clasp'. This photograph reveals that the house made – or certainly finished – their own-label handbags.

LEFT TO RIGHT, TOP TO BOTTOM — 'In all the important dressmaking forms, the salaried staff, first hands, saleswomen, clerks etc., in short, all those who are in direct touch with the public, receive the midday meal and sometimes an evening meal as part of the salary. The workwomen are generally paid by the day and their meal is not included... the house makes every effort to ensure good nourishment'. (Picken)[17]

The senior staff restaurant.

Chefs and kitchen staff preparing food for lunch.

Worth's 'Service des Parfums' delivery van with uniformed driver, parked in front of the house.

141

LEFT — Publicity photograph of Annette Mills wearing Worth's *sportif* daywear, 1927–8.
AAD/1990/4/251

BELOW LEFT — Publicity photograph of a Worth mannequin modelling golf sportswear, c.1927–8.
AAD/1982/1/79, vol.2

BELOW LEFT — A group of mannequins modelling evening dresses and a high-necked opera cloak, the successor of the *sortie de bal*, c.1927–8. Publicity photograph. AAD/1982/1/79

BELOW RIGHT — Publicity photograph of Worth house mannequins modelling the latest evening dresses, c.1927. AAD/1982/1/78

THE NEW SPORTS MODE

In 1927 American *Vogue* reported, 'The lion's share of smart, youth-giving novelties of detail is incorporated into the sports mode, in the clothes designed for actual sports and also, in that increasingly important group whimsically called sports clothes but really worn for all and sundry occasions not requiring an evening dress.'[18] The V&A Archive contains two large albums marked 'Publicity 1927–28', which include a photograph of Worth's golfwear. The box-pleated skirt (though not the shoes and socks) closely resembles the design of the *sportif* daywear worn by Annette Mills, a successful dancer and actress, aboard a yacht for a Worth publicity photograph. For the beach Jacques designed modern loose trousers and knits and for leisure at home, replacing the Edwardian tea gown, he created stylish satin ensembles (p.145, below left) and chinoiserie evening pyjamas.

The press continued to report extensively on Worth's evening gowns which, in line with prevailing trends, featured uneven hemlines and were notably less ornamented by 1927–8. The house retained its reputation for ceremonial wear, which was made to special order. Worth designed the dress worn by Her Highness the Begum Aga Khan for her presentation at court and also her wedding gown, which is recorded in an album of wedding photographs held at the Fashion Museum, Bath (Appendix 02). Judging by the huge audience that attended a Worth fashion show staged in 1928, the house remained extremely popular (see p.145).

SURVIVING THE DEPRESSION

During the 1930s the couture houses struggled to survive as the depression and tumultuous social and political circumstances impinged upon the lifestyles and finances of their clientele. The most famous couturiers started licensing their names (Schiaparelli endorsed Lightning Zips) or diversifying their output (Chanel designed costumes for Hollywood films). In 1937 Worth moved to smaller premises at 120 Faubourg Saint Honoré and a fourth generation (great-grandsons of the founder) ran the house with Roger, Jean-Charles's nephew, as designer and his younger brother Maurice (1913–1986) as business manager. A photograph of Roger's bride, Annette Collet, is included in the Worth album of wedding photographs. In 1935 the London branch relocated to 50 Grosvenor Street, with Mrs Charlotte Mortimer, a former mannequin at Reville, serving as director of the house and Madame Elspeth Champcommunal as head designer. Champcommunal had formerly worked as the first editor of British *Vogue* (1916–22), had run her own fashion house in Paris, and was also a practising artist. Henceforth her name was always acknowledged by the fashion press with reverence as Madame Champcommunal of Worth.

Wealthy women had always re-circulated the couture garments they no longer wore (the Empress Eugénie gave gowns she had worn just once to her ladies-in-waiting, who then wore them and in turn sold them on). In 1937 Jessica Mitford wrote to her sister 'Debo' (Deborah, Duchess of Devonshire), requesting a favour: 'You know my Worth satin dress that's been dyed purple? Well, I don't suppose I shall need a dress like that for ages by which time it'll be out of fashion; so I wonder if you could very kindly try & sell it for me? Being Worth & just newly cleaned and dyed it might fetch quite a lot… try & get about three to five pounds for it.'[19]

Worth continued to dress an elite international clientele and, as in the nineteenth century, the house continued to convey an aura of exclusivity while creating multiple models of the same design. This required meticulous administrative procedures, but occasionally errors were made. Grace Elvina, Marchioness of Kedleston, was a loyal Worth client. In 1937 she and her husband hosted a dinner party for the King and Queen of Spain at their London residence, Carlton House. 'As I went to greet the Queen of Spain when she arrived, I realized with a flash of horrified recognition that her dress was a replica of the one I was wearing myself. Both were made of white and silver brocade, by Worth of Paris, and they were absolutely identical.' Fortunately, she was at home, made her excuses and rapidly changed into another dress. 'I reproached Worth afterwards about this, and he candidly admitted that he had thought it safe to make identical dresses for the Queen of Spain and myself, because he knew I was unlikely to go to Madrid, and forgot that the Queen of Spain might very well dine with me in London.'[20]

BELOW, LEFT TO RIGHT –
Worth house mannequins wearing leisure trousers and knitwear, 1927–8. AAD/1982/1/79, vol.2

Her Highness the Begum Aga Khan, wearing a Worth dress for her presentation at court. Description on the reverse of photograph reads: 'A Worth court gown in gold and silver brocade with diamanté embroidery; the train was lined with gold lamé. Her tiara, a Cartier creation, was of diamonds.' Photograph by Caponier, Paris, c.1928. AAD/1990/4/250

OPPOSITE, CLOCKWISE –
Fashion show titled 'Groupe du Bal de la Couture'. Photograph by Agence Roll, 1928. AAD/1982/1/78

Madame [name illegible] wearing fashionable, floral-print, bias-cut evening gown with fur-trimmed jacket by Worth, mid-1930s. AAD/1990/4/254

Worth house mannequins modelling relaxed, at home evening wear, 1927–8. AAD/1982/1/79, vol.2

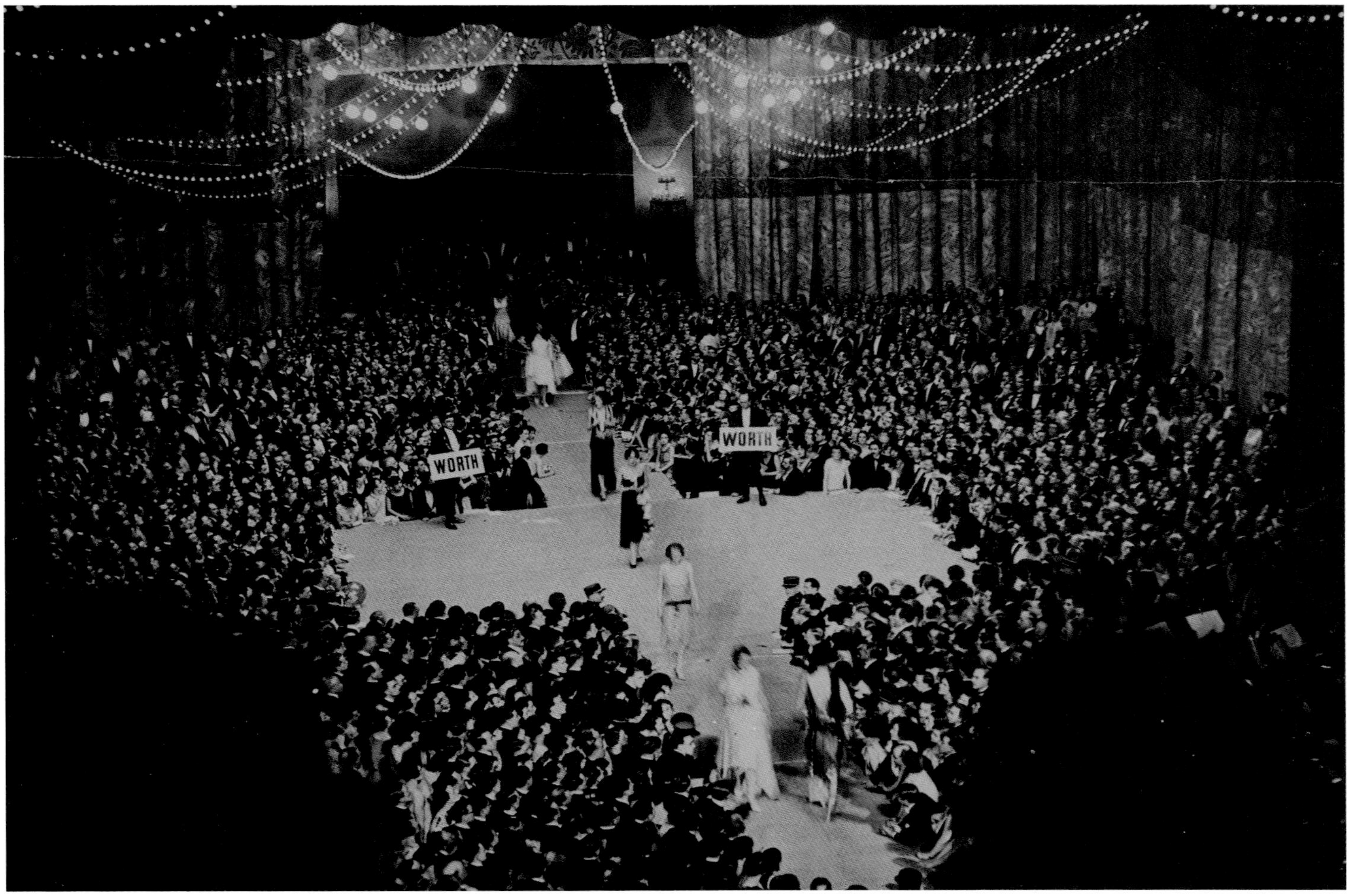
WORTH
WORTH

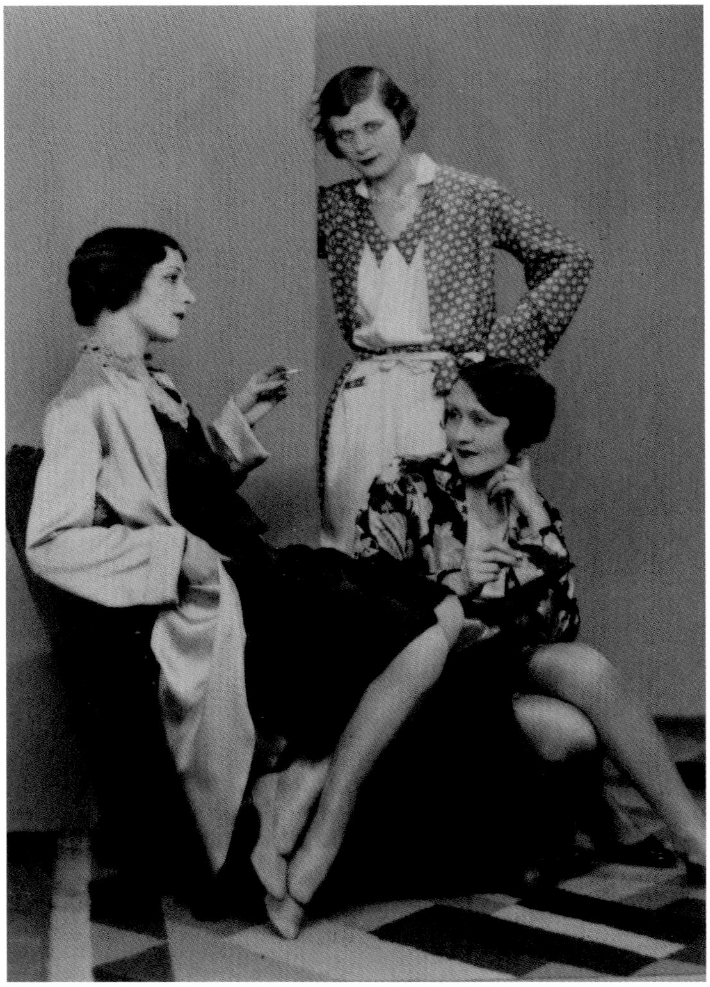

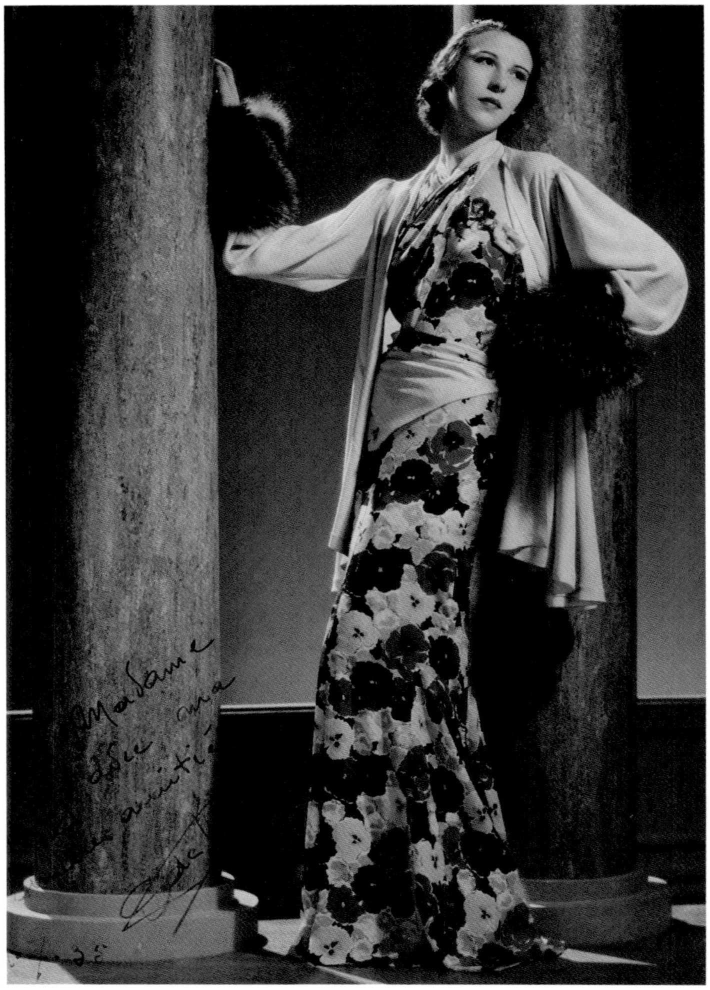

BELOW – Figurines dressed in daywear styles by Worth for the Théâtre de la Mode, Paris, 1945. AAD/1990/4/311

OPPOSITE, LEFT TO RIGHT – Figurines dressed in evening gowns by Worth for the Théâtre de la Mode, Paris, 1945. AAD/1990/4/315

Figurines dressed by Worth and displayed presumably in the rue du Faubourg Saint Honoré salon window, 1945. AAD/1990/4/308

SECOND WORLD WAR AND ITS AFTERMATH

Along with many of the Paris couture houses Worth continued to function throughout the Second World War. Dominique Veillon's research for *Fashion Under the Occupation* (2002) reveals that after an initial dip in business, by 1942 orders for couture clothing were revived by orders from the new rich, German clients and for stage costumes. Worth also enjoyed a good income from the business in Cannes, which became the fashionable centre of the free zone. In London, Hardy Amies (1909–2003), who went on to become one of London's most successful couturiers and dressmaker to the Queen, worked as a designer at Worth, which he juggled with his army career. The chairman and managing director of Worth (London) Ltd, Lieutenant-Colonel F.W. Pay, was also in the army. Working within austerity rulings, Amies' stylish tailoring formed an ideal foil to Madame Champcommunal's soft, feminine dress designs. In 1945 Amies set up his own house. Odette, Worth's fitter, left to join Amies, followed by her workroom staff, the *vendeuses* – a French woman called Marthe and Leonard the tailor. Such movement (or poaching) of skilled staff was not uncommon, although it cannot have helped Worth's early post-war business.[21]

Once peace was declared, Paris set about re-asserting its international fashion profile, but in this war the reputation of the industry had been tarnished by accusations of collaboration. Faced with shortages of luxury cloth, the creative industries joined forces, under the direction of the Chambre Syndicale, to present 'Le Théâtre de la Mode' in order to generate publicity for the couture industry and raise money for French and British charities. It made its debut at the Musée des Arts Décoratifs, Palais Louvre, in March 1945. The neo-romantic artist Christian Bérard was responsible for the overall design, which comprised 12 miniature 'theatres'; ballet dancer Boris Koschno created the *mise en scène* and the production was supervised by sculptor Jean Saint-Martin, who also made the wire figurines designed by illustrator Elaine Bonabel. Forty-one couturiers, including Worth, dressed 170 figurines, supported by 37 milliners, 21 hairdressers, specialist boot makers, jewellers, umbrella- and flower-makers. The couturiers are not credited for their individual contributions in the original catalogue, but photographs in the Worth archive record Worth's contributions. One shows romantic evening wear placed in 'Theatre Life' designed by Bérard; another displays tailored daywear, presented in the 'Paris Sketch' theatre, its scenery designed by Saint-Martin. Le Théâtre de la Mode toured to international cities, including Vienna and Stockholm, before finding its resting place in Maryhill Museum in Washington, United States. Some of the clothes – including designs by Worth – clearly anticipated new couturier Christian Dior's 1947 Corolle line – dubbed the 'New Look' – which sealed Parisian post-war fashion supremacy.

END OF AN ERA

In 1945 the London branch of Worth was acquired by Paquin, but continued to operate under its own name, as one of between 10 and 12 couture houses in London during the 1940s and 1950s. Fashionable and ceremonial dress designs continued to be produced from the late 1940s (pp.150-1), for which the V&A Archive contains a few watercolour and ink designs, though most from this period are held at the Fashion Museum, Bath. Roger Worth retired in around 1952 and

Maurice became sole director. Owen Hyde Clark, who had trained with the designer Maggy Rouff in Paris and at Bradley's in London, was appointed to design Worth's ready-to-wear collections in 1953. The following year the House of Worth in Paris was also purchased by Paquin but in 1956 it finally closed its doors and the Worth Archive was presented to the Victoria and Albert Museum.

As part of the Paquin group Worth (London) Ltd continued for another decade, providing fashionable clothing for a largely British following. In November 1957 journalist Alison Adburgham announced that Worth had introduced a wholesale line and opened two new departments within the Grosvenor Street premises in London's West End: Worth Boutique and Miss Worth. She noted, 'Nearly all the couturiers, in Paris as well as London, now do something in the ready-to-wear line; it is just a sign of the times.' During her interview with Mrs Mortimer, whom she credited for her 'vigilant up-to-dateness', the two women became uncharacteristically nostalgic, reflecting that it was almost a century since the House of Worth was established. Mrs Mortimer rued the introduction of man-made fibres, extolled satins so stiff they stood alone and sighed as she recalled the 'serene repose' of Edwardian women attired in diaphanous tea gowns. Together they decided that, 'It was gin that killed the tea gown', blaming the vogue for American cocktails, drunk at the time women would have previously worn their tea gowns, for its demise as 'clearly one could not drink gin in a tea-gown.'[22] Worth (London) Ltd ceased trading on 29 December 1967. Paquin sold the Worth name to Sidney Massin who re-launched Worth (London) Ltd in 1968. The times had certainly changed.

NOTES

1. American *Vogue*, 1 April 1916, 48c.
2. Woolman Chase 1954, p.160.
3. American *Vogue*, May 1926, p.34.
4. American *Vogue*, February 1925, p.80.
5. Picken 1924, pp.197–8.
6. Picken 1924, p.199.
7. Picken 1924, p.198.
8. Ibid.
9. Nystrom 1928, p.195.
10. Ibid.
11. Nystrom 1928, p.196.
12. Nystrom 1928, p.207.
13. Nystrom 1928, p.196.
14. Picken 1924, p.99.
15. Picken 1924, p.175.
16. Nystrom 1928, p.195.
17. Picken 1924, p.193.
18. American *Vogue*, 15 April 1927, p.57.
19. In a letter from Jessica Mitford (written at the Hotel des Basques, Bayonne) to her sister Deborah, Duchess of Devonshire (née Deborah Mitford), 6 April 1937, quoted in Mosley 2007, p.88.
20. Curzon 1955, p.136.
21. Amies 1954, pp.12–121.
22. Adburgham 1964, p.234. Originally published in *Punch*, 27 November 1957, p.234.

WORTH
120 FAUBOURG St HONORÉ

CANNES SUR LA CROISETTE   **LONDRES** 50 GROSVENOR STREET

ECHANTILLONNAGE TISSUS MODELES DEPOSES

COLLECTION AOUT 1947

- N° 1   BIJOU
- N° 7   ROMANTIQUE
- 2   LE CLUB
- 8   PAVILLON DAUPHINE   Tailleur   Blouse
- 3   INCROYABLE   Manteau   Robe
- 9   ENGADINE   Manteau   Jaquette
- 4   CHAMPS ELYSEES   Cape   Robe
-   Robe
- 5   COTE BASQUE   Manteau   Jaquette
- 10   FAISAN DORE   Manteau   Robe
-   Jupe   Blouse
- 11   REPORTER   Canadienne   Jupe
- 6   OLYMPIE   Manteau   Jaquette
-   Blouse
-   Jupe   Blouse
- 12   COURVAN   Robe

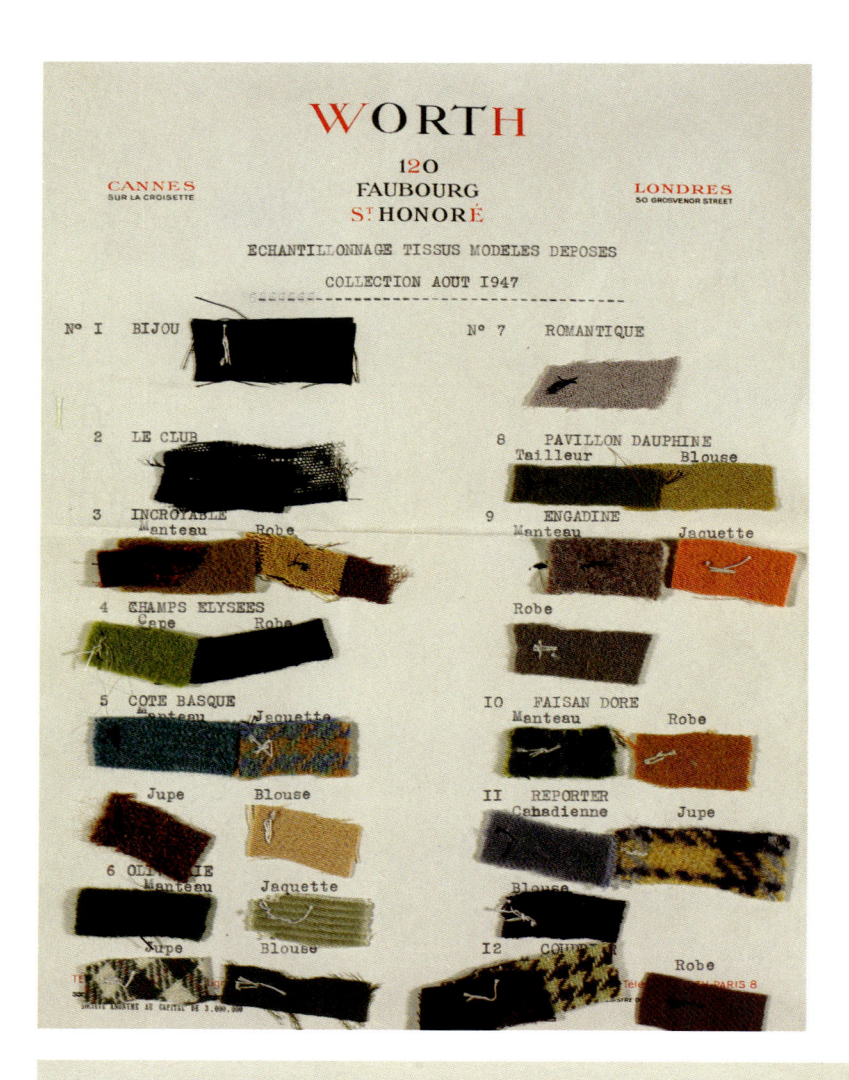

LISTE DE NOS MODELES DEPOSES   10 MARS 1948   PROTECTION ARTISTIQUE

Journée du   COLLECTION PRINTEMPS ETE 1948

N° PHOTOS ~~LETTRES~~	N° MODELES ~~TÉLÉPHONE~~	NOM DES MODELES ~~RENDEZ-VOUS~~	DESIGNATION ~~PREMIÈRES~~	REFERENCES TISSUS ~~PUBLICITÉ~~	~~PHOTOS~~	DIVERS
8	3678	PASSIONNEMENT	Ensemble d'après midi	nylon imp. blanc jaune et noir	BUCOL	
9 a.cape bis 9 s.cape	3733	PIERRES PRECIEUSES	Ensemble du soir	Robe crêpe saphir Cape mousseline fushia	COUDURIER BIANCHINI	
10	3681	GRISETTE	Robe de diner	Taffetas quadrillé n. et bl. imp. pois vert	LESAGE	
11 a.cape bis 11 s.cape	3687	COCCINELLE	Robe d'après midi et cape	lainage marine toile rouge pois bl.	REMOND LEONARD	
12 a.cape bis 12 s.cape	3750	ECRIN	Ensemble du soir	Robe crêpe parme Cape satin vert	REMOND LESAGE	
13 manteau bis 13 robe	3717	BAR DU SOLEIL	Ensemble de plage	Robe toile imp. bleu n. Manteau ratine grise	SOLABELLE MOREAU	
14	3737	MADAME CARDINAL	Robe du soir	moire cerise	SADEA	

OPPOSITE, ABOVE AND BELOW — Textiles used in Worth's Winter 1947 collection. AAD/2009/11/5/3

List of collection models, design details and fabric swatches for Worth's Spring 1948 collection. AAD/2009/11/6/2

BELOW — Worth house mannequins wearing striped and floral-printed summer dresses, c.1950. AAD/1990/4/328

astrakan
laine

col châle
beige
renard

OPPOSITE – Sketches for Worth's tailored designs, March 1948. AAD/2009/11/4

LEFT – Watercolour design for a Worth wedding dress, c.1948. AAD/2009/11/4/1

AU POLO
Robe d'après-midi de Worth

RENDEZ-VOUS VILLA GORI
ROBE ET MANTEAU, DE WORTH

N° 9 de la Gazette du Bon Ton.   Modèles déposés. Reproduction interdite.   Année 1924-1925. — Planche 6

DEUX HEURES DU MATIN
MANTEAUX, DE WORTH

N° 2 de la Gazette.   Modèle déposé. Reproduction interdite.   Année 1923. — Planche 9

AMALFI
ROBE, DE WORTH

LE PONEY FAVORI
Tailleur élégant de Worth

LE CHOIX DIFFICILE
Manteau du soir de Worth

LA COQUETTE SURPRISE
Robe du soir de Worth

LE PAYSAGE ROMANTIQUE
Costume tailleur de Worth

APPENDICES

APPENDIX 01:
THE WORTH ARCHIVE AT
THE VICTORIA AND ALBERT MUSEUM
Alexia Kirk, Victoria Platt and Daniel Milford Cottam

HOUSE OF WORTH LTD AND PAQUIN LTD
The House of Worth archive was given to the Victoria and Albert Museum in 1956 by the fashion house. The archive consists of photographs and paper-based material relating to both the House of Worth and the House of Paquin, and is divided between the V&A's Archive of Art and Design and the Prints and Drawings collection.

The material held in the Archive of Art and Design dates from 1825 to about 1952 and comprises over 90 volumes of photographs depicting daywear, outdoor wear, special occasion wear, as well as publicity photographs and photographs of the interior of the salons and shops. It also includes over 80 files of loose photographs, including wedding dresses and theatrical costumes, and a small number of design sketches for day, evening and outerwear; the latter date mainly from the 1940s. This material may be consulted in the Archive and Library Study Room in the V&A's study centre at Blythe House, near Olympia, in west London.

The main series of design drawings by both Worth and Paquin, bound and loose, is held in the V&A's Prints and Drawings collection, together with a large reference collection of printed fashion illustrations and theatrical and fancy dress designs. This material is accessible in the Prints and Drawings Study Room at the V&A and is described in the second half of this list.

PHOTOGRAPHS AND SKETCHES IN THE ARCHIVE OF ART AND DESIGN

PHOTOGRAPH ALBUMS: DAYWEAR, 20 VOLUMES, 1903-c.1916
Annotated and usually indexed. Containing a mixture of dresses, suits, skirts and blouses. AAD/1982/1/1 to 20.

PHOTOGRAPH ALBUMS: OUTDOOR WEAR, 20 VOLUMES, c.1899-c.1913
Annotated and usually indexed. Containing a mixture of coats, capes, boleros and jackets. AAD/1982/1/21 to 40.

PHOTOGRAPH ALBUMS: SPECIAL OCCASIONS, 22 VOLUMES, 1899-1914
Annotated and usually indexed. Containing a mixture of evening dresses, dinner dresses, ball gowns, tea gowns, 'corsages' and, occasionally, wedding dresses and 'déshabillés'. AAD/1982/1/41 to 62.

PHOTOGRAPH ALBUMS: THE COLLECTIONS, 15 VOLUMES, 1907-13
No annotations or index. Volumes of design photographs, season by season. AAD/1982/1/63 to 77.

PHOTOGRAPH ALBUMS: PUBLICITY, 2 VOLUMES, c.1927-c.1929
Annotated and numbered. Indexed by name of garment. AAD/1982/1/78 to 79.

PHOTOGRAPH ALBUMS: INTERIORS, 2 VOLUMES, UNDATED
Volumes of photographs of business and domestic interiors. AAD/1982/1/80 to 81.

LOOSE PHOTOGRAPHS: THE COLLECTIONS, 42 FILES, c.1900-49
The majority of the photographs appear to have been used for publicity purposes. AAD/1990/4/1 to 214.

LOOSE PHOTOGRAPHS: WEDDING DRESSES, 17 FILES, c.1920-c.1960
The photographs are mainly formal studio portraits. A few include grooms, bridesmaids and page boys. Many are annotated with name of the client and date of the wedding. AAD/1990/4/215 to 238.

LOOSE PHOTOGRAPHS: THEATRICAL COSTUMES, 1 FILE, UNDATED
Theatrical costumes: classical, oriental, historical, romantic styles, undated. AAD/1990/4/262 to 307.

LOOSE PHOTOGRAPHS: 'THÉÂTRE DE LA MODE', 1 FILE, c.1945
Record shots apparently of the travelling couture exhibition titled 'Théâtre de la Mode', which toured Europe in 1944-5. Miniature versions of garments displayed on wire dolls. Suits, coats, day dresses, evening dresses and wedding dress. AAD/1990/4/308 to 315.

LOOSE PHOTOGRAPHS: SHOP AND SALON INTERIORS, 3 FILES, c.1920-c.1930
Interiors of Biarritz, Cannes and London branches. AAD/1990/4/316 to 324.

LOOSE PHOTOGRAPHS: PUBLICITY, 2 FILES, 1900-c.1955
Scene from Worth's 'Incidents from everyday English life' display at the 1900 Exposition Universelle, Paris, and a fashion show. AAD/1990/4/325 and 329.

NEGATIVES: 1 FILE, C.1948-C.1949
'Cliches negatifs de 56 modeles'. AAD/2009/11/17.

PRINTS AND DRAWINGS: 5 FILES, 1826-c.1950
Prints from the historical archive of Paquin and Worth designs, including costumes, eveningwear and wedding dresses. AAD/2009/11/1 to 4 and AAD/1990/4/333.

SKETCHES: COLLECTION FOR DAY, EVENING, AND OUTDOOR WEAR, 5 FILES, *c*.1948

Design sketches by 'Paul', 'Helene', 'Jean' and 'Madeleine'. Includes textile samples. AAD/2009/11/9 to 13.

SKETCHES: PATTERNS FOR TEXTILES AND WINDOW DISPLAYS, 3 FILES, *c*.1920-*c*.1945

Sketches of textile patterns and a set design for Paquin perfume. AAD/2009/14 to 16.

LISTS OF COLLECTIONS AND TEXTILE SAMPES: 4 FILES, 1940-9

Records of collections: appearances in the press, sketches for dresses, letters and collections lists with textile samples. AAD/2009/11/5 to 8.

PHOTOGRAPH PACKAGING: 3 FILES, *c*.1939

Envelopes and photograph wrappers. AAD/1990/4/330 to 332.

DESIGNS, FASHION PLATES AND ILLUSTRATIONS IN THE PRINTS AND DRAWINGS COLLECTION

FASHION DESIGNS: PAQUIN, 1897-1953

Designs for Winter 1897-Summer 1939 bound in volumes. E.18 to 9276-1957.
Loose designs for Summer 1944-Winter 1953. E.22467 to 22865-1957.

FASHION DESIGNS: WORTH, *c*.1865-75; 1920-56

Design books (3), *c*.1865-75. E.22392 to 22394-1957.
Designs for Winter 1921-Summer 1955 bound in volumes. E.9277 to 21029-1957.
Loose designs for Worth, 1920s-40s. E.22196 to 2204, 22207, 22208, 22213 to 22216, 22232 to 22241, 222873 to 23024-1957.

DESIGNS: MASQUERADE AND THEATRE COSTUMES, PROBABLY FOR WORTH, *c*.1865-*c*.1925

Designs (65) by Léon Sault, Jules Marre, Jules Helleu and others. Masquerade costumes, *c*.1865 to *c*.1880. E.22035 to 22099-1957.
Costume designs (91), mostly by Jean-Charles Worth, *c*.1920-25, E.22100 to 22189-1957.

FASHION ILLUSTRATIONS: WORTH AND PAQUIN, *c*.1920-*c*.1950

Original illustrations by Jean de Haramboure, Pierre Mourgue, Enrico Sacchetti, Fanny Fern Fitzwater and others, for publication or promotional purposes. E.22190 to 22195, 22205, 22206, 22209, 22210 to 22212, 22217 to 22231, 22242 to 22250, 23025, 23026-1957.

REFERENCE MATERIAL: USED BY WORTH AND PAQUIN, *c*.1595 TO *c*.1930

Large group of fashion plates and costume prints, both loose and bound in volumes; also including some original drawings and designs. Mainly 18th and 19th century. E.20327 to 23047, 21193 to 21375, 21409, 21421, 21429, 21581 to 21583, 21600, 21604 to 21608, 21610 to 21673, 21694, 21695, 21705, 21713, 21728 to 22034, 21718, 22251 to 22391, 22395 to 22397-1957.

MISCELLANEOUS: WORTH, *c*.1930

Two decorative papers used for lining dress boxes, *c*.1930. E.23052 to 23053-1957.

APPENDIX 02: THE WORTH ARCHIVE AT THE FASHION MUSEUM, BATH

Rosemary Harden and Ben Whyman

The Fashion Museum is one of the world's major museum collections of historic and contemporary fashionable dress and has been located in the Assembly Rooms in the Georgian city of Bath since 1963. The museum collection – which today numbers in excess of 80,000 objects – is designated as a collection of outstanding national significance, with objects ranging from exquisite pieces of seventeenth-century embroidery to cutting-edge 21st-century fashions by top international designers.

The museum was founded as the Museum of Costume by Doris Langley Moore, a writer and costume designer (she designed the costumes for the 1951 film *The African Queen*), as well as a leading scholar on the work of the poet Lord Byron. Mrs Langley Moore frequently referred to herself as 'The Collector', and her life's work spent collecting and presenting examples of historic dress, and the documentation that contextualized it, has established her as one of the pioneering figures in the study of the history of fashion.

It was Mrs Langley Moore's friendship and professional relationship with James Laver that led to the acquisition by the Museum of Costume of the remaining bound photograph albums, press-cutting books, drawings, photographs, bound registered designs, and a library of art history books, which is now known as the Worth-Paquin Archive. The material was passed to Doris Langley Moore for the Museum of Costume (which at that date had still to secure permanent premises in the Assembly Rooms, which were then being re-built following war-time damage) by the Victoria and Albert Museum in 1959. Mrs Langley Moore was thrilled with the donation, writing, 'As the quantity of stuff you have been so good as to send is unexpectedly large, I have not had time to examine it all yet, but from what I can see it will be most valuable to us… I am most anxious, when the Museum has at last solved its fearful problem of premises, to inaugurate a library for students, to be run in conjunction with the collection of costumes, and this is a fine contribution.'[1]

Today, some 50 years later, the Fashion Museum remains true to Mrs Langley Moore's founding vision by welcoming students, researchers, curators and all those who are interested in discovering the breadth and depth of this outstanding fashion archive collection.

THE WORTH-PAQUIN ARCHIVE

The archive includes 40 leather-bound volumes of photographs from the Worth archives dating from 1902 to the 1950s (as listed here): 13 contain images of 'Costume' (1903–11); 10 contain 'Manteaux' (capes and coats) (1902–11); 12 contain images of '*robes de bal*' (evening and ball gowns) (1902-12); and 5 contain images of 'Wedding Gowns' (1920s to the 1950s), worn by the brides themselves, including Mrs Roger Worth, the wife of C.F. Worth's great-grandson. The Museum also houses a number of boxes of original drawings, the majority of which were created for collections from the 1930s, 1940s and 1950s. This archive includes near or complete sets of drawings from one collection, with fashion show notes (names and descriptions of each model), cloth samples and designs for a number of collections from the late 1940s. There is also a number of black outline drawings or facsimiles of designs from the 1900–1920 era, and drawings of designs for hats, jewellery, theatrical and masquerade costume, and ski wear.

WORTH VOLUMES

Worth-Models Costumes 1: 1903
Worth-Models Costumes 2: 14 January–23 April 1904
Worth-Models Costumes 3: 1904
Worth-Models Costumes 4: 1905
Worth-Models Costumes 5: 04 December 1905–10 August 1906
Worth-Models Costumes 6: 06 April 1906–02 April 1907
Worth-Models Costumes 7: 20 July 1907–January 1908
Worth-Models Costumes 8: 28 March 1908–29 January 1909
Worth-Models Costumes 9: January–July 1909
Worth-Models Costumes 10: July–December 1909
Worth-Models Costumes 11: 26 November 1909–21 July 1910
Worth-Models Costumes 12: 1911–12
Worth-Models Costumes 13: 1910–11

Worth-Models Manteaux A: 22 January–19 September 1902 (no inventory)
Worth-Models Manteaux B: August 1902–May 1903 (no inventory)
Worth-Models Manteaux 1: 24 April 1903–13 January 1904
Worth-Models Manteaux 3: June 1904–September 1905
Worth-Models Manteaux 4: 27 June 1904–06 June 1906
Worth-Models Manteaux 5: 15 March 1906–25 April 1907
Worth-Models Manteaux 6: 07 April 1906–23 March 1908
Worth-Models Manteaux 7: March 1908–January 1909
Worth-Models Manteaux 8: 21 December 1908–07 February 1910
Worth-Models Manteaux 9: 17 January 1910–20 February 1911

Worth-Bal 1: 19 May 1903–05 January 1904
Worth-Bal 1A: 1902–3 (no inventory)
Worth-Bal 2: 15 May–06 December 1904
Worth-Bal 3: 1904–5
Worth-Bal 4: 25 November 1905–18 August 1906
Worth-Bal 5: 05 December 1905–20 August 1907
Worth-Bal 6: 1907–8
Worth-Bal 7: 1908–9
Worth-Bal 8: 13 January 1909–09 July 1909
Worth-Bal 9: 10 July 1909–18 February 1910
Worth-Bal 10: 1910–11
Worth-Bal 11: 1911–12

Volumes of wedding dresses by Worth 1920s–40s:
Worth 1
Worth 2
Worth 3
Worth 4
Worth 5

A number of boxes of loose drawings of Worth (with occasional Paquin illustrations):
- drawings of hats
- line drawings: 1920s, 1930s, 1940s and 1950s designs. Also, a number of black outline drawings/facsimiles of designs from the 1900–1920 era, stamped with the following: 'Ste Anne au Capital de 5 Millions, Modèle Déposé, Priere de Renvoyer ce Dessin'
- Worth and Paquin designs, miscellaneous: jewellery, theatrical/masquerade, ski wear, specific collections; show notes, samples, designs: Tendance Hiver 1948–9; Printemps/Été 1949 (list of models [72] and material samples); Février 1947 (list of models [76] and material samples; Spring 1947 (same as previous); Madame Delroy – 3 Paquin designs with material samples attached to each design.

SCRAPBOOKS OF PRESS CUTTINGS RELATED TO WORTH 1926-56

Worth – Publicité Juillet 1926–Novembre 1927
Worth – Publicité 1927–30
Worth – Publicité 1929–35
Worth – Publicité Parfums Janvier 1930–Août 1933
Worth – Publicité 1930s
Worth – Publicité 1935
Worth – Publicité Decembre 1935–Decembre 1938
Worth – Publicité Janvier–Novembre 1938
Worth – Publicité Janvier 1947–Janvier 1948
Worth – Publicité Fèvrier–Octobre 1954
Worth – Publicité 1953–6

NOTE
1. Letter from Doris Langley Moore to Graham Reynolds, Keeper of Prints and Drawings, Victoria and Albert Museum, 2 September 1959.

LEFT TO RIGHT –
Wedding dress worn by the Marquise de el Cinares, 1920s
Fashion Museum, Bath and North East Somerset Council

Wedding dress worn by the Comtesse de Fleuview, 1930s
Fashion Museum, Bath and North East Somerset Council

APPENDIX 03:
THE PENNINGTON-MELLOR COLLECTION OF HOUSE OF WORTH HAUTE COUTURE c.1885-1914

E-J Scott

In 2006 a trunk containing women's clothing was opened, for the first time in almost 70 years, at Southside House, the home of the Pennington-Mellor family, in Wimbledon, London. Textile conservator Zenzie Tinker was brought in to evaluate the contents and immediately recognized that 19 of the heavily creased, and in some cases disintegrating, garments were from the House of Worth. They had been sent to Southside House in 1939 by Hilda Pennington-Mellor (1876–1967), who foresaw the Nazi occupation of France and wanted to safeguard her family's personal possessions. The Worth garments date back to the 1880s and were worn by Hilda and her mother Anna (1845–1929), who had subsequently preserved them as holders of deeply personal memory. This fascinating collection, currently being conserved by Tinker, is probably the largest surviving collection of Worth clothes worn by two generations of women from one family.

Like the Worths, the Pennington-Mellors enjoyed the benefits of social status that their wealth enabled. And, they, too, constructed carefully their social identities. John Pennington-Mellor's industrial fortune was self-made and Anna was a divorced American. In 1872, the same year the newly-wed couple arrived in Biarritz, John Pennington-Mellor co-founded the English Club. He even imported foxes to establish the English hunting tradition in the Basque region. Making their adopted home permanent, the Pennington-Mellors built one of southern France's most impressive mansions, Villa Françon (completed in 1878), in the tradition of English vernacular revival architecture. Jean Dumoulin, Directeur de la Federation Aquitaine des Caisses d'Allocations Familiales, confirms that, 'At the end of the nineteenth century, the name Françon was known in the courts of Europe, it was an estate visible to the whole resort and an elegant rendezvous for aristocrats and rich industrialists.'[1] Villa Françon was not only the hallmark that established the couple's social standing in Biarritz; it also became a fulcrum of Biarritz society.

Without title, and facing the social impediment of Anna's divorcee status, the family would not have been permitted to attend the Court of Queen Victoria in London. In Biarritz, however, they were welcomed into social circles at the pinnacle of high society and dressed accordingly. The family entertained lavishly at their magnificent home, with Anna Pennington-Mellor and her daughter receiving their guests attired in their splendid Worth gowns. At their annual fox hunt balls, the Pennington-Mellors frequently hosted royalty (including the Prince of Wales, Alfonso XII, Elisabeth of Austria, crowned both Empress of Austria and Queen of Hungary, and Anna's friend, the Queen of Serbia), politicians (including the British prime minister, Mr Campbell-Bannerman) and successful entrepreneurs (such as banker and British Vice Consul, Edmund Hook Wilson Bellairs). According to the *Courier de Bayonne*, at their ball in 1906, 'Madame Mellor looked charming in white, diamonds and superb lace'.[2]

Anna Pennington-Mellor's peach coloured brocade urban walking jacket is almost identical to tailored jackets pictured in the Worth photograph album for 1889–1901. And, during her conservation research, Janet Wood at Zenzie Tinker Conservation recognized a very similar design illustrated in Janet Arnold's *Patterns of Fashion 2: Englishwomen's dresses and their construction c.1860–1940* (1972). Arnold states, 'The sleeves are full over the shoulder with small pads to support them, and are very characteristic of these years.'[3]

The Pennington-Mellors' graceful evening dresses, the popular, highly fashionable and modern urban walking *jaquette*, and creative fancy dress costumes, all bear testimony to the design talent of Jean Worth. This collection is fascinating, romantic and intriguing, while being informative, didactic and historically insightful.

THE PENNINGTON-MELLOR COLLECTION OF WORTH DRESSES COMPRISES:

Fancy dress costume (bodice and skirt) in peasant or gypsy style. Green, blue and maroon coloured silk velvet, with gold metallic beaded chains at front and gold baubles on sleeves. The narrowness of the skirt suggests a date of c.1883.

'Van Dyck', fancy dress costume for a girl (8–12 years old), light blue silk (bodice and skirt). Blue silk, trimmed with cream lace on collar and cuff, silvery metallic lace edgings. Cream silk bows centre front with metallic tassels, c.1886–8, but meant to be reminiscent of c.1640–60.

Cream coloured silk velvet evening dress (bodice, skirt and train), finished with corded silk design work and tulle sleeves, c.1894–5.

'Night & Day', fancy dress (bodice and skirt). Contrasting midnight blue and yellow velvet, silk, silk tulle, crêpe, metallic thread, feathers, gold and silver fringing. It is decorated with a real stuffed bird, a crescent moon and scattered butterflies, bats, stars and roses, c.1897.

Peach coloured urban walking jacket in wool broadcloth with cream silk brocade. High stand collar and pleat inserts at back in cloth of gold. Ribbed silk lining with woven satin spots, c.1889. Peach wool bodice with cord appliqué, c.1900.

Hooded peach wool daywear cape, c.1900.

Cream silk evening cloak, c.1900.

Black silk and lace evening dress, trimmed with diamanté and pearl chain, diamanté and shoulder caps, finished with hanging silver and diamanté and pearlized acorns, c.1900–2.

Black and cream striped, chiné weave, Lyons silk evening dress with pink and green floral design, c.1901.

Cream silk bodice featuring grey fan design and high standing lace collar, c.1905–6.

Black brocaded silk evening dress, c.1908.

Black silk and lace evening gown with long, lace sleeves and high, boned collar. This dress has not yet been removed from its box and so can only be approximately dated to *c*.1908. Black silk crêpe dress with cream coloured tassels and glass beads, *c*.1910–12. However, according to Elizabeth Ann Coleman, its House of Worth label – no. 76167 – suggests it is 1906.

Cream silk evening dress trimmed with cream lace, *c*.1910. Cream and purple silk evening dress with sequins (an identical matching sequin design, for a different garment dated 1906, was found in the V&A Worth Archive), *c*.1910–12.

Midnight blue silk velvet opera coat, trimmed with chinchilla fur, with high collar and cuffs, *c*.1927.

Chiné weave bodice. Unviewed.

Grey silk day dress. Unviewed.

This research formed part of an extensive study of this collection undertaken for the author's unpublished dissertation, 'The Pennington-Mellor Collection of House of Worth Haute Couture, *c*.1883–1927: Forgotten, Found and Revealing', directed by Professor Lou Taylor, at the University of Brighton.

By kind permission of the Pennington-Mellor Munthe Charity Trust and Zenzie Tinker Conservation Limited.

NOTES

1. Jean Dumoulin, 'The Estate of Françon, Biarritz', *Domaine de Françon Biarritz*, edited by Hubert Cahuzac, Anne-Marie Fayol, Brun Fayolle-Lussac, Jean-Paul Grao, Genevieve Mesuret, Jacqueline du Pasquier (Bayonne, 1991), p.9.
2. Jean-Paul Grao, 'John Pennington-Mellor and His Family', *Domaine de Françon Biarritz*, cited note 1, p.48.
3. Janet Arnold, *Patterns of Fashion 2: Englishwomen's dresses and their construction c.1860-1940* (London, 1972), p.40.

Worth *jaquette*, design number 18980 in Worth Album marked 'Jaquettes', 1899-1901
AAD/1982/1/40

APPENDIX 04: PERFUME
Ben Whyman

The House of Worth was one of the first fashion houses in the world to produce, trademark and sell perfume. Charles Frederick was averse to perfume and disliked being surrounded by the fashionably heavily-scented clientele in the salon (he complained of migraines because of it).[1] It was Charles Frederick's son, Jean, who initiated plans to develop a Worth perfumery. The *Dans la Nuit* scent was trademarked in December 1920 and given to esteemed clients or sold to others within the salon, making Worth the third design house (after Paul Poiret and Maurice Babani) to create a scent (before Chanel's Number 5, trademarked in 1921). It was not until 1924 that the name 'Worth' was trademarked as a producer of perfumes and scent publicized and sold widely.[2] A relationship was forged between the house and René Lalique, the glass designer and manufacturer, who created bottles for Worth's perfumes until the 1940s. The bottle for *Dans la Nuit* was created after Lalique saw paintings that Jean had brought back from a holiday in Italy. The watercolours, depicting the soft Italian night sky, inspired Lalique to create a bottle of deep blue glass with clear glass stars, through which the amber liquid appeared, resembling 'the bowl of heaven, midnight blue glass with a sprinkling of stars through which light sprinkles…'.[3] The success of this perfume was so great that Lalique had to outsource bottle production 'to many glassworks in the Bresle valley to manufacture flacons using molds that he furnished'.[4]

A series of scents followed, including *Vers le Jour* (1925), *Sans Adieu* (1929), *Je Reviens* (1932) and *Vers Toi* (1934). These first five perfumes released by Worth comprise a fragrant love poem: *Dans la Nuit* ('in the night'); *Vers le Jour* ('just before dawn'); *Sans Adieu* ('without goodbyes'); *Je Reviens* ('I come back'); and *Vers Toi* ('to you'). For *Je Reviens* Lalique designed one of his first modernist bottles: 'A fluted blue glass cylinder, its neck steps up in three segments to meet an aqua button stopper…'.[5] The design was altered by Lalique in 1952 due to customers having difficulty opening the stopper.

The Fleurs Parisiennes series of scents was launched in 1929: *Oeillet* (carnation), *Jasmin*, *Rose*, *Lilas* (lilacs), *Gardénia* and *Honeysuckle*. *Projets* was launched in 1935 and *Imprudence* in 1938. Worth also created special, one-off scents including *Cadeau de Pâques* ('Easter Gift'), the bottle of which was registered by Lalique in March 1928 (only 200 of the white [clear] egg-shaped glass bottles with a low-relief pattern made up of the letter 'W' were made), and *Le Parfum des Anges* ('Scent of Angels'), created for the Oviatt department store, Los Angeles, in 1927.[6]

The House of Worth launched *Spotlight* in 1943, *Requête* ('By Request') in 1944, and in around 1948, *Eau de Cologne Naturelle* and *Cologne Chest*. The unique bottle for *Requête* was one of the first designs by Marc Lalique (son of René), a flattened sphere with scalloped edges outlined in blue enamel.[7] After the couture house closed in 1967, Les Parfums Worth was purchased by the Société Maurice Blanchet. *Monsieur Worth* was launched in 1969 and *Fleurs Fraîches* in the early 1970s. *Requête* was re-launched in 1976. *Miss Worth* was launched in 1977, *Worth Pour Homme* in 1980, and *Monsieur Worth* was re-launched the same year. *Dans la Nuit* was re-launched in 1985. In 1992 Les Parfums Worth was sold, to become part of International Classic Brands, and *Sans Adieu* was re-launched in 1995. The company was then acquired by Lenthéric in 1999, and now forms part of Shaneel Enterprises Ltd. *Worth by Worth* was launched in 2002, *Je Reviens Couture* in 2004 and *Courtesan* in 2005. Due to changes in the legal use of certain ingredients, the formulas for perfumes that have been re-launched have been revised.

NOTES
1. R. Stamelman, *Perfume: Joy, Obsession, Scandal, Sin: a cultural history of fragrance from 1750 to the present* (New York, 2006), p.95.
2. C.M. Lefkowith, *The Art of René Lalique* (New York, 2010), p.338.
3. Quoted in press dossier, Worth Archive, n.d.
4. Lefkowith, cited note 2, p.346.
5. M.L. Utt, G. Utt and P. Bayer, *Lalique Perfume Bottles* (London, 1991), p.72.
6. Utt, Utt and Bayer, cited note 5, p.104.
7. Utt, Utt and Bayer, cited note 5, p.111.

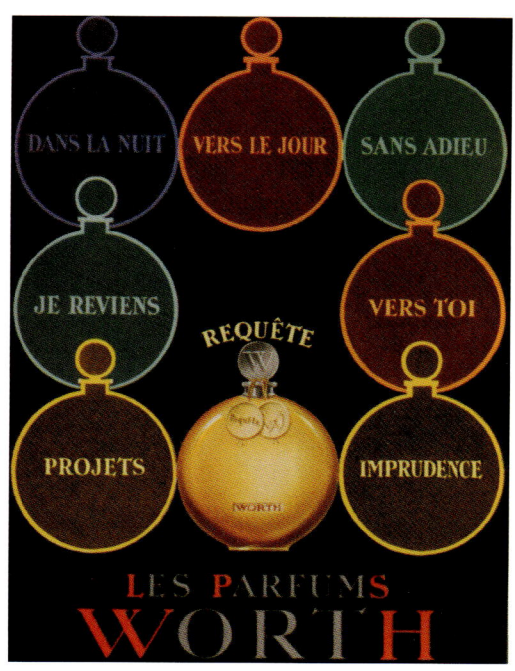

APPENDIX 05:
THE WORTH PARIS ARCHIVE: OBITUARIES AND PERSONAL LETTERS ON THE DEATH OF CHARLES FREDERICK WORTH

Ben Whyman

Jean Worth wrote of his father's obituaries and letters of condolence: 'We have two albums as big as dictionaries filled with these messages and newspaper articles. They came from kings and queens, aristocrats and peasants, the bourgeois and the artists and paupers and millionaires'.[1]

The House of Worth Archive holds these two, heavy black leatherbound volumes that report on the death of Charles Frederick Worth from public and personal perspectives. One volume contains newspaper and press clippings of obituaries for Worth, commentary on his rise from printer's apprentice to become one of the world's first – and most famous – haute couturiers, his legacy as a dressmaker, and reflections from journalists who had interviewed him. It contains over 1,200 clippings from American, French, British and other European newspapers, of which a majority are dated 14 March 1895, although they extend into July of the same year. Worth is commonly described as the 'famous man dressmaker' or 'man-milliner'. He is described as calm and pleasant, stout and genial, 'with a peculiarly low-toned voice and very quiet manners'.[2] Paris's *Figaro* newspaper (14 March 1895) highlights that Worth was a stickler for etiquette, 'and often expressed his disapproval in the plainest of terms of those ladies who presented themselves in underskirts that had lost their first freshness.' London's *Pall Mall Budget* (14 March 1895) comments that dress fittings for clients were revealing affairs: 'When he was ready the lady was shown into his presence, undressed behind a screen, clothed in the new gown, and then paraded before his critical eyes. He commented aloud, standing on the hearthrug, and pointing at her with his scissors; occasionally, even, fixing a pin in her here and there.' It also states that Worth 'was a good deal more than a dressmaker; he was an artist. He recognised that the dress and the dressed are not two, but one.' But both newspapers go on to note that his reputation had lately waned, 'sober Republicans finding fault with his flamboyant taste' (*Pall Mall Budget*).

The second volume contains letters, telegrams and calling cards, personally addressed to Worth's wife and sons, from devoted clients and employees wishing to express their condolences. The letters (numbering at least 340) capture personal memories about Worth, his creativity and his working practices. There are over 140 calling cards and some 110 telegrams. One letter, written by Annie Chapman of Godalming, Surrey, as one 'who greatly regrets your sad loss', describes how she worked as a Worth seamstress up until 1879. Margot Asquith, Countess of Oxford and Asquith and wife of Herbert Henry Asquith, a prime minister of England, notes Worth 'was a unique figure and the kindest of men'. In a letter addressed to Mr Worth (one of Charles Frederick's sons), an unknown customer (name unreadable) relates: 'You are too young to remember, that I was one of your poor father's earliest clients, and the interest he had in adding by his art… to the beauty of my youth, and [unreadable] to the dignified appearance of my middle age, was unfailing and unchanged. I was much touched by the continued interest he manifested toward my child, and the minute care he gave, when she also came, in her turn, as I had, to be prepared for her marriage. And that was the last time I ever saw him. He then promised to compose for me especially an old lady's costume, the style of wh. [which] need never be changed.'

NOTES
1. J-P. Worth 1928, p.179.
2. *Kensington Society*, London, 14 March 1895.

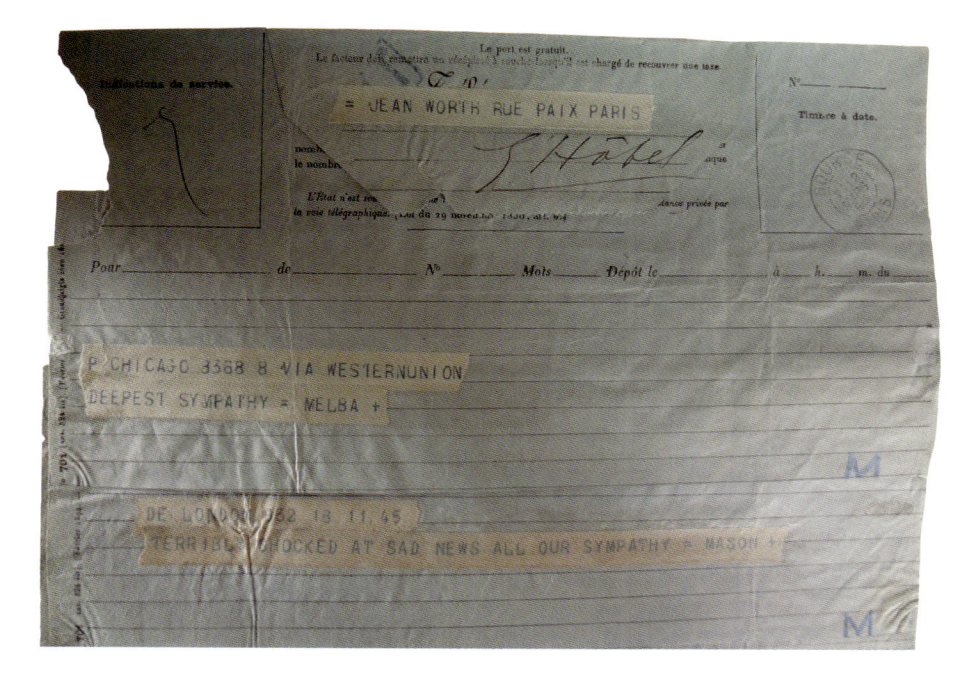

OPPOSITE, LEFT – *Dans la Nuit* perfume flacon, 1924 to c.1940, designed by René Lalique. Described in Utt, Utt and Bayer's book *Lalique Perfume Bottles* (1991) as 'simple and elegant, appropriate and evocative', this flacon was produced by Lalique from the 1920s to the 1940s, the design of both bottle and stopper varied by numerous subtle design permutations. Worth Paris Archive - Guardian, Dilesh Mehta

OPPOSITE, RIGHT – Poster, 1940s, from the Worth Paris Archive. Although Les Parfums Worth is renowned for its unique flacon designs, especially those created by the Lalique glass factory, the generic shape with which the Worth name has become synonymous is that of the flattened spherical bottle in which so many of its scents, including *Dans la Nuit, Je Reviens, Vers Toi, Vers le Jours, Sans Adieu* and *Projets*, have been sold. Worth Paris Archive - Guardian Dilesh Mehta

LEFT – Cable of condolence sent to Jean Worth by Dame Nellie Melba, the opera singer, dated 12 March 1895. Worth Archive - Guardian, Dilesh Mehta

CLOCKWISE – A personal letter addressed to 'Dear Mr. Jean [Worth]', from Margot Asquith, Countess of Oxford and Asquith. Worth Archive – Guardian, Dilesh Mehta

Album of obituaries dated 11 March 1895. Worth Archive – Guardian, Dilesh Mehta

Letter of condolence written by Annie Chapman, a former seamstress at Worth. Worth Archive – Guardian, Dilesh Mehta

OPPOSITE, LEFT TO RIGHT – A half-page signed photograph of the designer, dated 20 March 1895. Worth Archive – Guardian, Dilesh Mehta

One obituary, dated 13 March 1895, recalls an interview with Worth about a favourite client, Mrs Brown Potter (whose photograph is housed in the V&A Archive). Worth Archive – Guardian, Dilesh Mehta

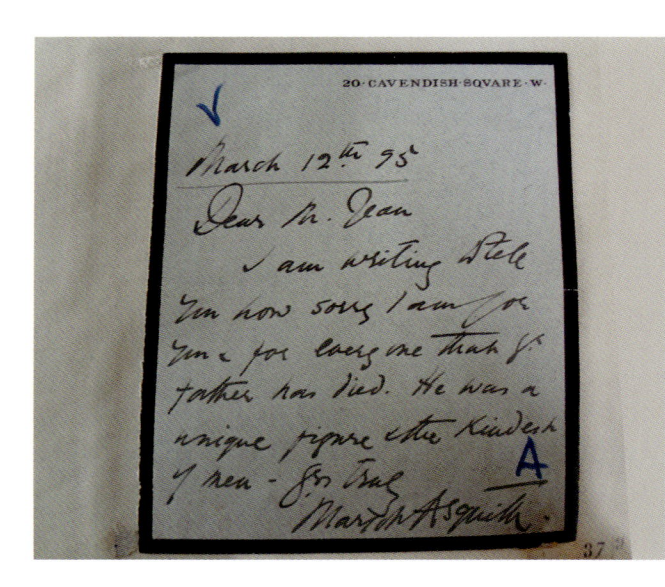

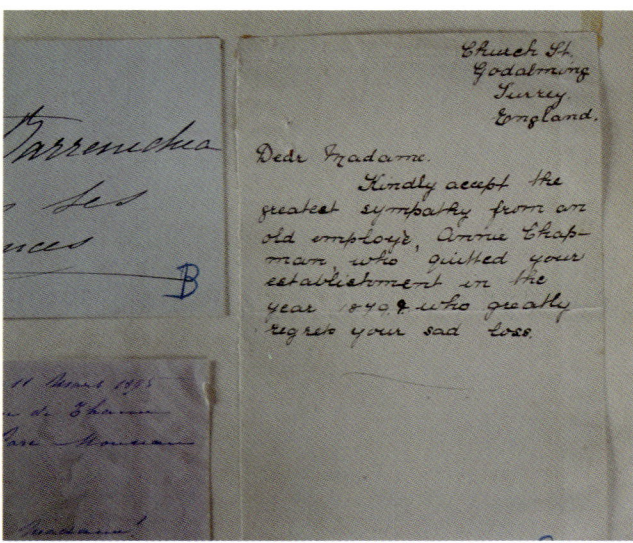

164 — APPENDICES

Sketch 20 Mars. Londres

THE LATE M. WORTH.

Home Journal 13 Mars. New York

The Passing of Worth.

Worth, the famous man dressmaker, of Paris, is dead. His humble beginning is well known. At the present time his establishment employs about 1,200 persons, and turns out between 6,000 and 7,000 dresses and between 3,000 and 4,000 cloaks a year. M. Worth was assisted by his sons.

"Who," asked a visitor recently, "are your best customers?"

"Well," replied Worth, "we send model dresses to all parts of the world, but I think Americans are the best clients."

"And your favorite figure to design for?"

"Ah! that's telling; but one of my ideals is Mrs. Brown-Potter. I consider her one of the most beautiful women I have ever seen."

"Do you think American women have good taste in their costuming?"

He answered: "They dress as well as any women in the world and have as good figures, which they are fond of displaying to the best advantage, and that is right. They exercise a large influence upon our fashions, and make and unmake to suit themselves."

CHRONOLOGY
Valerie D. Mendes

1825
Charles Frederick Worth is born, 13 October, at Bourne, Lincolnshire, England.

1838
Apprenticed to Swan and Edgar (a letter of condolence, dated 1895, from J. Ritchie notes: 'I was with him at Swans from 1842 to 1844'). Possibly works briefly for other London firms including Lewis and Allenby.

1845
Leaves London for Paris, works in a small dry goods store, possibly La Ville de Paris.

Later engaged by Maison Gagelin-Opigez, Chazelle & Cie (which becomes Opigez-Gagelin & Cie), rue de Richelieu, dealing in fabrics, shawls and mantles. Eventually made head salesman, or *premier commis*.

1851
Marries Marie Vernet, a fellow employee and *demoiselle de magasin* at Gagelin, who later becomes her husband's assistant and model. Worth starts to design gowns for the company, modelled by his wife.

The Great Exhibition of the Works of Industry of All Nations is staged in London, 1851. Gagelin exhibits 'India' shawls and gowns, probably by Worth, and is awarded a medal.

Louis Napoléon Bonaparte declares the French Empire restored.

1853
Emperor Napoléon III marries Spanish Countess Eugénie de Montijo. Her trousseau apparently incorporated fabrics by Gagelin.

Worth's eldest son Gaston-Lucien is born (known as Gaston).

1855
Opigez-Gagelin et Cie wins a first class medal at the Exposition Universelle, Paris, for a white train embroidered in gold and innovatively draped from the shoulder rather than the waist. Worth has been credited as the designer. The company is praised in the report on the exhibition for elegant 'vêtements pour femmes'.

Henry Creed opens Paris branch in the rue Royale, making riding habits for Empress Eugénie.

MID-1850s
Increasing numbers of patents are taken out for lightweight cage crinolines of whalebone or sprung steel hoops. Empress Eugénie was associated with the popularity of crinolines, or 'crinolinomania'.

1856
Worth's son Jean-Philippe is born (known as Jean).

1858
Worth leaves Gagelin and forms a partnership with Swedish-born Otto Gustaf Bobergh.

Worth et Bobergh opens at 7 rue de la Paix; it was said to employ about 20 staff.

1860
Princess Pauline von Metternich introduces Worth's creations to Empress Eugénie (according to the Princess), who thenceforward patronized the house.

1860s
Worth et Bobergh reputed to employ some 1,000 workers. Listed in the Paris trade directory as Worth et Bobergh Maison Spéciale, Robes et Manteaux, Confectionnés, Soieries, Haute Nouveautés, Paix 7.

The company is designated an official supplier to the Empress Eugénie.

Worth buys land and builds a substantial villa or 'chateau fantastique' (*Le Figaro*, 11 March 1895) in Suresnes, then a small village overlooking the Seine, about 9km west of central Paris. Intended for spring and summer use. In Paris Worth and his family live at 1 rue de Berri on the corner of the Champs-Elysées. Worth's villa in Suresnes is later demolished by his sons. The extensive Hôpital Foch (40 rue Worth) now occupies the land. All that remains of the original 'chateau' is a monumental entrance with grill gate and pediment surmounted by a pair of architectonic snails.

1867
Hippolyte Taine's satire *Vie et opinions de M. Frédéric-Thomas Graindorge* lampoons Worth.

1868
The trade union Chambre Syndicale des Confectionneurs et des Tailleurs pour Dames is established. In 1910, it became the Chambre Syndicale de la Couture Parisienne.

In various capacities, each Worth generation is involved with French fashion trade unions (especially the Chambre Syndicale de la Haute Couture Française) and other official fashion organizations, working to improve standards and working conditions. They serve as presidents and vice-presidents (Gaston was the first president of the Chambre Syndicale de la Haute Couture and Jacques, Gaston's son, served two terms as president). They join committees arranging French fashion submissions to major international exhibitions.

1870-1
Period of warfare and socio-economic disturbance encompassing the collapse of the Second Empire, the Franco-Prussian War, Siege of Paris and the Paris Commune. Worth is reputed to have escaped the siege in a hot air balloon. He helps to organize ambulances, and workrooms are used as emergency wards. The house is closed for a time. However, the business survives.

Bobergh retires and returns to Stockholm with his wife, Thérèse. The company name is abbreviated to Worth and remains at 7 rue de la Paix.

1871
The journalist F. Adolphus is granted a rare interview with Worth at his villa in Suresnes. Adolphus intended to discuss the state of couture in difficult times but chiefly recorded valuable information about the villa (including Worth's extensive ceramics collection), the family and their domestic life.

1870s-90s
The name Worth, as a synonym for exclusive and expensive fashion, appears increasingly in fiction – most famously in Emile Zola's *La Curée* (1872), in which Worth makes an appearance as the couturier 'Worms'. Other references occur in works by 'Ouida' (the popular novelist Maria Louise Ramé), including *A House Party* (1878) and *Friendship* (1887), while Frances Hodgson Burnett devoted an entire eponymous chapter to Worth in *Louisiana* (1880). The couturier is cited in the 1899 sonnet 'Sur mesure' by Philippe, 'Marquis de Massa', and in novels such as *Une Parvenue* (1881) by Guy de Charnacé and *Le Chien Perdu* (1872) by Arsène Houssaye.

1874-5
First Gaston, and then Jean, formally enter their father's employ.

1881
Charles Poynter Redfern, London dressmaker, opens a Paris branch in the rue de Rivoli.

1884
Chambre Syndicale de la Haute Couture Française is established.

1889
Date of the earliest photographs in the V&A's collection of Worth Photograph Albums (Museum numbers AAD/1982/1/1 to AAD/1982/1/81 and AAD/1990/4/1 to AAD/1990/4/333).

'WORTH MAISON SPECIALE robes et manteaux confectionnés, soieries, haute nouveautés, Paix 7'. Entry (under 'couturières') in the Paris Annuaire-Almanach du commerce et de l'industrie. Didot-Bottin, p.1172.

1890
Charles Frederick Worth (now 65 years old) reduces his working hours but reputedly never stops going into 7 rue de la Paix.

1891
The House of Paquin (destined to take over Worth) opens at 3 rue de la Paix.

1893
Worth v. Bradley. Worth sues Mrs Bradley trading in London as a dressmaker and corsetier under the name Worth et Cie. Counsel for Gaston states that Charles Frederick Worth had 'long ceased to take any part in the business'. This conflicts with the story that he continued to go into rue de la Paix until his final illness.

1895
10 March at Suresnes: unexpected death of Charles Frederick Worth, aged 69. Pinned to a letter in the album of personal condolences is an extract from *Vanity* (New York, 14 March): 'Worth is dead. The delicate hand and designing brain that composed so many pictorial poems in the shape of feminine fashion is still at last …'. Worth's body taken to rue de Berri where he lay in state in the grand salon. His funeral service at the Protestant Temple de l'Etoile is attended by some 2,000 mourners. Worth interred in the family tomb, Suresnes (destroyed by bombing in 1940).

Gaston and Jean Worth inherit the company and later in March donate to various charities including Société de Secours Mutuels la Couturière and the Association de l'Aguille in honour of their father.

Jean Worth asserts that the company 'rose like the phoenix from its own ashes. Gaston was born with a genius for finance' (*A Century of Fashion*, 1928).

Gaston Worth's exemplary report on the French fashion industry, *La Couture et la Confection des Vêtements de Femme*, is published in Paris soon after his father's death.

1896
Paquin becomes an incorporated company in England.

1900-1
Jean creates eighteenth-century interior settings at the Exposition Universelle, Paris, inhabited by wax mannequins displaying 'incidents from English life' in garments ranging from a maid's uniform to a court presentation gown.

At the same exhibition, an enormously popular display, 'La Collectivité de la Couture', of 52 couture ensembles by 20 top Paris houses is organized by the Chambre Syndicale de la Confection pour Dames et Enfants. Worth exhibits a sky-blue silk damask gown with court train, and a white satin and pink chiffon *robe de bal*, layered with black tulle applied with Worth's hallmark cloud forms in black velvet, the whole enlivened with 'rays' of sparkling diamantés. The show's final ensemble is a typically luxurious coat by Worth of velvet embroidered with chenille, lined with ermine and trimmed with sable. The Chambre publishes a booklet as a 'souvenir durable de cette manifestation industrielle'.

Gaston is elected president of the committee as well as the jury for Classe 85 at the exhibition.

Gaston (then honorary president of the Chambre Syndicale de la Couture) receives the Légion d'honneur. The official papers (Archives Nationales, dossier 19800035/0212/27814) describe him as a 'confectionneur pour dames' and list his membership of prestigious French organizations involved with fashion, textiles and commerce.

The House of Worth is recognized as an Ancien Notable Commerçant.

1901-2
Paul Poiret (appointed by Gaston) works for Worth.

1902
The first London House of Worth, with dressmaking workrooms, opens at 4 New Burlington Street.

1914
According to Edna Woolman and Ilke Chase (*Always in Vogue*, 1954), an anti-copying organization – Le Syndicat de Défense de la Grande Couture Française – is formed with Paul Poiret as president and Jacques Worth (then 32 years old) as vice-president.

1914-18
Towards the end of the First World War, workrooms at 7 rue de la Paix (designated Hôpital Militaire Auxilaire, no. 152) once again become emergency wards for the wounded.

1917
L'Autre Combat, a play co-written with A. Delamarre by Jean Worth, under the pseudonym Philippe Vernet (his mother's maiden name), is performed at the Théâtre Rejane in November. Published by Madon et Langlois, Paris, in 1921.

1920
Gaston retires, distraught and exhausted from his wartime duties.

The house branches out into perfume and registers *Dans la Nuit*.

1920s
Jean and Gaston are succeeded by Gaston's sons: Jean-Charles, who becomes designer for the house, and Jacques, who follows his father as business administrator.

New House of Worth Couture opens at 3 Hanover Square, London, with accessories, sports clothes and perfumes at 'their usual shop' (advertisement, c.1927) at 221 Regent Street.

Between the wars branches are opened at Cannes at Sur la Croisette (with modern streamlined salons) and Biarritz at 7 Place Georges Clémenceau (a 'heavy' interior with pseudo eighteenth-century touches and ornate furniture) to satisfy the holidaying, fashionable rich.

1921
Jacques Worth, a witness for Madeleine Vionnet in a case against unauthorized copying, makes a plea for improved laws to protect the work of couturiers.

1923
Jacques serves as president of the Chambre Syndicale de la Haute Couture and is largely responsible for establishing holiday pay in the couture industry.

House of Worth is founder member of L'Association pour la Défense des Arts Plastiques et Appliqués en France et à l'étranger – an anti-copyist organization.

1924
Gaston Worth dies aged 71 years.

Parfums Worth issues *Dans la Nuit*, followed by *Vers le Jour* (1925), *Sans Adieu* and the Fleurs Parisiennes perfume series: *Œillet*, *Jasmin*, *Rose*, *Lilas*, *Gardénia* and *Honeysuckle* (1929).

1926
Jean Worth dies aged 70 years.

1928
A History of Feminine Fashion is published posthumously. Jean Worth worked on these memoirs with the translator Ruth Scott Miller.

13 August, Jean-Charles Worth (Worth of Worth) appears on the cover of *Time: The Weekly News* magazine (New York).

1930
Jacques oversees the establishment of the Ecole Supérieure de la Couture.

Jean-Charles commissions the architects Jean Fidler and Alexandre Poliakoff to design his family home (Hôtel Worth) at Neuilly-sur-Seine. It takes elements from Mediterranean architecture and still features in surveys of Paris architecture.

1930s
Perfumes issued : *Je Reviens* (1932), *Vers Toi* (1934), *Projets* (1935) and *Imprudence* (1938).

1935
London branch relocates to 50 Grosvenor Street, with Elspeth Champcommunal as head designer. A fourth generation takes over: designer Jean-Charles retires and his nephew Roger assumes his role. Roger's brother Maurice becomes business administrator.

1937
The House of Worth, Paris, moves to 120 Faubourg Saint-Honoré.

1940s
Perfumes issued: *Spotlight* (1943), *Requête* (1944) and the eau de cologne *Naturelle*.

1941
Roger assumes role as head of the firm after the death of Jacques Worth.

1945
The London branch of Worth is acquired by Paquin Ltd but continues to operate under its own name.

Parfums Worth continues in Paris with Roger Worth on the Board of Directors.

1952
Roger Worth retires and is succeeded by Maurice.

1954
The House of Paquin takes over Société Anonyme Worth in an attempt to revitalize both labels. Both houses operate from 120 Faubourg Saint-Honoré

1955
At the annual meeting of Paquin Ltd (Court Dressmakers), it is proposed that the company should diversify because of the limited possibilities of dressmaking. By 1964 the former fashion house is mainly concerned with hire purchase and property development.

1956
Paquin Ltd closes 120 Faubourg Saint-Honoré and presents the V&A with the Worth-Paquin archive of photographs, designs, books and miscellaneous papers.

Worth (London) Ltd plans a Miss Worth department for ready-to-wear and accessories.

1958
James Laver organizes *The House of Worth. A Centenary Exhibition of Designs for Dresses* (1858-1958) at the V&A, displaying works from the Worth-Paquin Archive.

1960s
Worth (London) Ltd profits fluctuate. At the end of a year of substantial losses, Sir Leonard Dyer (chairman) remarks, 'An artistic joy can be a financial headache' (*The Times*, 24 March 1964).

1960s-2000s
Now a separate company, Parfums Worth revives earlier Worth fragrances, such as *Requête* (1976), and creates new blends, such as *Monsieur Worth* in 1966. In the 1970s *Fleur Fraîches* and *Miss Worth* (1977) are issued. A new version of *Monsieur Worth* is created in 1981 and a new *Dans la Nuit* in 1985. In the 2000s the company introduces *Worth by Worth* (2002), *Je Reviens Couture* (2004) and *Courtesan* (2005).

1962
Jean-Charles (who retired in 1935) dies, aged 81.

1967
Worth (London) Ltd ceases trading on 29 December. Paquin sells the name to Sidney Massin, who relaunches the company in 1968.

1999
Entrepreneur Dilesh Mehta takes over the House of Worth and re-energizes both the fashion and perfume branches. Giovanni Bedin is appointed head fashion designer.

2010-11
Bedin's first couture collection is released for Spring/Summer 2010 and his first ready-to-wear in 2011.

ACKNOWLEDGEMENTS

At the V&A's Archive of Art and Design we are most grateful for the professional and good natured support (the photograph albums are extremely heavy) provided, over the last three years, by Christopher Marsden, Eva White, Alexia Kirk, Nicholas Smith, Carys Lewis, James Sutton and Victoria West. Blythe House manager Glenn Benson always made us welcome, as did the security staff.

For their dedicated guidance and patience we are indebted to Mark Eastment, Director of V&A Publishing; our editor, Frances Ambler; Kate Phillimore, who helped with picture research; Rachel Daley, for her invaluable assistance in sorting the hundreds of images; and graphic designer Charlie Smith for her elegant concept.

For contributing valuable appendices we thank Rosemary Harden, Curator at Bath Fashion Museum; E-J Scott; Dilesh and Nikita Mehta; and Richard Brooks of the House of Worth; and Benjamin Whyman, Curation Project Manager, London College of Fashion.

At Bath's Fashion Museum, for their expertise and incredible generosity we acknowledge curator Rosemary Harden and her assistant Elaine Uttley.

We are grateful to Phyllis Madigson, Curator at the Museum of the City of New York. For their research input we have pleasure in thanking E-J Scott, Jennifer Rothrock, Holly Bruce, Anysa Cianni, Shonagh Marshall and Maude Bass-Krueger. For advice about the complexities of fur we are grateful to Basia Szkutznicka.

We both greatly appreciate the valuable input during the final stages of the book supplied by Amy's colleagues, Ben Whyman, and Laura Thornley, Administrator, Curation Office, London College of Fashion. Amy would also like to acknowledge Dr Frances Corner, Head of London College of Fashion. Valerie wishes to thank Peter, Sam and Joe Mendes for their forbearance, Dr John Stokes, Faith Evans and Loraine Fletcher.

The V&A's Furniture, Textiles and Fashion Department, led by Christopher Wilk, was supportive from the outset of this project and we are particularly indebted to the perceptive Edwina Ehrman, while the Word and Image Department kindly supported our research.

The extraordinary resources and helpful librarians at the V&A's National Art Library, the British Library and the London Library have eased our path. On a digital plain the Bibliothèque Nationale's Gallica (and partners) project has proved an eye opener, and we are indebted to all those who are responsible for this online phenomenon.

Without the skill and specialist knowledge of the V&A photographer Ken Jackson this monograph could not have been realized. Generous as ever, James Stephenson, former Head of V&A Photographic Studio, gave us expert advice.

**'FOR MY PARENTS, BRIAN AND JULIA'
AMY DE LA HAYE**

'TO DIANE AND ERNEST' VALERIE D. MENDES

GLOSSARY
Valerie D. Mendes

Basque (Fr.).
The skirt or tail of a blouse, coat or jacket. A slightly flared extension of the bodice below the waist.

Bodice.
Upper part of a woman's dress.

Bouquet de corsage (Fr.).
Cluster of real or artificial flowers attached to a bodice (*corsage*). Usually shortened to *corsage*.

Cachemire de soie (Fr.).
Light silk and fine wool with soft handling and excellent draping qualities.

Casaque (Fr.).
A long, fitted jacket with a slightly flared, deep basque.

Charmeuse (Fr.).
Lightweight, pliable satin-faced fabric with a low to medium lustre, much used for draped garments.

Décolletage.
Low-cut neckline of a woman's dress.

Decoupé (Fr.).
Cutwork.

Déshabillé (Fr.).
Negligee or undress. Used throughout the late nineteenth and early twentieth century to indicate informal at home wear.

Drap chamois (Fr.).
Usually woollen cloth with a nap imitating the suede-like finish of pliable leather made from the hide of the chamois (a goat-like antelope).

Duchesse.
Heavy, firm satin with a high lustre.

En princesse (Fr.).
Or princess line, indicating a garment without a seam around the waist. The panels of a princess gown are cut and sewn vertically, usually to skim the body and flare gently below knee level. Associated with HRH Queen Alexandra when she was Princess of Wales.

Engageantes (Fr.).
Deep, graduated layered flounces, or ruffles, of lace or muslin attached to sleeve edges.

Entre-deux (Fr.).
Literally 'between two'. Narrow insertion of lace or embroidery joining two panels of fabric. Much used in deluxe lingerie, blouses and lightweight garments.

Faille (Fr.).
A silk with a ribbed weave which is midway between the delicate rib of poult and the pronounced rib of grosgrain.

Fichu (Fr.)
French for neckerchief or kerchief. Draped scarf, neckpiece or shawl (usually of flimsy white fabric) worn around the neck and shoulders.

Flou (Fr.).
Dressmaking, as distinct from tailor-made garments.

Frou-frou (Fr.).
Literally, 'rustle'. An onomatopoeic term often used in association with multi-flounced garments in crisp silks such as taffeta which, in movement, make a rustling sound. Associated with the 1869 *Comédie Froufrou* by Henri Meilhac and Ludovic Halévy. A term attractive to playwrights, writers, musicians and poets. The saucy journal *Le Frou-frou* (1900s-1920s) was described as 'joyeux et léger'. In recent years the word has been appropriated by biscuits, blogs and an ambient music group.

Frogging.
Fastening of braid or fabric loop over a cylindrical button, around which silk or metal braid or cord is applied in ornate scrollwork. Derived from military uniform.

Guipure.
Term from the French with a variety of meanings from types of bobbin lace, in which the pattern is joined by bars without net grounds, to crochet edgings as well as embroidery, where the ground is cut away leaving the pattern joined by bars. Guipure, with bold patterns, became popular in the years flanking 1900.

Jabot (Fr.).
Frill (of a shirt or a dress). Longish frill or ruffle, often of lace or delicate white fabric which is fastened around the neck and cascades over the centre front of the bodice.

Karakul/Caracul/Astrakhan.
Persian lamb with distinctive curled hair.

Lamp shade skirt.
A flared skirt often with a wired hemline to retain the conical shape.

Liberty.
A plain, light silk, usually with a semi-lustrous satin surface. Not to be confused with Liberty (of London) printed silk.

Manteau (Fr.).
Coat, also mantle or cloak.

Mantle.
Cloak-like outer garment.

Moiré.
Fabric (often ribbed silk) with a rippled watermark achieved by passing the fabric through heated, engraved copper rollers or by chemical processes.

Mousseline glacée (Fr.).
Opaque delicate silk (chiffon) with a glazed finish imparting sheen.

Mousseline de soie (Fr.).
Chiffon. Opaque delicate silk.

Organza.
Very light, crisp, semi-transparent silk. Its cotton equivalent is organdie.

Ottoman.
A term loosely applied to mid-to-heavyweight silk with pronounced, usually horizontal ribs.

Paletot (Fr.).
Overcoat (as worn by both male and female). Usually short but generally applied to outer garments of various lengths and cut.

Pardessus (Fr.).
Overcoat. Generic term for outdoor garment. Of various lengths and cut.

Parure.
Matching set of jewellery (e.g. necklace and earrings) or decorative trimmings (e.g. collar and cuffs) for costume.

BIBLIOGRAPHY

Passementerie.
Trimmings. Generic term for braids, gimps, fringes, rosettes, tassels, cords and embroideries in silk and metal threads.

Peau de soie (Fr.).
A firm but soft silk with a dull satin surface.

Pékin (Fr.). Also Pekin.
Striped silk fabric, sometimes with slightly crisp handling. Also used as a generic term for striped textiles. In French a striped fabric is said to be *pékiné*. Name derived from place of origin.

Pompadour.
Eighteenth-century style of dress, fabrics, accessories and hairstyles etc, named after Madame de Pompadour, mistress of Louis XV.

Redingote.
French corruption of the English riding coat. Tailored outdoor coat or long jacket, fitted or semi-fitted.

Robe de cour. (Fr.).
Court dress.

Robe de bal. (Fr.).
Ball gown.

Rouleau/rouleaux (Fr.).
Roll.
Narrow tubular piping of bias-cut fabrics, sometimes with an internal cord or wadding for firmness. Used for applied decoration and edging as it is flexible and can be manipulated into intricate patterns.

Serge.
Worsted cloth used for tailoring. There are many types of serge and the term is often used loosely for worsted and woollen tailoring fabrics.

Soutache (Fr.).
Derived from the Hungarian *szuszak*. Narrow decorative braid, usually of two cords joined by a tight herringbone plait. Also known as Russian/Russia braid.

Sack back.
An eighteenth-century type of female gown. The back is arranged in box pleats at the shoulders and falls to a slight train.

Sortie de bal (Fr.).
Usually an ornate protective evening cloak or coat (often loose cut), worn over ball gowns.

Tulle.
Named after the town in SW France. An all silk net.

Vandyke.
Pointed zigzag-edged voile, or lace, or border for collars, sleeves, necklines etc. Inspired by costume details in portraits by Sir Anthony Van Dyck.

Voile (Fr.).
Veil.
Lightweight, sheer fabric which drapes well. Can be of silk, wool or cotton.

Voided velvet.
Velvet in which the pattern incorporates flat areas without velvet pile.

Zibeline.
Glossy, rippled cloth woven from lustrous worsted yarns. Made to imitate zibeline – the soft silky fur of the Siberian sable.

OF PARTICULAR RELEVANCE TO THE HOUSE OF WORTH

Adolphus, F., 'Mr Worth' in Blackwood's *Edinburgh Magazine*, vol.CLVII, May 1895, pp.790–7; reprinted in Adolphus, F., *Some Memories of Paris* (Edinburgh, 1895)

Anonymous, *A History of Feminine Fashion* (London, c.1928)

Beck, A. H., 'The House of Worth', *Leader* magazine, 28 January 1950

Belloc, Marie A., 'La Maison Worth: An Interview with M. Jean Worth', *The Lady's Realm*, November 1896, pp.134–6

Coleman, Elizabeth Ann, *The Opulent Era: Fashions of Worth, Doucet and Pingat* (New York, 1989)

De Marly, Diana, *Worth: Father of Haute Couture* (London, 1980; revised 1990)

The History of Haute Couture 1850-1950 (London, 1980)

Olian, JoAnne, *The House of Worth, the Gilded Age*, exh. cat., Museum of the City of New York, New York, 1982

Riley, Robert et al, *The House of Worth*, exh. cat., Brooklyn Museum, New York, 1962

Saunders, Edith, *The Age of Worth* (London, 1954)

Shonfield, Zuzanna, *The Great Mr Worth*, Costume, no.16, 1982, pp.57-9

'Worth of the House of Worth', *Time*, vol.XII, no.7, August 1912

Winterburn, Florence Hull, *Principles of Correct Dress* (New York and London, 1914); see chapters I-III by Jean-Philippe Worth

Worth, Gaston, *La Couture et la Confection des Vêtements de Femme* (Paris, 1895)

Worth, Gaston, 'Comment se Fait la Mode. Causerie d'un Couturier', in *Revue des Arts Décoratifs*, vol.XV1, Paris, 1896, pp.120-6

Worth, Jean-Philippe, 'Individuality in Dress', *Harper's Bazar*, January–March 1908

Worth, Jean-Philippe, *A Century of Fashion* (Boston, 1928)

FURTHER READING

Adburgham, Alison, *Shops and Shopping 1800-1914* (London, 1964)

View of Fashion (London, 1966)

Alexandre, Arsène, *Les Reines de l'aiguille. Modistes et Couturieres* (Paris, 1902)

Amies, Hardy, *Just So Far* (London, 1954)

Anand, Sushila, *Daisy: The Life and Loves of the Countess of Warwick* (London, 2008)

Andrews, Allen, *The Follies of King Edward VII* (London, 1975)

Arch, Nigel, and Marschner, Joanna, *Splendour at Court* (London, 1987)

Aria, Mrs *Costume, Fanciful, Historical and Theatrical* (London, 1906)

Aronson, Theo, *The King in Love: Edward VII's Mistresses* (London, 1988)

Asquith, Lady Cynthia, *Remember and be Glad* (London, 1952)

Asquith, Margot, *The Autobiography of Margot Asquith: 1* (London, 1920) and *The Autobiography of Margot Asquith: 2* (London, 1922)

Auchincloss, Louis, *The Vanderbilt Era: Profiles of a Gilded Age* (New York, 1990)

Balsan, Consuelo Vanderbilt, *The Glitter and the Gold* (London, 1953)

Banner, Lois W., *American Beauty: A Social History through Two Centuries of the American Idea, Ideal, and Image of the Beautiful Woman* (New York, 1983)

Bayles Kortsch, Christine, *Dress Culture in Late Victorian Women's Fiction* (Farnham, 2009)

Beaton, Cecil, *The Book of Beauty* (London, 1930)

The Glass of Fashion (London, 1954)

Beatty, Laura, *Lillie Langtry: Manners, Masks and Morals* (London, 1999)

Beckson, Karl, *London in the 1890s: A Cultural History* (London, 1992)

Beetham, Margaret, *A Magazine of Her Own? Domesticity and Desire in the Woman's Magazine, 1800-1914* (London, 1996)

Bennett, Helen, and Stevenson, Sara, *Van Dyke in Checked Trousers. Fancy Dress in Art and Life*, exh. cat., Scottish National Portrait Gallery, Edinburgh, 1978

Bentley-Cranch, Dana, *Edward VII* (London, 1992)

Bernard, Anne-Marie, *Le Monde de Proust vu par Paul Nadar*, (Paris, 1999)

Bigland, Eileen, *Ouida, The Passionate Victorian* (London, 1950)

Bloom, Ursula, *The Elegant Edwardian* (London, 1957)

Borgé, Jacques, and Viasnoff, Nicolas, *Archives de la Mode* (Paris, 1995)

Brandon, Ruth, *The Dollar Princesses: Sagas of Upward Mobility 1870-1914* (New York, 1980)

Breward, Christopher, *Fashioning London: Clothing and the Modern Metropolis* (Oxford, 2004)

Breward, Christopher, and Evans, Caroline (eds), *Fashion and Modernity* (Oxford, 2005)

Brown Potter, Cora, *Secrets of Beauty and Mysteries of Health* (New York, c.1910)

Buchan, Susan, Lady Tweedsmuir, *An Edwardian Lady* (London, 1966)

Buckley, Cheryl, and Fawcett, Hilary, *Fashioning the Feminine: Representation and Women's Fashion from the Fin de Siècle to the Present* (London, 2002)

Caffrey, Kate, *The 1900s Lady* (London, 1976)

Cannadine, David, *Decline and Fall of the British Aristocracy* (New Haven, CT, 1992)

Aspects of Aristocracy (London, 1994)

Carette, Mme, *My Mistress The Empress Eugenie or Court Life at the Tuileries* (London, 1889)

Chabanne, Laure et al, *Sous l'Empire des Crinolines*, exh. cat., Musée Galliera, Paris, 2008

Chapon, François, *Mystère et splendeurs de Jacques Doucet* (Paris, 1984)

Coates, Tim, *Patsy: the Story of Mary Cornwallis-West* (London, 2003)

Cohen, Lucy, *Lady de Rothschild and her Daughters 1821-1931* (London, 1935)

Cowles, Virginia, *Edward VII and his Circle* (London, 1956)

Crawford, M.D.C., *The Ways of Fashion* (New York, 1941)

Cunningham, Patricia A., *Reforming Women's Fashions 1850-1920* (Ohio, 2003)

Cunnington, C. Willett, *The Perfect Lady* (London, 1948)

Curzon, Mary, Marchioness of Kedleston, *Reminiscences* (London, 1955)

Davidoff, Leonore, *The Best Circles* (London, 1986)

De la Haye, Amy, and Mendes, Valerie, *Twentieth-Century Fashion* (London, 1999)

    Lucile (London, 2009)

De Laszló, Sandra, *A Brush with Grandeur: Philip Alexius de Lazló* (London, 2004)

De Stoeckel, Baroness, *Not All Vanity* (London, 1950)

Deslandres, Yvonne, *Paul Poiret 1879-1944* (London, 1987)

Devereux, G.R.M., *Etiquette for Women: a book of modern modes and manners by one of the aristocracy* (London, 1902)

Edes, Elisabeth (ed.), *The Age of Extravagance* (London, 1956)

Eliot, Elizabeth, *They All Married Well* (London, 1959)

Elsner, John and Cardinal, Roger, *The Cultures of Collecting* (Melbourne, 1994)

Ewing, Elizabeth, *History of 20th-Century Fashion* (London, 1974)

Evans, Caroline, 'The Enchanted Spectacle', *Fashion Theory: The Journal of Dress, Body & Culture*, 5:3, September 2001, pp.271-310

Forbes Hamilton, Lady Angela (St Clair Erskine), *Memories and Base Details* (London, 1922)

Forester, the Hon. Mrs C.W., *This Age of Beauty* (London, 1935)

Furbank, P. N. and Cain, A., *Mallarmé on Fashion: A translation of the fashion magazine La Dernière mode with commentary* (Oxford, 2004)

Garnier, Guillaume, *Paul Poiret et Nicole Groult*, exh. cat., Musée de la Mode et du Costume, Palais Galliera, 1986

Gaudriault, Raymond, *La Gravure de Mode Feminine en France* (Paris, 1983)

Gernsheim, Alison, *Fashion and Reality* (London, 1963)

Ginsburg, Madeleine, *Victorian Dress in Photographs* (London, 1982)

Glenn, Susan Anita, *Female Spectacle: The Theatrical Roots of Modern Feminism* (Cambridge, MA, 2000)

Greenhalgh, Paul, *Ephemeral Vistas: The Expositions Universelles, Great Exhibitions and World's Fairs, 1851-1939* (Manchester, 1988)

Gregory, Alexis, *The Gilded Age: The Super Rich of the Edwardian Era* (London, 1993)

Groom, Gloria (ed.), *Impressionism, Fashion and Modernity*, exh. cat., Musée d'Orsay, Paris/Yale, 2012

Hall-Duncan, Nancy, *The History of Fashion Photography* (New York, 1979)

Hawes, Elizabeth, *Fashion is Spinach* (New York, 1938)

Healy, Robyn, *Worth to Dior: 20th Century Fashion from the Collection of the National Gallery of Victoria*, exh. cat., National Gallery of Victoria, 1993

Hegermann-Lindencrone, Lillie de, *In the Courts of Memory 1858-1875* (New York, 1912)

Hegermann-Lindencrone, Lillie de, *The Sunny Side of Diplomatic Life* (New York, 1914)

Holden, W.H., *The Pearl from Plymouth. The first authentic biography of Cora Pearl* (London, 1950)

Holt, Ardern, *Fancy Dresses Described,* 6th edn (London, 1896; first published 1879)

Homberger, Eric, *Mrs Astor's New York: Money and Social Power in the Gilded Age* (London, 2002)

Hughes, Claire, *Dressed in Fiction* (Oxford, 2005)

Jachimowicz, Elizabeth, *Eight Chicago Women and Their Fashions 1860-1929*, exh. cat., Chicago Historical Society, 1978

Johnston, Lucy, *Nineteeth-Century Fashion in Detail* (London, 2005)

Join-Diéterle, Catherine et al, *Femmes de fin de siècle, 1885-1895*, exh. cat, Musée Galliera, Paris, 1990

Join-Diéterle, Catherine et al, *Au paradis des dames*, exh. cat., Musée Galliera, Paris, 1992

Jullian, Philippe, *La Belle Epoque* (New York, Metropolitan Museum of Art, 1982)

Kaplan, Joel H. and Stowell, Sheila, *Theatre and Fashion* (Cambridge, 1995)

Keppel, Sonia, *Edwardian Daughter* (London, 1958)

Kirkham, Pat (ed.), *The Gendered Object* (Manchester, 1996)

Kjellberg, Anne, and North, Susan, *Style and Splendour: The Wardrobe of Queen Maud of Norway* (London, 2005)

Koch, W. John, *Daisy, Princess of Pless 1873-1943* (Edmonton, 2002)

Kochno, Boris, for Le Chambre Syndicale de la Couture Parisienne, *Le Théâtre de la Mode* (Paris, 1945)

Lambert, Angela, *Unquiet Souls: the Indian Summer of the British Aristocracy, 1880-1918* (London, 1984)

Lambert, Miles, *Fashion in Photographs, 1860-1880* (London, 1991)

Land, Andrew, *Motoring Costume* (Princes Risborough, 1987)

Langley Moore, Doris, *The Woman in Fashion* (London, 1949)

    Fashion Through Fashion Plates (London, 1971)

Langtry, Lillie, *The Days I Knew* (London, 1925)

Latour, Anny, *Kings of Fashion* (London, 1958)

Laver, James, *Taste and Fashion* (London, 1937)

    Edwardian Promenade (London, 1958)

    Museum Piece (London, 1963)

    The Age of Optimism. Manners and Morals 1848-1914 (London, 1966)

Leslie, Anita, *Edwardians in Love* (New York, 1972)

Levine, Donald N. (ed.), *Georg Simmel: On Individuality and Social Forms* (University of Chicago, 1976)

Levitt, Sarah, *Fashion in Photographs 1880-1900* (London, 1991)

Lomax, James, and Ormond, Richard, *John Singer Sargent and the Edwardian Era* (London, 1979)

Lord, Walter, *A Night to Remember: Illustrated Edition* (London, 1976)

Lynam, Ruth (ed.), *Paris Fashion* (London, 1972)

McKibben, Ross, *Classes and Cultures, England 1918-1951* (Oxford, 1998)

Melba, Dame Nellie, *Melodies and Memories* (London, 1925)

Miller, Jonathan, *On Reflection* (London, 1998)

Morgan, Anne, *The American Girl: Her Education, Her Responsibility, Her Recreation, Her Future* (New York, 1915)

Mosley, Charlotte (ed.), *The Mitfords: Letters Between Six Sisters* (London, 2007)

Murphy, Sophia, *The Duchess of Devonshire's Ball* (London, 1984)

Nadelhoffer, Hans, *Cartier* (London, 2007)

Nicolson, Nigel, *Mary Curzon* (London, 1977)

Nystrom, Paul, *Economics of Fashion* (New York, 1928)

Paget, Walburga, Lady, *Embassies of Other Days and Further Recollections,* vols I and II (London, 1923)

Pastoureau, Michel, *L'Etoffe Du Diable Une Histoire des Rayures et des Tissus Rayes* (Paris, 1991)

Pearce, Susan M., *Interpreting Objects and Collections* (London, 1994)

Pearl, Cora (Eliza Emma Crouch), *The Memoirs of Cora Pearl*, authorized translation (London, 1886)

Peers, Juliette, *The Fashion Doll: from Bébé Jumeau to Barbie* (Oxford, 2004)

Pepper, Terence, *High Society Portraits 1897-1914*, exh. cat., National Portrait Gallery, London, 1998

Perrot, Philippe, *Fashioning the Bourgeoisie: A History of Clothing in the Nineteenth Century* (Princeton, 1994)

Picken, Mary, *Harmony in Dress,* Woman's Institute Library of Dressmaking (Pennsylvania, 1924)

Picken, Mary, *The Language of Fashion* (New York, 1939)

Picken, Mary and Miller, Dora Loues, *Dressmakers of France* (New York, 1956)

Pless, Daisy, Princess, *Daisy, Princess of Pless, by Herself* (London, 1929)

   More about Myself and Friends (London, 1930)

   From My Private Diary (London, 1931)

   What I Left Unsaid (London, 1936)

Poiret, Paul, *My First Fifty Years* (London, 1931)

Priestley, J.B., *The Edwardians* (London, 1970)

Pritchard, Mrs Eric, *The Cult of Chiffon* (London, 1902)

Quennell, Peter and Sage, Lorna, *The Last Edwardians: An Illustrated History of Violet Trefusis and Alice Keppel* (Boston, 1985)

Rappaport, Erika Diane, *Shopping for Pleasure: Women in the Making of London's West End* (Princeton, 2000)

Reeder, Jan Glier, *High Style: Masterworks from the Brooklyn Museum Costume Collection at the Metropolitan Museum of Art*, exh. cat., the Metropolitan Museum of Art/Yale, New York, 2010

Rennolds Milbank, Caroline, *Couture: The Great Designers* (London, 1985)

   New York Fashion: The Evolution of American Style (New York, 1989)

Ribeiro, Aileen, *Dress in Eighteenth-Century Europe 1715-1789* (London, 1984)

   Dress and Morality (London, 1986)

Roger-Milès, Léon, *Les Créateurs de la Mode* (Paris, 1910)

Rose, Jonathan, *The Edwardian Temperament: 1895-1919* (London, 1986)

Ross, Ishbel, *Crusades and Crinolines: The Life and Times of Ellen Curtis Demorest and William Jennings Demorest* (New York, 1963)

Rothstein, Natalie (ed.), *Four Hundred Years of Fashion* (London, 1984)

Ruffer, Jonathan Garnier, *The Big Shots: Edwardian Shooting Parties* (New York, 1977)

Sackville-West, Vita, *The Edwardians* (London, 1930)

Scart, Brigitte (ed.), *L'Atelier Nadar et la Mode 1865-1913*, exh. cat., L'Inspection Générale des Musées, France, 1977

Sermoneta, Duchess of, *Things Past* (London, 1929)

Sirop, Dominique, *Paquin*, exh. cat, Musée Historique des Tissus, Lyons, 1989

Sloane, Florence A., *Maverick in Mauve* (New York, 1983)

Souhami, Diana, *Mrs Keppel and her Daughter* (New York, 1996)

Splatt, Cynthia, *Isadora Duncan and Gordon Craig: The Prose & Poetry of Action* (San Francisco, 1988)

Sproule, Anna, *The Social Calendar* (Poole, 1978)

Stanley, Louis T., *The London Season* (London, 1955)

Steele, Valerie, *Fashion and Eroticism: Ideals of Feminine Beauty from the Victorian Era to the Jazz Age* (New York, 1985)

   Paris Fashion. A Cultural History (Oxford, 1988)

Stokes, John, *The French Actress and her English Audience* (Cambridge, 2005)

Taine, Hippolyte, *Vie et Opinions de M. Frédéric-Thomas Graindorge* (Paris, 1867)

Taylor, Lou, *The Study of Dress History* (Manchester, 2002)

   Establishing Dress History (Manchester, 2004)

Tétart-Vittu, Françoise, 'The French-English Go Between', *Costume*, no.26, London, 1992, pp.40-5

Thieme, Charles Otto, *Simply Stunning: 200 Years of Fashion from the Cincinnati Art Museum*, exh. cat., Ohio, 1988

Thompson, Paul, *The Edwardians: The Remaking of British Society* (London, 1975)

Tickner, Lisa, *The Spectacle of Woman: Imagery of the Suffrage Campaign 1907-1914* (London, 1987)

Trefusis, Violet, *Don't Look Round* (London, 1952)

Troubridge, Lady Laura, *Memories and Reflections* (London, 1925)

Troy, Nancy J., *Couture Culture* (London, 2003)

Uzanne, Octave, *Fashion in Paris: the various phases of feminine taste and aesthetics from 1797 to 1897* (London, 1898)

Veblen, Thorstein, *The Theory of the Leisure Class* (New York, 1899)

Veillon, Dominique, *Fashion under the Occupation* (Oxford, 2002)

Walkley, Christina and Foster, Vanda, *Crinolines and Crimping Irons* (London, 1978)

Walkley, Christina, *Dressed to Impress: 1840-1914* (London, 1989)

Warwick, Frances, Countess of, *Life's Ebb and Flow* (London, 1929)

   Afterthoughts (London, 1931)

Waugh, Norah, *The Cut of Women's Clothes* (London, 1968)

West, George Cornwallis, *Edwardian Heydays* (London, 1930)

Wharton, Edith, *The House of Mirth* (New York, 1905)

   The Age of Innocence (New York, 1920)

   A Backward Glance (New York, 1934)

White, Cynthia, *Women's Magazines* (London, 1970)

White, Palmer, *Poiret* (London, 1973)

Woolman Chase, Edna, and Chase, Ilka, *Always in Vogue* (London, 1954)

Wyndham Horace, *Chorus to Coronet* (London, 1951)

Zola, Emile, *La Curée* (Paris, first published 1872)

MAGAZINES AND NEWSPAPERS
Everywoman's Encyclopaedia

Femina

Harper's Bazar

La Gazette du Bon Ton

La Grande Dame. Revue de l'élégance et des arts

La Vie parisienne

L'Art et la Mode

L'Illustration

Les Modes

The Illustrated London News

The Lady's Realm

The Queen

Tatler

The Times

Woman at Home

Vanity Fair

Vogue

IMAGE CAPTIONS

BUCKLES [P.24]
ABOVE, LEFT TO RIGHT –
Evening gown, silk chiffon, 1907-8. AAD/1982/1/19
Afternoon ensemble, silk, 1905-6. AAD/1982/1/7

BELOW, LEFT TO RIGHT –
Day dress, fine wool and silk, 1908-9. AAD/1982/1/10
Afternoon gown, silk, 1908-9. AAD/1982/1/10

BOWS [P.25]
ABOVE, LEFT TO RIGHT –
Gown, Alençon lace, charmeuse and chiffon, 1909-10. AAD/1982/1/12
'Bleuet', afternoon ensemble, Vicuña and taffeta, 1912-13. AAD/1982/1/17

BELOW, LEFT TO RIGHT –
'Mireille, afternoon gown, various silks and lace, 1912-13. AAD/1982/1/18
'Papy', costume, wool and taffeta, 1912-13. AAD/1982/1/17

SLEEVES [P.48]
TOP, LEFT TO RIGHT –
Gown, fine wool and tulle, 1904. AAD/1982/1/3
Gown, chiffon and lace, 1905. AAD/1982/1/6
Jacket, zibeline, 1903-4. AAD/1982/1/27

MIDDLE, LEFT TO RIGHT –
Sortie de bal, taffeta and lace, 1904-5. AAD/1982/1/29
Jacket, taffeta and lace, 1904-5. AAD/1982/1/29
Costume, wool, 1903-4. AAD/1982/1/26

BOTTOM, LEFT TO RIGHT –
Jacket, wool, 1903-4. AAD/1982/1/26
Jacket, wool, 1903-4. AAD/1982/1/27
Coat, velvet and Russian sable, 1903-4. AAD/1982/1/27

BACKS [P.49]
TOP, LEFT TO RIGHT –
Costume, wool, 1906. AAD/1982/1/8
Gown, chiffon and lace, 1907-8. AAD/1982/1/9
Costume, wool, 1907-8. AAD/1982/1/9

MIDDLE, LEFT TO RIGHT –
Costume, wool, 1905. AAD/1982/1/6
Costume, silk, 1908-9. AAD/1982/1/10
Costume, wool, 1908-9. AAD/1982/1/10

BOTTOM, LEFT TO RIGHT –
Gown, silk and wool, 1908-9. AAD/1982/1/10
Grand manteau, wool and velvet, c.1900. AAD/1982/1/23
Coat, linen with insertion, 1906-8. AAD/1982/1/31

HISTORICAL AND WORLD [PP.74-5]
LEFT TO RIGHT – (front and back views)
Gown, fine wool, 1905. AAD/1982/1/6
Gown, velvet and silk, 1909. AAD/1982/1/11
Gown, chiffon and velvet, 1909. AAD/1982/1/11

LEFT TO RIGHT – (front and back views)
'Longchamps', evening ensemble, velvet and charmeuse, 1912-13. AAD/1982/1/18
Sortie de bal, velvet and organza, c.1901. AAD/1982/1/24
'Reynolds', afternoon gown, taffeta and chiffon, 1911-12. AAD/1982/1/16

BUTTONS [P.118]
TOP, LEFT TO RIGHT –
Costume, wool and velvet, 1907-8. AAD/1982/1/9
Costume, wool, 1905. AAD/1982/1/6

BOTTOM, LEFT TO RIGHT –
'Linette', gown, wool, 1912-13. AAD/1982/1/17
'Rafale', afternoon gown, charmeuse, 1913-14. AAD/1982/1/19

COLLARS [P.119]
TOP, LEFT TO RIGHT –
Coat, wool and lace, 1899-1900. AAD/1982/1/21
Jacket, wool and astrakhan, 1899-1900. AAD/1982/1/21

BOTTOM, LEFT TO RIGHT –
Coat, wool, 1904. AAD/1982/1/28
Jacket, silk, 1910-12. AAD/1982/1/35

LA GAZETTE DU BON TON [P.152]
ABOVE, LEFT TO RIGHT –
'Au Polo'. Vol. I, no. 8, June 1913, plate x
'Rendez-Vous Villa Gori'. 7e année, no. 9, 1924-5, plate 66

BELOW, LEFT TO RIGHT –
'Deux heures du Matin'. Vol. I, no.2, 1923, plate 9
'Amalfi'. Vol. II, no. 7, 1921, plate 54

LA GAZETTE DU BON TON [P.153]:
ABOVE, LEFT TO RIGHT –
'Le Poney Favori'. Vol. I, no. 11, September 1913, plate vii
'Le Choix Difficile'. Vol. II, no. 4, April 1914, plate 40

BELOW, LEFT TO RIGHT –
'La Coquette Surprise'. Vol. I, no. 3, 1913, plate viii
'La Paysage Romantique'. Vol. II, no. 7, July 1914, plate 68

INDEX

Page numbers in *italic* refer to the illustrations

A

actresses 125-6
Adburgham, Alison 147
Adolphus, F. 7
afternoon dresses 35, 41, 79, 98, 102-4, 106, 108-9
Aga Khan, Begum 143, *144*
The Age of Worth: the Gilded Age exhibition, New York (1982) 8
'Albano' 65
Alexandra, Queen (1844-1925) 79, 129
Alexandrine 13
Alma Tadema, Sir Lawrence 91
Amies, Hardy 146
Aria, Mrs 113, 126
Armani, Giorgio 46
Arnold, Janet 160
Arnould-Plessy, Jeanne Sylvarie (1819-1897) 125
Art Nouveau 21, 59, 91
Asquith, Margot 115, 163, *164*
Au paradis de dames exhibition, Paris (1992) 8-9
Audubon Society 55

B

Babani, Maurice 162
Bailey, Christopher 46
Balenciaga, Cristobal 42-6
ball gowns *38*, 91-2
bals blancs 91, 115
bals costumé 112, 113
bals poudré 112-13
Barbier, Georges 22
La Barucci (Giulia Beneni) 125
Beaton, Cecil 125
Bedin, Giovanni 9
Beer 22
La Belle Époque 6
Belloc, Marie A. 6
Beneni, Giulia (La Barucci) 125
Bérard, Christian (1902-1949) 146
Bernhardt, Sarah (1844-1923) 125
Bertin, Rose (1747-1813) 14
Beschoff 22, 23
Besnard, Jean 22
Biarritz 136, 160
Biba 54
Bida 85
Bigland, Eileen 31
Bismarck, Prince Otto von 16
Blatchford, Robert 114, 132
blouses *43*, 55
Bobergh, Otto Gustaf 8, 13, 16
Boldoni, Giovanni *129*
Bonabel, Elaine (1920-2000) 146
Bonnaire 6
Bonnard, Madame 13
Bonnat 85
Bordeux, Jeanne 125
Boston *Home Journal* 90
Boucher, François 28
Boué Soeurs 42
'Boule de Neige' *71*
Boutet de Monvel, Louis-Maurice 22
Bradley, Mrs 18
Bradley's 147
Breton, Claude 131
Breton, Jules 85

Breton, Pierre 131
Brissaud, Pierre 22
Broissard, Robert 30
Brooklyn Museum, New York 8, 114
Brown-Potter, Mrs James (1856-1936) 125-6, *127*, 164
Brummell, George 'Beau' (1778-1840) 52
Burberry 46
Burne-Jones, Edward 129
Burton, Sarah 42
Butterick 19

C

cache poussière 54
cage crinolines 15-16
calico balls 113
'Calipso' 98
Callot Soeurs 6, 21
Cannes 136, *137*, 146
'Caprice' *71*
Capucci 46
Cardin, Pierre 28, 46
Carette, Madame 7
Carter, Ernestine 8
Cartier 21
Cartier, Louis (1875-1942) 21
Cartier, Louis-François (1819-1904) 21
Castiglione, Comtesse de 114
Cavendish-Bentinck, Mrs 128
A Century of Fashion 8
Chambre Syndicale de la Couture Parisienne 19, 21, 22, 146
Champcommunal, Madame Elspeth (d. 1976) 143, 146
Chanel 162
Chanel, Coco 46, 136, 143
'Chanteler' *100*
Chapman, Annie 163, *164*
Chase, Edna Woolman 136
'Chasseur' 59, *73*
Cheruit, Madeleine 22, 136
Chez Grafton 13
Chicago Historical Society 8
Churchill, Lady Randolph 128
Cinares, Marquise de el *159*
Clark, Owen Hyde 147
clients 14-15, 121-33
coats *34*, *39*, *40*, *53*, 54-5, *54*, *56*, *66*, *67*, *72*
Coleman, Elizabeth Ann 8, 16, 19, 22, 31, 39, 52-4, 90
La Collectivité de la Couture 6
Collet, Annette 143
Condé Nast 23
conspicuous consumption 128
Cooper, Lady Diana (1892-1986) 91
copies 19
Corot, Camille (1796-1875) 16
corsetry 79
Costume 30
Costume Museum, Bath 30, 123, 158-9
costumes, tailored *32-3*, 55, *56-8*, *60-66*, *68-73*
court dresses 92-3, *92*
courtesans 125
couture à façon 14
Les Créateurs de la Mode 22, 37, 39, 136
Creed 52
crinolines 15-16, 125
'Cupidon' *87*
Curzon, Lady Mary 115, 123, *123*

D

'Danton' 59, *61*
day dresses 79, *80-81*, 85, 97, 99, 105, *107*
de Grey, Lady (later Marchioness of Ripon, 1859-1917) 131, *131*
Delamarre, Theodore 85
Delhi Durbar (1911) 123
demi-mondaines 125
Demorest, Ellen Curtis 19
Depression (1930s) 143
déshabillés *39*, 78, 79
design piracy 18-19
Designer Parfums 9
Deslandres, Yvonne 8
Devereux, G.R.M. 78, 79, 90
Devonshire, Deborah, Duchess of (1920-2010) 143
Devonshire, Louisa, Duchess of (1832-1911) 114-15, *117*
Devonshire, Duke of (1833-1908) 114-15
Devonshire House Ball (1898) 114-15, *117*
Dickens, Charles 7
dinner gowns *41*, 90-91
Dior, Christian 28, 46, 146
Doeuillet 21, 22, 23
Dolce & Gabbana 42
dollar princesses 128
Doucet, Jacques 6, 13, 21, 22, 132
dressmaking 77-93, *140*
    afternoon gowns 79
    ball gowns 91-2
    corsetry 79
    déshabillés 79
    design inspiration 85
    evening gowns 90-91
    morning dresses 78, 79
    princess gowns 79
    sorties de bals 91-2
    tea gowns 79, 85
    wedding gowns 92
Dudley, Lady 31
Dudley, Lord 31
Dumas, Alexandre 125
Dumoulin, Jean 160
Duse, Eleanora (1858-1924) *123*, 125
dust coats *39*, 54, *67*

E

Edward VII, King of England (1841-1910) 55, 93, 123, 129-32
Eight Chicago Women and Their Fashions 1860-1929 exhibition, Chicago (1978) 8, 128
Elizabeth I, Queen of England 13
Elizabeth II, Queen of England 115
embroidery 42, 59
'Espéranto' *84*, 85
Eugénie, Empress (1826-1920) 6, 15, 16, 112, 113, 122, 131, 143
evening gowns *17*, *18*, *39*, *45*, *84*-90, 90-91, *100-102*, 143, *143*
Ewing, Elizabeth 8
Exposition Universelle, Paris (1855) 13
Exposition Universelle, Paris (1867) 85
Exposition Universelle, Paris (1900) 6, 21, 22

173

F
fabrics 14, 19, 39, 52-4, 59, *148*
fancy dress 39, 111-17, *113*, *116-17*
Fashion Museum, Bath 30, 123, 158-9
fashion shows 145
Félix (Félix Poussineau) 6, 21, 23, 52
Felon 85
Femina 21, 23
Femmes fin de siècle 1885-1895 exhibition, Paris (1990) 8-9
Ferragamo 46
festivities, fancy dress 112-13
fiction, Worth in 126-8
Field, Julian Osgood 14-15, 31, 125
First World War 23, 59, 115, 136
Fleuview, Comtesse de *159*
flowers, fabric 91
Forbes Hamilton, Lady Angela (1876-1950) 19
Fortin, Marc-Aurèle 85
'Fortunio' *64*
Franco-Prussian War (1870-71) 16
French Revolution 58, 59
'Frileuse' *103*
'Fuchsia' *86*
furs 54, 55, *140*

G
Gagelin-Opigez, Chazelle et Cie 13, 15
Gainsborough, Thomas 91
'Gamine' *79*, *106*
Garnier, Guillaume 42
Gaultier, Jean Paul 42
La Gazette du Bon Ton 22, 23, *114*
Gérin, E. *64*
Germanisches National Museum, Nuremberg 39
Gérôme, Jean Léon 91
Ghesquière, Nicolas 46
Gibbs-Smith, Charles Harvard 30
Givenchy 28
'Glameuse' *101*
Goncourt, Edmond de 125
'Graziella' *79*, *83*
Great Exhibition, London (1951) 13
Greffuhle, Elisabeth, Comtesse de 21, 37, *38*, 92
Greffuhle, Mlle de 92
Grundy, Sydney (1848-1914) 131
Guiche, Duc de 92
Guillemin 85

H
hairstyles 39
Hall-Duncan, Nancy 37
Hardy 85
Harper's Bazar 14, 19, 23, 39, 52, 78
Haussmann, Baron Georges 6
haute couture 14
Hegermann-Lindencrone, Lillie de 92-3, 113, 123-5
Henner 85
Hermes 46
High Style exhibition, New York (2010) 8
A History of Feminine Fashion 8
Hogarth, William 122
Holden, W.H. 125
Holt, Ardern 113
The House of Worth exhibition, New York (1962) 8, 30
The House of Worth: A Centenary Exhibition of Designs for Dresses (1858-1958), London (1958) 30
Hurtaut et Magny 58

I
The Illustrated London News 52
Imans, Pierre 39
Impressionism, Fashion & Modernity exhibition, Paris (2012) 9, 37
Iribe, Paul 22

J
Jachimowicz, Elizabeth 8
jackets *12*, *36*, *43*, *54*
Jackson, Ken 37
Jacquet, G. 91
Jones, Henry Arthur 126

K
Kedleston, Grace Elvina, Marchioness of (1877-1958) 143
Keppel, Alice (1868-1947) 129, 132, *133*
Keppel, Sonia 132
Klein, Calvin 46
Koschno, Boris (1904-1990) 146

L
labels 19
Lafayette Studios 115
Laferrière 6, 23, 52
Lagerfeld, Karl 9, 46
Lalique, Marc 162
Lalique, René 162, *162*
Landelle, Charles Zacharie 85
Langley Moore, Doris 158
Langtry, Lillie (1853-1929) 7, 21, 39, *40*, 129-31, *130-31*
Lanvin 21, 22, 46
Latour, Amy 8
Laure, Mademoiselle 13
Laver, James 7, 8, 28-30, 31, 158
Lawrence, Sir Thomas 91
lay figures 21
Lebrun, Madame 91
ledgers 31
Leleux, Adolphe 85
Lepape, George 22
Leroy, Madame 13
Lewis and Allenby 13
lighting, photographs 37
literature, Worth in 126-8
Lloyd, Valerie 37
London 13, 22, 52, 136, 146
'Louis XIII' *40*
Louiseboulanger 136
Lyons 14, 19, 39, 52-4

M
McCalls 19
McCarthy, Martin 9
McCauley, Elizabeth A. 37
McCormick, Mrs Cyrus Hall (née Fowler, 1835-1923) 128
MacMahon, Maréchal (1808-1893) 16, 113
McQueen, Alexander 42
magazines 18-19, 22-3
Magidson, Phyllis 9
Mainbocher 9
Maison Belloir 93
Maison Savarre 128
Mallarmé, Stéphane 78
Manchester, Duchess of 128
mannequins and models 14, 33, 37-9, 54, *138*, *143*, *149*
Mannequins et Cires Artistiques 39

Manners and Rules of Good Society 91
mantles *47*, *96*, *103*
Marie, Grand Duchess (1853-1920) 122
Marie Antoinette, Queen of France 14, 39, *40*, 112, 114, 131, 132
Marlborough, Charles Spencer-Churchill, 9th Duke of 115, *117*, 128
Marly, Diana de 7, 8, 16, 33, 129
Martial et Armand 22
Marty, A.E. 22
masked balls 112, 115
Mason, Mrs 19
Massin, Sydney 147
'Matador' *41*
'Medicis' *87*
Mehta, Dilesh 9
Meissonier, Ernest 91
Melba, Dame Nellie (1861-1931) 126, *163*
Metropolitan Museum of Art, New York 39, 114
Metternich, Princess Pauline de (1836-1921) 14-15, 16, 122, 125
'Miguette' *81*
Milbank, Catherine Rennolds 8
military designs 59
Millais, Sir John Everett 129
Mills, Annette *142*, 143
mirrors 37
Miss Worth 147
Mitford, Jessica (1917-1996) 143
models see mannequins
Les Modes 23
Moltke, Helmuth, Count von 16
'Monique' *102*
Montespan, Madame de 115
Moore, Doris Langley 30
Moore, Mary (1861-1931) 125
Morgan, John Pierpont 128
Morgan, Junius Spencer 128
Morgan family 128
morning dresses 78, 79, *80-81*
Morris, May 113
Mortimer, Charlotte 143, 147
Mugler, Thierry 9
Muir, Jean 42
Müller, Florence 8
Murat, Princess 114
Murphy, Sophia 115
Musée des Arts Decoratifs, Paris 146
Musée de la Mode de la Ville de Paris 42
Musée de la Mode et du Costume, Paris 8
Musée de la Mode et du Textile, Paris 42
Musée d'Orsay, Paris 9
Museum of the City of New York 8, 9
Museum of Costume, Bath 30, 123, 158-9

N
Nadar, Félix (1820-1910) 37, 112
Nadar, Paul (1856-1939) 37, *38*, 112
naming the designs 55-8
Napoleon III, Emperor (1808-1873) 6, 13
National Gallery, London 13
Nattier, Jean-Marc 91
'New Look' 146
New York Times 114
Ney Soeurs 6
novels, Worth in 126-8
Nystrom, Paul 136, 138, 139, 141

O

Odette 146
Olian, JoAnne 8
Olivier, Lady (Vivien Leigh) 30
'Ostende' *105*
Österreichischen Museums für Angewandte Kunst 37
Otéro, Carolina 'La Belle' (1868-1965) 28, 31
Ouida (Maria Louise Ramé, 1839-1908) 31, 126

P

Paget, Lady (1839-1929) 19
Paget, Lady Mary 'Minnie' (1853-1919) 112, *113*, 115, *117*, 128
Le Palais du Costume, Paris 21
Palais Galliera, Paris 8-9, 42, 92
paper patterns 19
'Paquerette' *86*
Paquin 6, 8, 21, 28, 146, 147
Les Parfums Worth 136, 162
Paris Fashion Week (2010) 9
Patou, Jean 136
Pauwels 91
Pay, Lieutenant-Colonel F.W. 28, 146
Pearl, Cora (1837-1886) 125, *129*
'Pégase' *62*
Pennington-Mellor Collection 160-61
perfumes 136, *137*, *141*, 162, *162*
photograph albums 31-46
    anticipating the future 42
    classifying and conserving 31-3
    historical inspiration 39
    history of 30-31
    importance of the photographic archive 42-6
    lighting effects 37
    mannequins and models 37-9
    multi-purpose photographs 33-7
    photographing the collections 33
    splitting the archive 30
    marking the Worth centenary 30
Picken, Mary 136, 138, 141
Pilatte, Charles 16
Pingat 6
piracy, design 18-19
Poiret, Paul 21-2, 23, *32*, 42, 93, 162
'Postillon' *100*
Poussineau, Félix 21
Poynter, Edward 129
Premet 22
princess line 54, 73, 79, *109*
Pritchard, Mrs Eric 85
Proust, Marcel 92

Q

The Queen 21, 23, 54, 55, 79, 90-91, 92, 126, 131

R

Ramé, Maria Louise (Ouida, 1839-1908) 31, 126
Raudnitz 6
Ray, Man 136
ready-to-wear 136, 147
Redfern, Charles Poynter (1853-1929) 21, 22, 52
redingotes 40, 53, 54-5, *54*, *56*
Reeder, Jan Glier 8
Renaissance 39, 136
Riley, Robert 8, 16, 30
robes de bal *84*, *87*, 90, *90*, 91
robes de dîner 90-91, *101*, *102*
robes de mariée 92, *92-3*
Roger, Madame 6
Roger-Milès, Léon 54, 55-8
Romney, George 91
Rouff, Maggy 6, 147
royal clients 129-32
Roybet, Ferdinand 91

S

Sagan, Princesse de 113
Saint Laurent, Yves 46, 59
Saint-Martin, Jean (1899-1988) 146
San Francisco *Chronicle* 114
San Francisco *Report* 19
Sandoz, Adolf 39, 64
'Sans Gêne' *68*
Sargent, John Singer 132, *133*
Saunders, Edith 8
Schiaparelli, Elsa 42, 136, 143
Second Empire (1852-70) 13, 125
Second World War 146
Seeling, Charlotte 8
Settle, Alison 8
sewing machines 14
Simmel, Georg 128
skirts 20
Smith, Lord Justice A.L. 18
Snischek, Max 37
Société des Amis du Costume 28
Society for the Preservation of Birds 55
sorties de bals 91-2, *94-5*
Souhami, Diana 132
Sous l'Empire des Crinolines exhibition, Paris (2008) 8-9
sportswear 136, *142*, 143
Squier, Miriam Folline 16
Stevens 85
Stockman Frères 33
The Strand Magazine 37
stripes 55
Strong, Sir Roy 31
style anglais 52
Suresnes 7
Swan and Edgar, London 13
Sykes, Lady 79

T

tailoring 51-64, *140*
    costumes 55
    design inspiration 58-9
    fabrics 52-4
    full-length coats 54-5
    modernizing the look 59-64
    naming the designs 55-8
    stripes 55
    style anglais 52
    use of fur 54, 55
Taine, Hippolyte 7
tassels 79
tea gowns 79, *82-4*, 85
Tétart-Vittu, Françoise 16
textiles 14, 19, 39, 52-4, 59, *148*
'La Théâtre de la Mode' 146, *146*
theatrical costumes 39, 40
The Times 18, 19
Tissot, James 91
toiles 54
'Toscarina' *87*

travelling coats *34*, *39*, 54, 67
Trefusis, Violet 132, *133*
'Tripoli' *104*
Troy, Nancy 19
Turin International Exhibition (1911) 39

U

Uzanne, Octave 55

V

Valentino 46
'Van Lao' *35*
Vanderbilt, Consuelo (1876-1964) 91, 128, *129*
Vanderbilt, Mrs Cornelius (1845-1934) 114
Vanderbilt, Mrs William K. (1876-1935) 114
Vanity Fair 19
Vanloo 113
Veblen, Thorstein 128
Veillon, Dominique 146
Vernet, Marie Augustine see Worth, Marie Augustine
Versailles Ball (1913) 115
Victoria, Queen of England (1819-1901) 114, 129, 160
Victoria and Albert Museum, London 28-31
Victoria Eugenie, Queen of Spain 143
'Violetta' *102*
Vionnet, Madeleine 42, *45*
Vogel, Lucien 22
Vogue 23, 115, 125, 126, 136, 143

W

Ward, Edward 91
Warwick, 5th Earl of 132
Warwick, Frances ('Daisy'), Countess of (1861-1936) 114, *124*, 129, 132, *133*
Watts, George Frederick 129
wax mannequins 37-9
wedding gowns *17*, *34*, 92, *92-3*, 159
Wells 85
The Westminster Gazette 7
Westwood, Vivienne 42
Wharton, Edith (1862-1937) 126-8
Whistler, James McNeill 129
Wiener Werkstätte 37
Wimmer-Wisgull, Eduard Josef 37
Winterburn, Florence Hull 64, 91
Winterhalter, Franz Xavier 16, 90
The Woman at Home 115
Women's Tailoring Union 22
Wood, Janet 160
Worth, House of
    accounts books 31
    anticipating the future 42
    cage crinolines 15-16
    case against Mrs Bradley 18
    clients 14-15, 121-33
    design inspiration 58-9, 85
    design piracy and the fashion press 18-19
    dresses with interchangeable parts 59
    dressmaking 77-93
    employees 136, *138-41*
    fancy dress 111-17
    from 1914-1956 135-53
    historical influences 30, 58-9, 91
    in literature 126-8
    modernizing the look 59-64
    naming the designs 55-8